SANTA FE HIGH SCHOOL

MAFIA
PRINCESS

MAFIA
PRINCESS

Growing Up in Sam Giancana's Family

Antoinette Giancana and
Thomas C. Renner

William Morrow and Company, Inc.
New York 1984

Library of Congress Catalog Card Number: 83-63294

ISBN: 0-688-02620-6

Printed in the United States of America
12 13 14 15

BOOK DESIGN BY RICHARD ORIOLO

To my mother and father with loving remembrance and to those who made it possible, and to the doctor for what might have been . . .

—A.G.

TO NANCY
Who Never Lost Faith
and Has Sacrificed Much,
My Deepest Love Always

SMITHTOWN, N.Y.
MARCH, 1984

—T.C.R.

Foreword

Antoinette Giancana was an enigma to her father, her family, and to those who bowed and scraped to please the ruthless men who ruled the criminal world of Chicago for more than a decade. Instead of meekly obeying the dictates of the Mafia society she lived in, Antoinette, the eldest daughter of the late Sam (Mooney) Giancana, chose to defy them, which could have cost her her life had her father ever known just how far she had gone.

In the past she has said publicly that if she had been born a man, she would have followed in her father's footsteps and become a leader in the Mafia, that strange criminal organization which came to this country in the late 1800s from Sicily and has done more to sully the name of honest, hardworking, and proud Italian Americans than any other ethnic group in history. She might well have done just that, for there is in her life story a strange if subtle parallel between the path she followed in life and the path her father followed before he was assassinated in 1975.

I have always been intrigued with new and never-before revealed stories that deal with organized crime. Whether investigating or writing about premier federal informer Vincent Teresa and his worldwide exploits as a Mafia money mover, or about Wall Street swindler Michael Hellerman, I always tried to break new ground in reporting on organized crime. The Antoinette Giancana story follows in that tradition.

There have been books written about the wives and girl friends of so-called Mafia men. There has even been a story about the daughter of a low-level Las Vegas gangster. But in the more than quarter century that I have investigated, reported on, and written about organized crime, to my knowledge, there has never been a book written about the life of a daughter of a Mafia boss.

The children of Mafia leaders, particularly the daughters, generally know very little about the criminal lives of their infamous parents. That is by design. Not only are mafiosi chauvinistic by tradition, they are extraordinarily protective when it comes to their families, especially their daughters. Sam Giancana was no exception.

Though he had only a sixth-grade education and the morals of a male mink, and was probably responsible for the death of scores if not hundreds of men, Sam Giancana was almost puritanical when it came to his family.

From the moment Antoinette was born to the day her father was slain, the inner world of the Mafia was kept secret from her. When she was a child, her father was confined to a federal prison in Indiana. She was told that he was away at "college." For years she led a cloistered existence in the private Catholic schools of Chicago and Indianapolis where her father's criminal life was never discussed, but where for the privilege of ensuring that his daughter's education be free of media harassment and where she would associate with those in a higher social class, Sam Giancana made exorbitant contributions.

But there were glimpses—throughout the flashes of violence followed by funeral after funeral of dinner guests, of family friends—of a fat, jovial man who, though a killer, saw the need to keep a small child's Christmas fantasy of Santa Claus alive. In these fleeting moments, Antoinette Giancana knew that she was different, that in the secret world of the Mafia she was royalty, a princess.

She knew it when she was ushered into the dressing rooms of international stars such as Frank Sinatra, Jimmy Durante, Jerry Lewis, and Tony Martin. She knew it when tough, gravel-voiced enforcers went to excesses to please her father and his family. She knew it when she visited a Las Vegas casino and the owner had a diamond initial pin, identical to the one worn by his wife, made for her. And she knew it when dress designers and sales supervisors from famed clothing stores came to her home to design clothes for her mother and for her.

But with all the trappings of wealth and luxury, Antoinette Giancana lacked the one thing that all daughters want most desperately from their fathers . . . love. Perhaps because this love was denied her, she became a rebel among those bound up in the traditions of Mafia life.

This then is the story of Antoinette's life with her father . . . of her defiance of Mafia tradition and the consequences. In order to tell her story she had to examine with me thousands of pages of federal documents (obtained under the Freedom of Information Act) that detailed—by surveillance, informants, and electronic listening devices—her father's criminal life, a life that she never fully understood, or consciously believed existed.

She did not, for example, consciously believe that her father ordered the murder of other men until she read conversations in which he had participated detailing such murders. She did not know that her father had plotted with representatives of the Central Intelligence Agency to assassinate Cuban Premier Fidel Castro and several of his aides until it became public knowledge.

Her story is explosive, daring, sometimes sordid, and often tragic. She reached the heights as a Mafia princess with what amounted to a royal wedding; and she reached the depths with a sordid back-room abortion conducted in desperate fear of discovery by her father. She is consumed by terrible guilts, resulting from the deaths of her mother and father, and by overwhelming desires and a need to be loved, often by whoever is handy and strikes her immediate fancy.

Her father was slain in the cellar of what was once her home, but for more than a year prior to his death they had not talked. She was, for all intents and purposes, disowned, shunned not only by her father but by many members of her immediate family. Strangely enough, members of the crime family that Sam once led have treated her with respect at functions she has attended since his death.

The fortune that law-enforcement officials estimate Sam Giancana earned as a boss . . . $25 million or more . . . is hidden in time and secret accounts and Mafia transactions, none of which were shared with Antoinette, the eldest of Sam's three daughters. She has lived in flophouses, on welfare, and on food stamps. She has attempted suicide, been ignored by her family, and even by her sons; she has been cheated out of what little money she had by unscrupulous men, and been harassed in her attempts to open a restaurant-cocktail lounge in Schiller Park, Illinois.

Through it all, Antoinette Giancana has managed to maintain a thoughtful sensitivity toward others less fortunate than herself. She has nursed people dying of cancer in her small apartment and in a hospital, and she has talked many who are desperate and depressed out of commiting suicide. Each year for a week before Christmas and on Christmas Eve, she has worked as a volunteer for YULE, Chicago's hot line for people in need of comfort, understanding, and companionship during the Christmas holidays. She remembers that YULE was there six years ago to help her when desperation and depression overwhelmed her.

In the end Antoinette Giancana is a Mafia princess in every sense of the word. She may have broken the Mafia's traditional rules, but she has lived with a pride in her name, in her family tradition, and in the man who never was able to give her the one thing she wanted most . . . the love of a father. Hers is a remarkable story, a new and significant chapter in the lore of the strange, violent, and secret world of the Mafia.

—THOMAS C. RENNER

Contents

Foreword 7

The Havana Connection 13

Daddy, I Love You 27

The Mob Santa Claus 35

Careful Sam 41

Sweet Angeline 51

Sam and the Church 59

Speak Softly 69

That's Entertainment—Part I 83

That's Entertainment—Part II 99

Sex and the Mafia Princess 117

Farewell, Sweet Angeline 129

The Trojan Horse 145

The Slippery Fox 175

Travelin' Sam, the Casino Man 197

A Filly Named Phyllis—Part I 209

A Filly Named Phyllis—Part II 229

Sam and His Shadow 245

The Fall of the House of Giancana 261

Epilogue 283

Appendix: Chicago Crime Directory 291

Index 299

1

The Havana Connection

10/14/60

AIRTEL

TO: DIRECTOR, FBI
FROM: SAC [Identity censored by FBI]
SUBJECT: SAMUEL M. GIANCANA, aka
TOP HOODLUM—AR [Anti-Racketeering]
(00: CHICAGO)

[First seven lines blanked out]
CASTRO and Cuba were discussed. Subject said that
CASTRO was to be done away with very shortly. [Identity censored] registered doubt about this happening,
then GIANCANA assured them it was to occur in
November and that he has met with the assassin on
three occasions. [Blanked out] "assasin" was the term
used by GIANCANA. GIANCANA said he last met with
the "assasin" on a boat docked at the Fontainebleau
Hotel, Miami Beach, Florida, and that everything has
been perfected for the killing of CASTRO. GIANCANA
said that the "assasin" has arranged with a girl, not further described, to drop a "pill" in the drink or some food

of CASTRO's. GIANCANA also told [identity censored] that CASTRO is in advanced stages of syphilis and is not completely rational. [Two additional lines are blanked out.]
3—Bureau
1—Chicago
1—New York (109-74)
1—New York (02-793)
FRG: ald   (SENT DIRECTOR)
                  (10/18/60)

There was not even the slightest resemblance between the sun-tanned, balding, middle-aged man who twisted nervously in his chair in front of me and the media stereotype of a gravel-voiced Mafia "godfather." In fact, I can't think of anyone who looked less like the public's conception of a Mafia boss than my father in May of 1961.

There was no paunch on his lean, five-foot, ten-inch frame, thanks largely to the special diet of broiled steak with lemon juice and tomatoes that he followed religiously when his weight began edging modestly above the 160-pound mark. He didn't speak in broken Italian, and muscle-bound killers didn't enter a room, kissing his ring or hugging him while mumbling words of respect in his ear.

At fifty-two, Sam (Mooney) Giancana, the Chicago Mafia's successor to Prohibition gangster boss Al Capone, was more interested in maintaining a youthful appearance than in presenting a movie image of a mafioso.

Sam worked at looking young and, except for his balding head and graying hairline, he usually succeeded. He wore a carefully constructed, lifelike toupee that cost him more than a thousand dollars. When he wore it, it made him look ten years younger.

My father liked that. He liked looking younger. He liked feeling younger. Above all, he liked proving he was young with those so-called glamour queens whom he succeeded in bedding from Los Angeles to New York. Of course, all that female chasing had its disadvantages too. It drew agents of the FBI around him like flies . . . and all those agents made his job as Chicago's most powerful and influential hoodlum that much more difficult.

It was on a bright, sunshiny May afternoon in 1961 when I recall walking into his cellar conference room in what had once been my home at 1147 South Wenonah Avenue, Oak Park, Illinois. While I knew my father was under surveillance by the FBI and other agencies, I had not the slightest idea that he had been plotting with the CIA and various hoodlum friends, including Florida's notorious Santos Trafficante, to assassinate Fidel Castro.

Sam had almost a collegiate look to him as he leaned back in his high-backed, half-wing Romweber chair. His sharply creased blue slacks matched his tailored light blue, open-neck sport shirt perfectly. Glistening from his beltline were golden initials, "S M G," attached to a solid-gold key chain that disappeared inside his right-hand pants pocket. On his left wrist was a thin, rectangular gold watch with diamond chip numerals, and between his fingers he held a gold swizzle stick, given him by my mother, to stir his drink with. A slipper dangled precariously from his left foot.

He acknowledged my presence with a frown. I remember vividly feeling a chill course its way up my spine as he flicked an imaginary speck from his slacks while his cold, piercing brown eyes looked at me as if they were X-raying my mind.

I kissed Sam lightly on the cheek and sat down directly across from him in a chair identical to his in this, his very private conference room. It was a soundproof room where some of the nation's most notorious and powerful crime leaders had often gathered and changed the course of events in the glittering casinos of Las Vegas, or on the bustling streets of New York, or on the floodlit sets of Hollywood's movie studios. For as long as I could remember there was a Jekyll and Hyde quality to my father's character, and I often wondered how he managed to master such a dual life.

When I was a small child, Sam had cuddled me in his arms, bounced me on his knee, and spent hours decorating our Christmas trees and putting toys together for me. And as he did those things . . . those loving and thoughtful acts . . . he was also deciding whether men should live or die on the streets of Chicago.

Here in this room, dressed in casual attire, relaxing before me, was a man who struck chilling fear from the streets of Cicero, Illinois, to the cocktail lounges of Chicago and the sunbaked beaches of the Caribbean.

Sam was a man who could be as graceful as a gazelle whether

walking across a street with his shoulders pulled back and his head held high, or lifting steaming strands of spaghetti from a platter with an almost maestrolike movement of his arms and hands. Yet, when charged with anger, his eyes would flash with fury and his natural grace would give way to the violent, almost animallike action and brutality of Chicago's underworld jungle, where men were tortured while hanging on meathooks in a warehouse or gunned down on the steps of a courthouse.

The newspapers, television, the FBI, the Chicago police, all at one time or another described my father as the most powerful and fearsome godfather west of New York from the day he ascended the Chicago Mafia throne of leadership until perhaps a year or two before he was assassinated in 1975 in the very cellar he and I were sitting in that day in May, 1961.

My father was a man who had learned the arts of murder and terror first as a member of a neighborhood ghetto gang in an immigrant area in Chicago known as "the Patch," and had refined later working for and with the violent thugs Chicago spawned during the days of Prohibition.

Sam had been closely allied with members of the infamous Al Capone gang first through his youthful friendship with Vincenzo DeMora, better known to the Chicago press as Jack McGurn, Capone's most feared machine-gun-toting assassin. And as my father grew in stature, he worked for many of Capone's successors, including Frank Nitti, Paul DeLucia, better known in Mafia and police circles as Paul (The Waiter) Ricca, and Anthony (Joe Batters) Accardo. Sam learned his trade so well that he followed in their footsteps to the top of the criminal ladder.

My father had always prided himself on his ability to handle a car, to take the wheel and with the deftness of an experienced Indianapolis 500 racing driver, make it do tricks at dangerously high speeds. I can recall riding with Sam and hearing him almost scream with laughter as he wheeled around corners, rubber burning and brakes screeching, to shake a tail of federal agents or local police. Sometimes, after he had eluded them, he would race up a side street and down another until he came up behind his confused pursuers, honking his horn with obvious delight as he peeled off down another street to lead them on another wild chase, laughing all the time.

The almost fiendish delight with which he engaged law-enforcement officials in such chases was the result of a craft he had learned as a youth as a "wheelman," a driver, for young killers and had fine-tuned while acting as chauffeur for Paul Ricca and Anthony Accardo when they led the remnants of the old Capone mob. But that was in the past, and now, as we sat together in the privacy of his conference room, Sam was the constant target of surveillances by the FBI, by the Chicago police, by law-enforcement agents from one end of the country to the other. No matter where he went—whether to Florida, the Bahamas, the Caribbean, or Mexico—Sam was always watched. He had no privacy on the street or even in a bedroom with a woman, and the tension that such a lack of privacy produced was showing now as we sat together. He looked tired and drawn, and there was an edge of irritation to his voice as we talked.

"Why don't you just quit, Dad?" I asked. "You've got all the money you'll ever need. Is it worth all this running . . . being followed constantly, harassed wherever you go?"

His eyes narrowed as he glared at me. He put down the glass of juice he was drinking down on a tray and waggled a finger at me.

"For chrissake, Annette, what the hell do you know about anything?" he snapped. "You don't understand. Mind your business. What I do is none of your business."

I didn't understand. He was right about that. I knew nothing about the Mafia, or "the Outfit" as it's called in Chicago, except what I had read in the newspapers, and I had been told since childhood that newspapers never told the truth, particularly when they referred to Sam's activities. The only things I really knew were things I sensed or saw when I was in the presence of some of the underworld figures who worked for Sam, or when I was around entertainers who bowed and scraped and fell all over themselves to please him. So I suppose when I opened my mouth and suggested that my father quit as a boss, I sounded like a fool. It never dawned on me that the only way Sam could quit was to die.

Sam fell silent again, staring off into some space behind me, withdrawing into that world I was seldom able to penetrate and almost never able to discuss with him. That other world of violence and secret conferences and international travel was never shared with me, my sisters, Francine and Bonnie, or even my mother.

I changed the subject and decided to talk to him about a newspaper story I had just read about Castro and Cuba. The story was about the Bay of Pigs invasion disaster and about President John F. Kennedy's role in it. For a month newspapers, radio, and television had devoted huge amounts of space and time describing the April 17 invasion by American-trained Cuban exiles. There were stories about the Central Intelligence Agency and about Havana hotels and their casinos that were no longer run by criminals like my father.

I knew Sam had made many trips to Cuba, and naïvely I wanted to share some information I had learned and at the same time find out how what had happened in Cuba had affected some of his investments and other business opportunities I had heard he was planning. On many occasions when I was in Florida either with my mother, with Sam, or with friends, Sam would leave our summer home or the hotel where we were staying, like the Fontainebleau, to make a quick trip to Cuba. At times he would be with other men when he made those trips.

One of those men was Johnny Roselli, a rather handsome, polite, and soft-spoken man, who was murdered after my father was killed. Roselli had testified before a U.S. Senate committee investigating assassination plots of international leaders by the CIA. My father, I learned later, was scheduled to testify before the committee, then headed by Senator Frank Church of Idaho, just before he was murdered in 1975. I've always felt very strongly that the subpoena requiring Sam to appear before that committee was the death warrant that led to his murder.

But now as I talked to Sam, I knew nothing about international plots, the CIA, or how they might relate to Sam. In truth, it would have been incomprehensible to me that he would work for or deal with anyone in government unless he had bought and paid for them. And I had no way of knowing how deep a hatred he held for Castro because it was a subject he had never discussed with anyone in our family.

What I knew came from what I had overheard when Sam talked to some of his friends or when some of his friends would make casual remarks to me.

*   *   *

One such casual remark concerned Sam's investments in shrimp boat businesses that both he and Anthony Accardo had in Cuba and in Mexico. They were large businesses, and I suspect Sam and Accardo had several million dollars invested in them, although I could never attach a reliable price tag to the overall business when I was researching my father's estate assets following his death. Not even the FBI or the Internal Revenue Service were able to establish how much money was involved, but their records suggest it was considerable and well hidden behind corporate fronts.

"You know, Dad," I said, "I have an article here that you might be interested in. It's about Cuba and how a lot of people have investments there that they may lose."

Sam's head snapped up from a magazine he had begun looking at. I had his interest now, his real interest, for the first time since I'd entered the room. Sam had a habit of ignoring things I had to say. He ignored or patronized most women, except my mother, in serious discussions. It was an irritating habit, one that stirred an often reckless abandon on my part to force him to pay attention to me, to help me feel that I was somebody, not a machine to be turned on and off at his whim.

His face colored slightly as his eyes focused on the article I held in my hand. I began reading excerpts from the article to him. They concerned Meyer Lansky, a Jewish figure in organized crime whom my father knew quite well, and casinos that Lansky and other so-called organized-crime people had interests in. Although the article didn't name my father, he was one of those who held a considerable interest in Havana's once popular casinos.

The article didn't mention Sam's shrimp boat business, but I did. "Didn't you and Accardo have a big shrimp business in Cuba?" I asked.

As Sam stared at me, I had the sense that if looks could kill I would have been dead on the spot. I clearly remember noticing that the knuckles of his hands were almost white from gripping the arms of the chair so tightly.

"How many times you gotta be told?" he snapped. "You never talk about my business . . . you don't speak about my friends and what we do. You understand? Keep your mouth shut about things you don't understand."

I understood all right. Business, "family business" of the mob, was not a subject for discussion within our family. It was forbidden, a real no-no. The subject was there and yet it wasn't. What he really meant but never said was that if my sisters and I knew too much about his business affairs, we could be subpoenaed and sent to jail if we didn't talk. Worse, we could be hurt or Sam himself, despite his power as a boss, could be embarrassed, hurt, or even eliminated if the information we had could seriously affect the mob and its investments.

One of those capable of taking such violent action was Anthony Accardo.

Accardo was a man of immense power and influence in Chicago's underworld. He had once been a bodyguard and an enforcer for Al Capone, and Sam had been Accardo's driver during the violent heyday of Prohibition and illegal booze.

When Accardo stepped down as boss and went into semi-retirement, my father moved up as operating boss of the crime family. But even in retirement, Accardo maintained an influence on Sam and the crime family and received a considerable return on investments he had made while running the Chicago mob. One of those investments was in the shrimp business with Sam.

I recall that Sam and Accardo frequently traveled to Florida, sometimes taking their families with them, and then left Florida's sunny beaches on so-called fishing trips to Bimini and other parts of the Caribbean. I know that Accardo was an avid fisherman and that he loved to catch marlin and tuna, but I never really believed that all the trips they made together from Florida or to Mexico were for fishing.

Accardo is not a particularly lovable man. He has a certain amount of polish when he decides to display it, but it isn't the old-school, European polish that others like the late Paul (The Waiter) Ricca exuded.

Basically Accardo was a rather simple and often crude and cheap individual. He used to hold an annual Fourth of July bash for Chicago's mob at his home. At one such barbecue I attended with my father, I made the mistake of taking a dip in his pool and leaving the pool door open.

"Hey you!" he shouted across the room, knowing full well what my name was. "You live in a barn? Shut the damn pool door."

I could have died right there. My father was standing next to him. Nearby was Ricca, once Capone's right arm. My mother and a dozen or more other godfathers with their wives and children stood with him, and I was being singled out by this mafioso for committing the cardinal sin of leaving open the door to the pool. I could feel everyone's eyes on me. Somehow I kept my cool, dried myself off, and casually closed the door looking right at him with my eyes telling him to go straight to hell. I never said a word, just turned on my heel, and left the presence of the "great one" to change. As I left the room, I noticed a sort of wry grin on my father's face. I was never certain whether he was grinning because I had been chewed out or because I had shown presence in the face of Accardo and given him a "Mafia look" that he understood . . . a look I suppose I had inherited from my father, whose eyes would narrow and chill you to the bone when he felt the need to do so.

The press and some members of the mob who came to my father's home often referred to Accardo as "Joe Batters" or "Big Tuna." I don't know how he got those nicknames, but I've often been amused by the fact that my father's friends who talked about "Joe Batters" among themselves were very careful to call him Mr. Accardo, or if they were on a higher perch in the pecking order of the mob, to address him as Tony when in his presence. There was always a lot of chitchat about him when he wasn't around, but when he was present they fell over themselves bowing and scraping and practically licking his boots. All but Sam. He stood as an equal with Accardo and any of the other former Capone mob members who had reached the higher echelons of Chicago's underworld. Accardo might look down on others, make them feel subordinate, but he never acted superior in the presence of my father, or in the presence of Paul Ricca. Ricca had been a boss of the mob after Capone's death and the suicide of Frank Nitti.

I still don't know many of the details of Sam and Accardo's shrimp business. I did know that they both had put a lot of money into it. They had a large number of boats and processing plants in Cuba and Mexico, and it had been a very profitable venture in Cuba until Castro came to power. Then it was seized like so many other businesses Americans had invested in.

The seizure in Cuba cost Sam and Accardo millions of dollars, but it represented only a fraction of the losses they sustained from investments in the Havana casinos. Those casinos were the golden lode whence the profits flowed into the Chicago mob's treasury—and into the coffers of other crime families across the country.

Those losses made Sam a bitter man when the subject of Cuba came up.

I had been chilled by my father's outburst, but my silence was only temporary. So often I tried to have normal, average discussions with him and was always left with a sense of being invisible, of having nothing of significance to say, of being so boring to my father that he had to ignore me.

For some reason I really wanted his attention that day. I wasn't ready to be shunted aside and told to shut my mouth like I was a child who should be seen and not heard. If I couldn't talk about his business, then maybe I would get his attention with something more provocative. Maybe he would listen and take his eyes off that magazine if I talked about Castro. I should have known better, I suppose, but I was starved for Sam's attention.

I should mention that my father had never shown an appreciation for my choice in men. Whomever I went with, whoever I admired, even the man I had married were all subjects of his derision. Perhaps there was one exception . . . the time I dated Anthony Tisci, a young lawyer Sam wanted me to marry and whom my sister Bonnie later married. Tisci was a protégé of my father's, a man for whom he had big political plans when he worked as an aide to Sam's congressional puppet, former Representative Roland Libonati. My failure to marry Tisci was never forgotten.

Sex was a forbidden subject in my father's presence. He had made that abundantly clear over the years, and as a result I had for the most part kept my liaisons with men secret. Sometimes I slipped and spoke of the attraction some men held for me. Sam usually ignored my remarks, told me to shut up, or walked out of the room.

Now here I was once again being ignored by him, longing for his attention, even if it was negative. It seemed to me that the ideal subject to draw some response would be Fidel Castro, the man who had caused him so many financial difficulties. How was I to know . . . how could I know that Sam had been involved in a plot with the CIA to murder Castro? It was beyond my wildest imaginings at the time.

So it was in complete ignorance of the depths of Sam's hatred of Castro that I began remarking about what a handsome and virile man Castro was . . . how I was attracted to him . . . how if I wasn't married and a mother, I would have liked to have met and spent some time with him.

The married daughters of crime bosses don't or shouldn't admire the physical and sexual attributes of men other than their husbands, certainly not in the presence of their fathers. They are supposed to be decorative and obedient, and to become dutiful wives to Italian stallions approved by Poppa. On all counts I had failed to conform, and my outspoken admiration for Castro was typical of the nonconformist acts I was known for.

I expected a reaction, of course, but nothing like what followed.

Suddenly Sam leaped from his chair and almost instantaneously was at my side, ripping the paper from my hand and slapping my face.

"Don't ever mention that bastard's name in this house again . . . ever!" he screamed.

Sam was like a wild man. His face was flushed, almost beet red, and his arms flailed wildly in the air as wheeling away from me, he paced up and down, mumbling in Italian, all the while scuffing his slippers at the floor as if he were kicking at some invisible enemy.

"That son of a bitch . . . that syphilitic bastard . . . do you have any idea what he's done to me . . . to our friends?" he shouted.

I shook my head in shocked disbelief. I was actually frightened by his anger. I'd seen him angry before, but never this way. I was trembling now, not knowing what his next move would be or what I should do.

The more he ranted about Castro, the angrier he got. He was almost in a frenzy as he screamed at me. His face was so flushed I thought he was going to have a stroke. The veins in his neck and his forehead swelled and pulsed as he continued to shout at me, pounding on the table as he did so.

"Goddamit, Annette, you don't know anything about anything," he yelled. "I lose a bundle because of this bastard and you're talking about him like he was some goddam movie star. Where the hell are your brains? Get the hell outta here, Annette. Get outta here before I kill you."

I knew enough at that moment to give him no further argument. I just turned on my heel and hurried from the room. As I did, I could feel a cold sweat break out across my forehead. As I look back now, I think I had come very close to being killed, daughter or no daughter.

It wasn't until fourteen years later, when Sam was subpoenaed by Senator Church to testify with Johnny Roselli that I began to see how much he had been involved in the plot to kill Castro. Twenty-one years later I read an FBI document dated October 18, 1960, that finally revealed how deeply he had become enmeshed in international intrigue.

AIRTEL

TO: SACS, New York
    2—Chicago
    2—Miami (Enclosures)
FROM: DIRECTOR, FBI (109-584)
SUBJECT: ANTI-CASTRO ACTIVITIES
INTERNAL SECURITY—CUBA
    [Word blanked out] airtel 10/14/60 captioned "SAMUEL M. GIANCANA, aka TOP HOODLUM—AR," copy enclosed for Miami.

New York and Chicago should closely follow this matter and should immediately advise Bureau if any additional data is received regarding alleged plot against CASTRO. In particular, if information should be received indicating that GIANCANA plans travel to Miami area or other trips which could be to contact individuals implicated in alleged plot, Bureau and interested offices should be expeditiously advised and recommendations should be furnished concerning close coverage of GIAN-

CANA with view to identifying any contacts he might make regarding this matter, including physical surveillance. Chicago should promptly advise if it has received any information indicating recent travel on GIANCANA's part to Miami or other areas, such as Mexico, which might indicate possible contacts with anti-CASTRO elements. Chicago should also review appropriate records to determine if GIANCANA has recently made any long-distance phone calls to persons who might be involved in the alleged plot against CASTRO.

Miami should immediately furnish its comments regarding possible identity of person who allegedly met with GIANCANA at boat docked at Fontainebleau Hotel, Miami Beach. However, any inquiries conducted concerning this matter by Miami should be discreet so as not to jeopardize [identity censored] or alert individuals possibly involved to the Bureau's interest.

Future correspondence concerning alleged plot against CASTRO should be submitted under instant caption.

How had my father reached such a position in the underworld where the CIA was negotiating clandestinely with him through intermediaries to plot the murder of Castro while keeping the FBI, the U.S. Department of Justice, and even President of the United States John F. Kennedy in the dark? *Had that plot and the resulting publicity led to my father's assassination, and was it the underworld or a government-hired assassin who killed Sam Giancana in the basement of our home?*

To find some of those answers I've had to look back at both my life and that of my father, and piece together not only his life of crime, but mine as a Mafia boss's daughter. I've had to read thousands of pages of government documents, and I'm still fighting to gain access to others the government has withheld from me. And even as I write this with my co-author, I am learning about my father, with whom I lived and who I watched later placed in the family mausoleum. I am learning and realizing that unlike most daughters, I never really knew my father, never understood him, until now.

2

Daddy, I Love You

I was just a little over four years old when my father was committed to the United States penitentiary in Terre Haute, Indiana. He had been operating an illegal whiskey still in a remote little town called Garden Prairie, Illinois, with twelve other men when Uncle Sam's revenue agents swept in and caught everyone cold.

That was in February, 1939. On October 16, Sam was sentenced to four years and fined $3,700. Less than ten days later, Sam left home, kissed my mother, little Bonnie, my baby sister, and me good-bye, and left for the federal prison at Leavenworth, Kansas. A year later he managed somehow to be transferred to Terre Haute where he became prisoner number 104.

I suppose the transfer from Leavenworth to Terre Haute was arranged to ease the terrible visiting hardship imposed on our family. Transportation to Kansas was rather slow from Chicago in those days and money was scarce.

I'm sure there were other reasons for the transfer, not the least of which was Sam's hatred of Leavenworth. I had a glimpse of that hatred years later.

I was in school at the time and I had just bought a book called *My Six Convicts*, a really amusing story about the lives of some inmates at Leavenworth. It wasn't the type of book I would normally have read, but some of my friends at school had bought it and said it was funny. One girl in particular had laughed about it in class and had read a few excerpts to me that I thought were funny. So I bought the book and brought it home.

One evening, I was sitting in the living room reading the book and chuckling to myself about it. At that time, I still had no idea that Sam had ever been imprisoned at Leavenworth. Sam entered the room, noticed my amusement, and asked me what I found so funny. I began relating to him some of the anecdotes in the book.

His friendly mood suddenly darkened, and with a rasp to his voice, he snapped, "That's enough . . . I don't wanna hear any more. It's a lotta crap. It's a bunch of lies. There's nothing funny about that place. Leavenworth is a lousy rotten place and I don't wanna hear any more."

Sam seemed to get angrier the more he talked about it, and I didn't understand. I asked him what was the matter. "It's just a book, Dad, with a lot of funny stories," I said.

"I said it's a lotta trash," he shouted. "That's not the way things really are. What the hell are you reading crap about prisons for anyhow? You shouldn't be reading such books."

By this time he was in a rage and stormed out of the room. I didn't realize it at the time, but he had just told me he'd been in Leavenworth and he knew what prison life there was really like. He hated confinement, and life at Leavenworth and even Terre Haute had been hard and held bitter memories for him.

None of that, of course, is reflected in his prison records or in the FBI documents I acquired, but those records do show that while Sam was at Terre Haute he wrote letters to Bonnie and me.

The truth is that Bonnie was not much more than a baby at that time and I couldn't read or write. Neither of us received those letters, and until I read the FBI documents I never knew he had written to us. I realize now that those so-called letters were really instructions sent to my home and then passed on to his criminal associates. Our home on West Lexington Street was an address that would not be suspect. Letters to his children would not be inspected or censored. What better way to give orders to criminal associates carrying on his work and following his orders?

While the memory of that particular moment in time is somewhat vague, I do remember quite vividly wondering why my daddy had to leave our home for a long time and where he was going. I recall running to my mother after he had left, pulling at her dress for attention, and asking her about why he left with tears running down my cheeks.

"Doesn't Daddy love me anymore?" I asked, sobbing. "Is it because I've been a bad girl again?"

Mother's eyes were red and teary as she looked down at me from the kitchen sink. She wiped her hands, knelt, hugged me quite hard, and assured me that Sam loved me.

"Daddy's going to college," mother explained. She paused, stroked my hair, and held my hands in hers. She looked so frail and tired. "Daddy's going to be gone for a while to learn new things. He just wants you to be a good girl and go to school and learn things so that you can show him how much you've learned when he gets back."

In a way, prison was a college of sorts for Sam. He certainly learned from it. It was there, I found out later, that Sam met the policy rackets king of Chicago's South Side, a man named Edward Jones. Jones was a black gambler who was in jail for evading taxes, and he apparently bragged about the money he and his brother had made in a racket that thrived on the pennies, nickels, and dimes of the black ghetto's poverty-stricken people. All that bragging gave Sam ideas . . . ideas about using his associates, all members of a gang he grew up with known as the "42s," to seize control of the black policy rackets.

My father was not an educated man. He had only completed the sixth grade before he began hustling on the streets of Chicago. But he had an amazing grasp of simple mathematics. He memorized numbers, adding, subtracting, multiplying in his head, almost like a computer. Press the right button, and out came the right numbers for the right occasion. On the streets it prevented police from catching him with evidence, and it was something he used to figure what he and his friends could do to increase their power and influence in the Chicago underworld if they took over that city's black policy rackets. It would later prove to be a very violent scheme, one that would result in the slaying of one of his and my dearest friends, Leonard Caifano.

Sam's life began in poverty, as did the lives of so many children of immigrants. I don't offer this as an excuse for what he became; it's just a simple fact.

My grandfather, Sam's father, Antonio Giangana, came to this country from Castelvetrano, Sicily, in 1905 at the age of twenty-four and at the height of Chicago's Italian immigrant explosion. His first wife, Antonia DeSimmona, followed him to America a year later in December, 1906, after the birth of their first child, my late aunt Lena.

My grandparents were desperately poor and lived in a tenement in the Patch, a section west of Chicago's Loop on South Aberdeen. My aunts and uncles told me it was a poverty-stricken immigrant ghetto that mixed a bazaarlike trade in Italian food specialties—fruits and vegetables, fish and meats, flour and eggs—with the tragic struggle for survival on dirty streets and squalid living quarters where disease and death were an everyday occurrence. One of those deaths was that of Sam's mother, who died at Mary Thompson Hospital from internal bleeding caused by a miscarriage. Another was that of grandfather's second wife, Mary Leonardi Giancana, who was killed by a car in front of their home as she dashed from the stoop to grab Sam's stepbrother, Charlie, then four years old. Sam was eighteen at the time and, I've learned from relatives and government records, the very active and violent head of a street gang known as the 42s.

Chicago's Bureau of Vital Statistics provided the FBI with a birth certificate reflecting the fact that my father was born May 24, 1908, under the name Gilormo Giangana. I find that interesting because we celebrated my father's birthday on June 15, and the birth and baptismal records I have from the Holy Guardian Angel Church on West Arthington, Chicago, show my father's birth date as June 15, 1908, under the name Momo Salvatore Giancana. As far as Dad was concerned, there was only one name he lived by unless he was in hiding and that name was Sam (Momo) Giancana.

My father never talked about his life in the Patch or of his career with the 42s. Secrecy about his life as a criminal was a way of life for Sam. He wanted respectability for his family, and for as long as I can remember, he hid behind a facade of legitimacy and tried to keep all his children in the dark about his role in the underworld. Never once did he admit to me or my sisters that he was a mafioso. The closest he ever admitted to being engaged in criminal acts was that he was a gambler. That was it. What he did was "business," and it was none of our business what that business was.

What I learned about my father's youth and his treatment of his father I learned from aunts and uncles at family gatherings. What they gave me were glimpses of Sam's past filled in partially by what I've read in records and by the media. The glimpses from my relatives are of a Sam Giancana whom the media and writers and government documents never really understood or had access to.

My grandfather Giancana was an honest, hardworking immigrant street peddler who spoke English with a thick Italian accent. He might have become a legitimately wealthy man through his labor and backbreaking toil if it hadn't been for Sam and the trouble he was constantly getting into.

Grandpa dealt in the Patch, selling watermelons stacked in hay to keep them from bouncing and breaking in the horse-drawn wagon he owned. When he wasn't selling watermelons, he was carrying ice, but never once did Sam help him in his business, nor would Grandpa have wanted his help.

I can still hear the musical strains of his voice as he peddled his wares on Lexington and California streets in the neighborhood where I was born, and later on South Monitor where we moved as Sam's stature and fortunes improved.

Grandpa would walk down the streets and into the narrow alleys hollering to the tenants in the two and three flats above: "Watermelon for sale . . . getta you watermelon now. Watermelon for sale . . . itsa fresh." And when he was carting ice in the very early morning hours, he would call out for his ice customers with the same musical quality in his voice. The ice was always covered by a canvaslike cloth to slow the melting, and Grandpa would chop it up with his icepick with the skill of a cutting machine, carve out the right-sized block, throw a cloth over his shoulder, and hoist it up with his ice clamps to bring it to the apartments of people who needed to cool their iceboxes. Before the sun was very high in the sky, Grandpa was sold out and off peddling some fruits and vegetables.

He supported Sam and all his children that way—eight of them, two by his first marriage and six by his second—and eventually became so well known and respected that he had his own little neighborhood store. But while Grandpa was hustling to scrape pennies and nickels together by hard labor, my father was busy doing his own hustling to make a fast and easy dollar as a street thief and wheelman and enforcer, and his hustling more often than not landed him in jail. Whenever that happened, and

it happened quite frequently, Grandpa would have to gather together what little money he had saved to buy a new wagon or
another horse and pay it out to cover Sam's fines or his bail or
some other debt he had incurred.

I remember one of my aunts telling me that Sam was the apple
of Grandpa's eye, the favorite son who could do no wrong no
matter what others said, no matter how many times he was arrested, and Sam was arrested more than twenty times by the time
he was eighteen years old. No matter.

"There wasn't anything your grandfather wouldn't do for Sam,"
my aunt said. "The police, they would arrest Sam and they would
tell Grandpa Giancana that Sam would stay behind bars until he
got bail money and a lawyer. Your grandfather would get very,
very upset and he'd say: 'My Mooney . . . I gotta getta him outta
the jail. Hesa no should be in jail. Hesa a good boy. I gotta getta
him out.' And get him out he would even if it meant spending the
last dollar left in the house for food."

My father didn't care, my aunt said. He'd get a bawling out
from Grandpa, who sometimes would even hit him on the side of
the face. It didn't faze Sam. As soon as Grandpa turned his back
and went out to work, my father was back on the streets with his
friends, stealing and robbing and burglarizing. My father was arrested under a variety of names: Gincana, Gincanni, Gencani,
Ginncana, and even his true name, Giancana.

The worst of those arrests in those early years was on September 17, 1926, when my father was indicted for murder. The indictment came as a result of my father being the wheelman for
several other members of the 42s as they robbed a middle-aged
barber named William Girard. Sam's friends shot Girard when he
resisted, and Sam drove off before they escaped, but not before
he had been seen by some cab drivers. Girard died the next day,
and Sam and his friends were arrested. Somehow Grandpa raised
the money to free his son, and two weeks later he had to come up
with even more money to pay for the funeral of Sam's step-
mother, Mary Leonardi, when she was killed saving Charlie.

My father was never tried for that murder, nor were his friends.
One of the key witnesses against the teenagers who had killed
Girard was shot and killed, and his wife said she was unable to
identify any of those she had previously identified. Police said the
witness, an Alex Burba, had received calls repeatedly from my

father and his friends, suggesting he shouldn't testify. After Burba died, other witnesses had memory lapses or left town. So my father continued to terrorize businessmen with his friends and fellow members of the 42s, and Grandpa continued to believe that his son was really a good boy who got in trouble because he was in bad company. These same boys of the 42s became the nucleus of the gang with which Sam ruled Chicago long after Al Capone was dead and buried: Sam Battaglia, Felix (Milwaukee Phil) Alderiso, Marshall and Leonard Caifano, William (Willie Potatoes) Daddano, Rocco Potenza, and others later terrorized all of Chicago with Sam, becoming household words in the media and familiar faces in my home before and after I was born.

Grandpa suffered in other ways because of Sam. An FBI background report on my father dated April 11, 1958, quotes from an unidentified law-enforcement memorandum dated July 15, 1946. That report contained a clipping from the *Chicago Tribune* dated September 27, 1928, concerning the bombing:

> . . . for the second time in 11 days of the ice cream plant of A. Giancane, 1510 Taylor St. Following the first bombing of this place, the police surmised that it was in retaliation for the slaying of Edward Divis, west side gangster. Sam Giancane, son of the ice cream manufacturer, and Dominic Caruso, son of the old Giancane's business partner, had been mentioned in the investigation of the Divis murder, but they had never been found.

The police memo quoted by the FBI report went on to say that Sam had been held for two days after the bombing and then released. The police memo also said that Sam "was a known racketeer—that he was a candidate for the leadership of the '42 gang.' The police further indicated that they suspected that Giancana had shot one Tony Russell with a shotgun a short while before and that they were desirous of holding the prisoner until they could locate Russell."

On July 25, 1954, Grandpa Giancana died, just three months after my mother died. It was a traumatic moment for me and for Sam. In spite of the fact that he caused Grandpa so much grief, Sam really loved the old man. To the day he died, Grandpa was and had always been a simple, wonderful, Old World Sicilian immigrant with a deep sense of honor and love of family, of honesty, and of generosity.

With all that generosity and love you would have thought some of the qualities would have rubbed off on my father. They didn't. The only thing Sam inherited was Grandpa's fastidiousness. Where Grandpa was very gentle and kind, Sam was always cool and calculating. Where Grandpa constantly demonstrated his love for his children and grandchildren, Sam demonstrated annoyance at our presence and a coldness that froze our emotions. Where Grandpa gave what he had out of love, Sam gave to buy your silence or salve his conscience.

I recall vividly occasions when Sam would visit Grandpa and give him some money. Grandpa didn't want it, but he wouldn't insult his son even if he didn't like the way he got his money. Without Sam knowing it, Grandpa would wiggle his finger at me or at my sister Bonnie, and one of us would climb up on his lap. He would hold a finger to his lips to indicate silence and that we were sharing a secret as he slipped some of the money Sam had given him into our hands or our coat pockets. He would hug us, love us, and tell us stories, and later I would think, Oh, what a wonderful world this would be for me if only Sam had been like Grandpa.

Grandpa had nothing to do with the rackets or Sam's underworld businesses, but when he was waked it seemed most of Chicago's underworld turned out to pay their respects. Theirs were the names that made politicians dance, hoodlums quake, and businessmen cower: names like Anthony Accardo, Milwaukee Phil Alderiso, Dominic Brancato, Jake (Greasy Thumb) Guzik, Joey Glimco, Ross Prio, and scores of others. Some came to the Cermak Funeral Home in Cicero, Illinois, to pay their respects. Others, many of them politicians and judges as well as hoodlums, avoided police surveillances by visiting and sitting with Sam at a nearby cocktail lounge known as Joe Corngold's.

In death as in life, Grandpa was a man of honor, not in the Mafia sense of being a member of the secret criminal society, but in the literal Italian sense of being a man who had earned respect from his peers because of hard work and his deeds. I am sure that many of those in the mob who attended Grandpa's funeral did so out of deference to my father's station in the underworld. But I also know that many more came to Grandpa's wake and funeral because they respected the man even if he disapproved of them and their occupations.

3

The Mob Santa Claus

Our neighborhood was primarily Italian and while it was relatively poor, it was always clean, not like the Patch. Our home, a red brick three-flat (three-floor) house at 2822 West Lexington Street, was always spotless, a center of activity, a place where my relatives would congregate and where Sam's friends would frequently visit and were made welcome. Several years ago when I visited it to recall those early days, I found that the warm, solidly built home I had lived in was gone, and the neighborhood, now black, was reminiscent of a bombed-out city. Once attractive two- and three-flat homes had been stripped bare, filthy skeletons with smashed windows or burned-out interiors. Mother Cabrini Catholic Church, where I had gone to Mass as a child with my mother, was closed, and the tavern Sam had frequented bore no resemblance to the way it looked.

Gone were the pushcarts, as was the smell of Italian delicacies from almost every household, filling the air with a warm, pleasant ambrosia. In its place was a stench from garbage-strewn alleyways where I had once played in safety, and there was a chill in the air, not from the cold of Chicago's winds, but from the fear that permeated the area. No longer were there chattering women and nodding old men who waved from the building stoops, nor were there laughing, squealing children playing contentedly on the streets. In their place were sullen faces, hate-filled eyes, a sense of hopelessness in a desolate battlefield filled with glass and garbage and broken dreams. I remember thinking, A war has taken place here and the face of poverty is much different, much worse than I remember it to be.

There was a great difference between the poverty of that ravaged neighborhood I had once called home and the Depression poverty I recall living through as a child. What sticks out in my mind was that while everyone was poor, some more than others, there was still a joy, a happiness, a security to the area, never a sense of fear. Many families had a tough time just surviving, but they managed to have food on the table and clothes to wear, even if they were homemade or hand-me-downs. And I never heard people complain of their misfortune or demand government support. People scratched and scraped and clawed their way to survival in those days. How time changes life and the quality of living.

While I had a sense of poverty, of things being scarce at times, I also remember that even though my father was away and not bringing home candy and other goodies like he used to, I never had to wear any hand-me-down clothes, nor did Bonnie, and there was always plenty of good wholesome food on the table. Even at four years of age, I knew that other children in my neighborhood had far less than I did. I was also aware that they had something I didn't have . . . fathers who came home from work, played with them, tucked them in bed, and told them stories. They had a luxury I wanted more than anything else—and it was unattainable.

Mother didn't work. Sam would never have permitted it whether he was home or in prison. Still, there was always money in the house to buy whatever was needed. At four I had no understanding of where the money was coming from.

Later, I understood how we survived so well. Part of the money we lived on came from my mother's parents, Francescantonio DeTolve and his wife, Maria, as well as from her brothers Michael and Joseph. But the bulk of it came from Sam's criminal friends, men who grew up with him as members of the 42s, the teenage street gang, and now were members of the remnant of the old Capone mob.

Our chief benefactor, the man who came each week with an envelope for my mother, was Fat Leonard Caifano, a gregarious, jovial, friendly man whose chief mission in life while Sam was away was to make sure that my father's family was well taken care of.

Fat Leonard was a bookmaker, a loan shark, and an enforcer for my father. They had been close from the younger days when as members of the 42s they shared in the burglaries and protection rackets of the Patch. Fat Leonard was a loyal soldier, who fell over himself to please Sam.

Even at four, I knew that Christmas, 1939, was going to be a bleak holiday with my father away at "college" and no chance of his paying us a surprise visit. Mother told me not to expect much from Santa Claus. It is hard for a child to understand why one year Santa would bring toy pianos and dolls and frilly dresses, and glorious, tall gaily lit Christmas trees and the next year bring nothing.

Before Sam left, he had taken me to see an ice show, they call it the *Ice Capades* now, to watch Sonja Henie. Whenever we went to a show like that, no matter how poor we seemed to be, Sam always managed to have box seats for all of us in the first row at center stage. He had the right connections even then, and he was just starting up the ladder of criminal enterprise.

At that ice show my father promised that one day he would buy me a pair of silver skates so that I could learn to skate like Sonja Henie. But Daddy was gone now, and there would be no ice skates unless . . .

One night I knelt by my bed and asked God to let Santa Claus bring me skates for Christmas so that I could learn to skate well enough to make my father proud of me when he returned home. I just had to have those skates. I even begged my mother to get them for me if Santa Claus forgot. "Please, Momma, that's all I want," I said. "I promise I'll be a very good girl."

My mother smiled weakly at me. "Maybe next year," she said softly.

About a week or so before Christmas, Fat Leonard stopped by the house to bring the envelope and pay his respects to my mother while making sure that everything was all right. Mother, of course, said things were just fine. Not little Toni. I piped up

that I wanted ice skates so I could be a great skater and make my
father proud of me, but that Momma had said Santa Claus might
not bring them and that she couldn't afford them with Daddy
away.

Mother was mortified. At that moment I'm not sure whether
she wanted to hit me or send me to bed, but she kept her composure and said nothing.

I looked at Fat Leonard and just smiled. He was a huge man.
That's how he got his nickname, Fat Leonard—he must have
weighed four hundred pounds. There were rolls of fat everywhere. However, Fat Leonard was an exciting, funny, friendly
man. He could be dull, like so many of those who worked with
Sam, but with me he was always chuckling, kidding me, making
me feel important. And despite his enormous weight, he had a
good-looking face with twinkling eyes and a broad, infectious
smile.

Nothing more was said that day. I just continued praying a lot,
asking God to let Santa Claus come to our house and bring the
skates.

The day before Christmas I looked longingly at the little table-
top Christmas tree with its blue lights and lead ornaments that
Mother had set up. Why, I wondered, did we have such a small
tree this year. Other kids had bigger trees. I'd seen them through
their windows. No matter. As long as Santa Claus brought me the
ice skates.

Early that evening, I remember hearing a "Ho, ho ho," and
seeing a big fat man in a red suit and a white beard come into our
living room and leave several gaily wrapped presents under the
tree. He left as quickly as he had come before I could get up the
courage to leave the hallway by my bedroom.

After he had disappeared, I ran into the living room and as
Mother watched with a smile, I shouted: "You see, Momma, you
see . . . Santa Claus did come . . . he did!"

Without waiting for her to answer, I began examining each of
the gifts under the tree until I found an odd-shaped box. There
was a card tied to it and I recognized my name on it. I shouted
with glee and tore off the wrapping. When I pulled open the top
of the box, there lay a beautiful pair of white figure skates with
gleaming silverlike blades.

I cried and cried and cried. Hysterical tears, tears of joy. "I got my skates! I got my skates!" I shouted at the top of my lungs. "I'm going to be the neatest girl in the neighborhood."

I guess for as long as I live I will never forget that moment or the fact that the man in the red suit was Fat Leonard. He had bought those skates for me. He had rented the red suit and played Santa Claus so that a little girl wouldn't lose her belief in Santa Claus. It is hard even now to realize that Fat Leonard was one of Sam's professional killers, a man who lived by the gun and eventually died by it.

I didn't see Fat Leonard much after my father was finally discharged from prison. Occasionally he and his wife would come to our home with his brother, John Michael Caifano, better known as Marshall Caifano. Both had grown up with my father. Both were uneducated men, barely completing the fifth grade of elementary school. Of the two, Marshall Caifano was the most intelligent and handsome and important. He had grown in importance with my father in the 42s gang and, like Sam, had a long record of arrests. Now serving a twenty-year federal term for racketeering, Marshall had also spent time in jail for burglary, fraud, and larceny, and he had been a suspect in a number of murders. He even won a sort of media recognition by being cited for contempt when he refused to answer questions put to him by the U.S. Senate's labor-rackets committee headed by Senator John McClellan. As the years progressed, the Caifano brothers were among my father's most trusted associates, and Marshall was Dad's most feared enforcer. Fat Leonard might have reached an equally important role in the mob if it wasn't for a shooting that took place in June, 1951. That was when I heard that he had been killed.

No one told me much about how Fat Leonard died, but I learned later he had been killed while trying to kidnap a black policy rackets hoodlum named Theodore Roe whom my father wanted out of the way. Roe had killed Fat Leonard to save himself, and a year later Roe would also be dead on Sam's orders.

The deaths of both men might never have happened if Sam hadn't learned about Chicago's lucrative black policy rackets in Terre Haute federal prison from the talkative black racketeer Edward Jones. From the day that Jones began bragging to him about the profits of his business, my father plotted and schemed with his gang members and his mob superiors to take control of the black policy rackets.

My father's scheming ended with the death of Roe, but on June 21, 1951, Fat Leonard's wake was held, two days before my sixteenth birthday. The funeral parlor was small and it was jammed with people. I remember being sickened by the sweet smell of the huge wreaths of funeral sprays and bouquets. Everything about the wake seemed so grotesque. People were standing in the small room, next to the body in the coffin, chitchatting about Fat Leonard's death, about how Roe would pay for this, about the weather outside, about a hundred other inane things. No one seemed to care about the pain felt by his family. That pain was salved by the envelopes stuffed with cash that were given to his immediate family.

While my father was deeply saddened by Fat Leonard's death, he couldn't show up for the public wake because he was being sought by the police for questioning. Yet after the family and friends had left, Sam managed to slip in unnoticed during the night to pay his respects. They had been very, very close, and Sam was determined to say good-bye to an old and loyal friend in his own way even if he was being hunted.

I had very different memories for which I mourned Fat Leonard's brutal death. For once, I shared something of my father's pain, a pain brought on us all by the ruthlessness of his life with the Mafia.

4

Careful Sam

From the time he first held me in his arms to the moment he walked out the door of our home to go to "college," I idolized my father. I cherished any moment I had with him and I tried hard to please him. More often than not I failed.

I was born Annette Giancana at 3:50 A.M. on June 23, 1935, at Mother Cabrini Memorial Hospital. At that time, Sam and my mother lived at 2822 West Lexington Street, Chicago, Illinois, a predominantly poor but clean ethnic Italian neighborhood.

Annette was a name I hated as I grew older, so later I changed it to Antoinette because it sounded better and had a more sophisticated ring.

Mother was not a physically strong woman, and from the beginning our family physician and friend, Dr. Eugene J. Chesrow, was concerned when he discovered she was pregnant. His fears were justified. Not only did Mother have a difficult pregnancy, but I arrived two months early and weighed in at only three pounds, a weight that in those years was considered dangerous.

The best account of the time of my birth came from one of Sam's closest friends, Chuckie English.

Chuckie English was born Charles Inglese in November, 1914. He was a handsome, rugged man with dark brown eyes and a lean, muscular body; he stood about five feet ten inches, rather tall among the Mafia men who dealt with Sam.

Chuckie was a cherished friend of Sam's. FBI records reflect the fact that he had arrests for extortion and counterfeiting phonograph trademarks, and that in the 1958 Senate labor-rackets hearings he had repeatedly invoked the Fifth Amendment when questioned about extortion, labor racketeering, beatings, and assaults. He was also identified as a Chicago mob soldier in the Valachi trial and in the 1983 hearings of the U.S. Senate Subcommittee on Investigations. Numerous newspaper accounts have identified Chuckie English as a West Side loan shark and labor racketeer—the man who led the mob invasion of the jukebox business. I knew Chuckie from his many visits to the house and from his operation of a business owned by my father, Lormar Distributing Company, which controlled the distribution of jukeboxes and records throughout Illinois. Chuckie was also very active politically and boss of Chicago's Twenty-ninth Ward. He also oversaw the Chicago Mafia's control of a huge Arizona real estate enterprise that was heavily involved in everything from land ownership to the infiltration of that southwestern state's jukebox and restaurant industry.

Until I was out of my teens, I thought of Chuckie and his wife, Laura, as "family." They weren't just friends to Sam or to my mother. They were like uncles and aunts. It was Chuckie and Laura who told me of Sam's reaction to my birth.

The Englishes' bedroom was adjacent to my mother and father's in our three-flat home on West Lexington Street. Chuckie was working for my father with the remnants of the 42s and the Capone gang.

The Englishes had helped my mother during her pregnancy and consoled Sam when he worried over her fragility. Chuckie told me that Sam's greatest fear was that something would happen to my mother and that I might not be born alive. Dr. Chesrow had warned him of such a possibility without telling my mother.

Once my father was sure Mother was safe, and that I was alive and with a good prognosis for survival, he returned to our home in the wee hours of the morning and climbed into the Englishes' bedroom through the window. It was still dark, the air was stifling, and the windows didn't have screens on them. Once inside, they recollected that he sat on the edge of their bed, shouting at them, waking them from a sound sleep, announcing that he had a little girl.

Sam spent hours talking to them about me, his firstborn, and later to Grandpa Antonio Giancana. He talked only briefly to my mother's family, the DeTolves, who had never really liked Sam and opposed his marriage to my mother.

It wasn't long after I came home with Momma from the hospital that I took ill, came down with pneumonia. The doctors said I had to have mother's milk to survive, and Momma was unable to supply it.

"Sam turned the world upside down to get you the milk you had to have," Chuckie told me. He used friends, he pulled strings, he used the political connections of friends, and finally he acquired enough clout to move the Chicago Board of Health to act to provide the necessary milk at the city's expense.

I was a little more than four years old when Sam decided the family needed a vacation in Rhinelander, Wisconsin. Though my memories of that time are somewhat fuzzy, pictures from family albums and recollections of close relatives project an image of Sam as a handsome, slim, street-wise hustler with a full head of hair, carefully tailored clothes, and a flashy car.

Wherever Sam went, he went first-class. Our car was an expensive, convertible roadster, popular in that era of Chicago gangsterism and Sam's proudest possession. He kept the car so polished that its chrome running boards sparkled and you could see your reflection in the door. There was, in fact, nothing subdued about Sam's appearance and demeanor. He was clearly a young man moving upstairs fast and he wasn't afraid to let the world know it.

When we went to Rhinelander, no expense was spared. We stayed at a luxurious hotel, where we had a suite of rooms, including separate bedrooms for Momma and Dad and for Bonnie and me, together with separate baths and a sitting-living room complete with a fully stocked bar.

It turned out to be a wonderful time, with Sam and Momma taking me shopping, swimming together at an almost private beach, and picnicking, something I had never done before. It was a happy time and I tried my damnedest to please.

Life seemed so free and easy that I was totally unaware of any danger that might be present. Of course, at that age I knew nothing of Sam's operating a still, or being involved in robberies, or of any criminal activity of any kind.

Danger was the furthest thing from my mind when late one Saturday morning I heard a knock at the door of our suite. Momma and Dad were still in their bedroom and Bonnie was playing in the playpen in our bedroom. There was a second knock followed by a man's voice on the other side of the door announcing rather cheerfully, "Breakfast is served."

Without further thought, I went straight to the door, opened it, and let the man wheel the table of food into the main sitting room. As the waiter set the table, Sam came into the room from his bedroom. For an instant, he turned white as a sheet. He ducked back into his room and returned with my mother to pay the waiter.

Almost before the door had closed on the waiter, Sam was raging.

"Never, never open the door to a stranger again!" he shouted. He upended me and gave me a thorough spanking to bring the lesson home. Then he stalked off without eating, mumbling something about how I was going to "get us all killed one day."

I, of course, didn't realize until years later that pretending to be room service was a technique often used by professional killers to get at their victims in hotels or motels. I also didn't understand that men like my father who work in an organized criminal atmosphere live constantly with the fear that someday, somewhere, someone is going to try to kill them. So many in the old Al Capone mob had been killed receiving flowers, eating in restaurants, answering doors without checking first who was in the hallway or on the front stoop.

Sam had learned from the example set by Anthony Accardo. Accardo was suspected by the FBI and the Chicago police of having a role in the St. Valentine's Day massacre in 1929, when seven members of the rival Dion O'Banion gang were machine-gunned in a Chicago warehouse by members of the Capone gang. One of the suspected killers was Jack (Machinegun) McGurn, who was known as Vincenzo DeMora when Sam was a member of the 42s. DeMora was one of those who had brought Sam into the Capone gang because of his talents as a wheelman and his reputation for keeping cool under pressure. Seven years after that

massacre on St. Valentine's Day DeMora was killed in a public
bowling alley by men armed with machine guns, who after they
were through left a comic valentine on his body.

It was this kind of pressure, the subconscious knowledge that
your best friend, perhaps even a relative, might be the one sent
to kill you, that prompted supercaution on my father's part. His
rule of thumb, his formula for survival in the early years, was:
Trust no one, take no chances. Time and again as my life progressed, I had glimpses of that caution, that fear when I was
with him.

Our homes on West Lexington and, later, in Oak Park were
places where Sam's associates of years past and present frequently
congregated. Men like Fat Leonard and his brother, Marshall
Caifano, Sam DeStefano, Sam (Teets) Battaglia, Albert (Obie)
Frabotta, Joey Glimco, or Paul (The Waiter) Ricca, all former
members of the 42s, the Capone gang, or the expanded Chicago
mob, were visitors and close friends of my father's. Friends or
not, Sam never greeted them at the door himself, and he never
permitted me to answer the door when they knocked.

That left a lasting impression on me as a child. There were so
many precautions Sam took at home and away from home.
Momma, no matter how weak or ill she might be, always had to
descend the stairs of our two-flats or three-flats and check on the
caller through a speakerphone before opening the door.

I recall her peeking out through the window curtains to see if
she recognized who it was. Even when she knew the visitor, she
would still crack the door slightly to get a better view before letting the person in. If it was someone she didn't recognize, she
would get the name through the speakerphone, asking Sam if he
knew the individual and if he wanted to speak or meet with him.
If Sam said no, Momma would simply tell the caller Sam wasn't at
home. Then she would laboriously climb those stairs back to our
flat. By the time she reached the top floor, she would be out of
breath and her heart pounding a mile a minute. It made me so
angry with my father when I saw her like that while he sat non-
chalantly by the window, apparently unconcerned about her
physical state, looking out, scanning the neighborhood, trying to
spot something or someone strange to the area.

Sam and Momma were equally careful about telephone calls.

They were always screened by Momma. Sam would never answer the phone, only my mother. She would ask who it was, repeat the name loud enough for him to hear, and watch as he nodded his head yes or no, indicating he would or wouldn't talk to the caller.

Caution seemed to prevail wherever we were. Even as a small child I noticed that before entering a restaurant or any other public place, Sam would always drive around the block at least once or twice to survey the area, see if he saw anything out of the ordinary. Once satisfied things were in order, he would lead us inside, scanning the entire eating area, searching out faces he might recognize. If he saw somebody he knew and wanted to acknowledge him, he would nod or have the waiter discreetly carry a message or a drink to the proper table. And when we sat down, Sam would never allow us to be near a window, and he insisted that his seat be situated so that his back was to the wall and he could have a clear view of the entrance.

My father's suspicions, his paranoia about strangers extended even to the friends that I or my sisters, Bonnie and later Francine, had. It was very difficult for me, for any of us to have real friends because of Sam's demands for privacy. Everyone I knew was carefully screened. I learned very quickly in life that kids from our neighborhood, whether on Lexington Street, or later on South Monitor, or in the suburbs of Oak Park, were not to be allowed inside the house unless they had been personally checked out and okayed by Sam.

I suppose he didn't want kids around who might blabber about the expensive furniture, chinaware, silver, or crystal. Too much talk about how we lived or what we had might lead tax agents to our door and that was the last thing Sam wanted . . . trouble from tax agents. Al Capone was caught by tax agents, and my father learned from that.

Whatever the reason, it was very embarrassing for me and my sisters. It appeared to us that Sam had a complete résumé on every youngster and his or her parents that I brought to the house. He knew about their fathers and what they did for a living; about their mothers and how they acted; about their families and the friends they associated with. If he decided for some reason that he disapproved of some child, either because of parents or ethnic background—and Sam had prejudices against everything from blacks and Jews to Greeks and Hispanics—I not only couldn't have that child to my home, I couldn't be seen with him or her.

I was always amazed at how much Sam knew about my friends and their families. I learned later that he had his criminal associates gather information like they were private detectives, and this information was frighteningly accurate. He would tell my mother that the father of one child was an alcoholic or a petty thief, or that my friend's mother was sleeping around with other men. He seemed to know how often they breathed or had sex, or when they came home or ate or how much money they had. They didn't know it, but they had no privacy.

I was isolated, like some fairy-tale princess, from people around me. It was almost as though if they weren't "family," either my natural family or Sam's "crime family," they weren't acceptable. As a result, for many years until I was a senior in high school and later in college, I had no really close friends. I hated that kind of life, but until I was older I didn't dare question his rule.

My failures in maintaining proper security at home and in the selection of friends weren't the only ways in which I didn't please Sam when I was a young child. One of my most serious mistakes took place when I was very young and trying to please him by helping Momma clean house.

Sam was a collector of antiques, particularly bisque and porcelain figures. He became such an avid collector that after he died, his collection of Meissen porcelains, Dresden china, Venetian mirrors, rare oil paintings, and antique music boxes were sold at auction at the Chicago Art Galleries in June, 1976. This event was the talk of the town and drew art lovers from throughout the Midwest as well as the East.

Sam's collecting had begun back on West Lexington Street before he went to jail. It continued up to the year he died. He loved going antiquing, and it was during his travels, first around the Chicago area and later through the capitals and off-the-beaten-track towns of the United States, Europe, and Central America, that he developed an almost fanatical bug for rummaging through shops. As he grew older, long after he was paroled from prison on December 14, 1942, he became an art collector.

He would walk into a store, see a painting he admired or a figurine that had classical lines, and he would announce: "I gotta have this painting . . . it looks great."

In the beginning he might not have understood the paintings he admired. They just looked great. They reached something inside of him . . . triggered a hidden emotion. Once that trigger was pulled, Sam would move heaven and earth to acquire the painting or figurine or art work that attracted and moved him so deeply.

I think my father, with the right education and study, could have been a connoisseur of art. When I started going to Ladywood School for Girls, an expensive Catholic finishing school for young women in Indianapolis, Indiana, Sam became more conscious of the finer things in art and literature, in chinaware and bisqueware. He became almost obsessed with the need for understanding different forms of culture. It was like a rebirth for him . . . a new being.

Sam went through stages in the development of his art tastes, particularly in paintings. Early on he liked realistic paintings of people and things and places he could identify. Toward the end of his life he favored the contemporary, the cubistic, the abstract.

There was one phase in particular that I remember vividly every time I walk through my own apartment. On my walls are several paintings of children with tears in their eyes that he acquired in Mexico. These paintings affected him deeply because of the pain and sadness they reflected, the same pain and sadness he saw in the eyes of children whenever he traveled in Mexico. When I was with him once in Cuernavaca, a rather large Mexican town popular with wealthy tourists and where the people were either very rich or lived in poverty, Sam would drive into the city and throw out bags full of pesos to the poor children and adults lining the streets, begging and staring sullenly at the rich gringos.

"How the hell can people live that way?" he would ask. "Why don't they help themselves . . . why doesn't their government help them? Those kids are starving, and the parents just stand around, letting them beg. They should be out hustling . . . not the kids." He would smile as he watched them scramble for the money and stuff it in their pockets.

Despite these moments of compassion, Sam could demonstrate

a different side to his character when he was being served a sumptuous meal amid the lavish surroundings of his own wealth. As he savored a particular dish that only the very rich could afford, he would smirk suddenly and say, "I wonder what the poor people are eating tonight."

Once the meal was over, Sam would go up to his room and look through his telescope into the valley where the poor people lived. He would sit for hours watching them.

While Sam saw the beauty, the grace, the delicacy of the figurines and china that he sought out in antique shops, he also thought of them as investments. They were articles he could give to his children so that they could sell them and never have to pay taxes if they played their cards right. I remember his saying one evening, as he looked at his growing collection, that one day they would all be very valuable and we would all benefit from them.

His fine-arts collection also gave him something no one else in Chicago's Mafia had, a touch of class, of culture. It set him apart from the rest of the thugs.

One of the figurines Sam treasured the most in those early days on West Lexington Street was that of a girl holding her skirt . . . a blue skirt. It was a very expensive figurine he had found in an antique shop. It stood on a register, which would normally regulate the air flow but was covered and closed off to accommodate the figurine.

It was late in the morning and Momma was busy doing something in the kitchen when I got the notion to show her that I knew how to dust and that I could be a real helper. I figured if I helped her and did a good job she would tell Sam and he would be proud of me.

So I began cleaning the entire room, just as she had done many times. Everything went super until I reached the register where the figurine stood. As I dusted it, it slipped from its perch and fell to the floor, breaking into a million pieces.

Momma came running into the room. She hardly got the words "Oh, my God" out of her mouth before Sam arrived behind her. He looked at the pieces of porcelain on the floor, then at the register, and then at me.

Without a word, Sam took off his belt and as I started to run, he scooped me up from the floor, turned me over his knee, and spanked me with the belt until there were red welts on my bottom.

As I sobbed uncontrollably, trying to tell my mother that it was an accident, that I was just trying to help, she turned on me in surprising anger, saying coldly, "Don't touch anything, you hear! Don't touch *anything* without asking." Sam, once he had finished beating me stormed out of the house without saying another word.

His compassion, though displayed liberally to the stricken children of Cuernavaca, was never extended to his own. A broken figurine seemed to mean more to him than a broken child.

5

Sweet Angeline

My mother was the only person in the world whom my father truly cherished and loved.

They say opposites attract. That was certainly true of Sam Giancana and Angeline DeTolve. No two people could have been more different when they met.

Sam, of course, was a three-star hellion, a street tough whose reputation as a leader of the 42s was well known both to the "good" families and to those whose values were somewhat shady. He was known as a thief, a boy who taunted shopkeepers, challenged the police, was a suspect in murders, and ran around with loose girls. The values of a strict Catholic upbringing were traditional among most immigrant Italians in the Patch. They held little meaning for Sam, who by the age of eighteen had probably violated all the Ten Commandments, not to mention the laws of society.

Mother, on the other hand, came from a family steeped in the traditions of the Catholic Church. Grandma Maria and Grandpa Francescantonio DeTolve came from a southern Italian region known as Basilicata. Grandma DeTolve was an orphan and had been raised in a convent in Italy before she came to the United States. It was in the convent where she learned embroidery, and it was probably from that background and her deep religious convictions that she provided each of her children with sheets embroidered with little red crosses.

My mother was one of three daughters. Her sisters' names were Rose and Anna. The DeTolves also had four sons, Joseph, Andrew, Michael, and Anthony. All were raised in the strict traditions of the Church and the old Italian ways. Mother and her sisters, until they were fourteen, were educated at Our Lady of Pompeii parochial school by nuns who taught them to be devoted practitioners of the faith.

As a young girl, Momma was very carefully watched over by her mother. Careful control of the movements, associations, and growth of their daughters was a DeTolve resolve. They were a poor but proud family who wanted to provide a future for their children. Their sons were also watched carefully, although the family strings were a bit looser. In any event, Grandpa DeTolve was extra careful not to allow his sons to become involved or mixed up with street gangs such as the 42s, or with any of their members.

When Grandpa DeTolve came to this country, he worked as a laborer in the construction industry, carefully saving his money to become a man of substance, a man of property. Among the construction projects he worked on was the Chicago and North Western Railway Station. On Saturdays and Sundays, he sold balloons to children in an area outside the Patch. It was from this side occupation that he became known as the "balloon grandpa." It was also from this extra job that Grandpa DeTolve earned considerable sums of money, enough to buy a twelve-flat apartment house, which he maintained and from which he earned sufficient funds to educate his family and help his sons get into legitimate business ventures.

In her youth my mother was an outstanding athlete. She played softball, a not-very-common sport for young women of her time, and she was a remarkable swimmer. She became so good, in fact, that she was judged the top swimmer for her age group in Chicago, swimming across and back a major lake to win that distinction. Then, quite suddenly, her athletic prowess came to an end. Doctors discovered Mother had rheumatic fever, a disease that caused damage to her heart and left her with a handicap that frequently resulted in illness and hospitalization and restricted her ability to raise her own children. Despite these limitations, despite the danger of too much physical exertion, which caused her to become bedridden, my mother managed to keep a spotless house.

I remember quite clearly watching Momma, sick and weak as she was, spend hours scrubbing the kitchen floor, the windows, the cabinets, the stove, and the refrigerator. When she was through in the kitchen, she moved on to another room, scrupulously cleaning every nook and cranny until everything sparkled.

When she wasn't cleaning, she was cooking, preparing full-course meals, beginning with homemade soups and appetizers, on to a wide variety of Italian dishes and salads, and finishing off with desserts of fresh homemade pies. Her meals were prepared for the family, five of us after Francine was born, but somehow when Sam decided to bring friends to dinner, and that was quite often, Momma managed to stretch what she had and still satisfy everyone's appetite.

More often than not, Momma was too exhausted to keep an eye on her children. Frequently I was sick, and more often I was in mischief. Francine had serious vision problems requiring doctors and special education. Only Bonnie was healthy and probably the most obedient of all of us. The net result was that I was farmed out to aunts and uncles so that Momma could rest before Francine was born, and then I was sent to parochial boarding schools when I became of school age. The same was true of my sisters as they grew older. Momma did what she could, but frequently there were days when she needed rest, and relatives picked up the slack to ease her burden by babysitting one or more of us at their homes.

Sam first met my mother before he began serving his first major jail sentence on March 26, 1929, at Joliet State Penitentiary. He had been arrested by the Chicago police under the name of Sam Gincanni. The charge was attempted burglary, but by the time he pleaded guilty, his name had been changed to Sam Gincana.

This was not the first time he had been arrested. There had of course been the charge of murder mentioned earlier. He was indicted by a grand jury for that crime on September 17, 1926, but was never tried because of the murder or disappearance of or loss of memory by key witnesses. Police and FBI criminal records show that as a result of fingerprint identifications, my father was arrested under the name of Gencani on September 25, 1925. That charge was auto theft and he was sentenced to thirty days in the Chicago House of Correction. He was just seventeen. In January, 1926, he was fined ten dollars for motor-vehicle larceny, and in June, 1927, was found not guilty on another larceny charge. In January and March, 1928, Sam was found guilty and fined on two disorderly-conduct charges. The year 1929 appears to have been his most eventful. On February 15, he was accused of burglary and larceny, and five days later he was arrested again on charges of robbery. This was followed by a charge on March 12 of attempted robbery, which resulted in a jail sentence.

It was this damning record of arrests and criminal activity that prompted Illinois Judge John J. Sullivan to sentence Sam to a term of one to five years in the toughest prison in Illinois, a penitentiary that took in veteran criminals who were not considered candidates for rehabilitation. Sam served forty-five months inside Joliet, where some of Chicago's most notorious criminals served their time.

Sam's criminal life was like a red flag in the face of an angry bull for a man like Grandpa DeTolve. Sam was the epitome of the street tough the DeTolves abhorred. He drove a sporty car, wore expensive and typical gangster-style clothes, including wide-brimmed hats. To the young women of the Patch, men like that were exciting; they represented an adventurous flight from the parental discipline, poverty, and loneliness of their uneventful lives. For my mother he had a strange fascination when he was introduced to her at a soda fountain.

Momma talked to him on occasion when she was in the company of other girls. She even thought he was attractive and quite polite. But even the mention of his name at home drew a torrent of admonitions from her parents to steer a different course from his. Momma tried, but my father was persistent. He had already fallen for her. She was respectable, from a fine family, a young lady quite different from the girls he was used to being with. I suppose her aloofness and her family's strenuous opposition to him intrigued him even more. However, before he could really campaign for her attention, he went to jail.

Between the time Sam went to prison and the time he returned to the Patch, my mother had met a young man my family remembers only as Solly, and she had become engaged. Solly, it turned out, was one of Chicago's biggest jewel thieves. I'm not sure that the DeTolves or my mother really knew that until later . . . after Solly was killed on New Year's Eve on an icy pavement in an automobile accident.

Emotionally my mother almost became a cripple. She saw no one, practically became a recluse in her home, and kept Solly's picture and mementoes of their romance with her wherever she was. It was during this period in 1933 that my father was freed from prison and when he learned of my mother's sorrow, began making low-key attempts to see her. Out of her loneliness, I was told by relatives, out of a need for some companionship and understanding from someone she knew outside the family, at first she agreed to see Sam and then go out with him under the proddings of friends of his whom she knew.

From the beginning Grandpa DeTolve threw every roadblock he could in the path of the budding romance. He made it abundantly clear to Sam that he didn't like him and didn't want him to go out with my mother. That didn't deter Sam and, in a way, it made Mother all the more rebellious.

After all, Mother was a beautiful twenty-four-year-old woman with as perfect a figure as one could ask for. Despite her fragile health caused by the rheumatic fever, she still swam, she danced and engaged in many strenuous activities, all designed to maintain her figure and rebuild her strength. Many boys wanted to date her, but none dared to chance a confrontation with a man like Sam.

Because of Grandpa DeTolve's strenuous opposition, many of the dates between my mother and father took place clandestinely at the homes of her girl friends. They all knew and liked Sam, and they all did their best to help the romance flourish. In the meantime, Sam stayed out of trouble with the police, although he continued his criminal activities in gambling and making illegal alcohol.

My aunts and uncles told me that their romance followed a rocky course for months with opposition from mother's family causing the most problems. But by late July, 1933, Grandpa De-Tolve agreed to the marriage, and the wedding took place in church on September 23, 1933. By Mafia standards it was a very modest wedding. Mother had a lovely but not particularly expensive white gown, a small wedding party, and a traditional Catholic ceremony. The costs of the wedding, which family members called a "peanut wedding" because of its size, and the reception at the DeTolve family home on Polk Street were borne by my aunt Rose DeTolve and her brother Joseph. To the bitter end, my grandparents refused to help with the wedding, even though they knew it was inevitable.

From the day I understood what love was as a child, I knew there was a special relationship, a warmth between my parents that I didn't share, that only they felt, and I resented it. I suppose that resentment was the result of my being sent away to religious boarding schools, but even before then I had a sense of being left out.

There was one thing I did share with them, and that is what I call the "last supper syndrome." I really became aware of it as a teenager, but when I look back, I realize it was there whenever Sam was home and not in prison.

As I think of those moments, it's as if my mother were the wife of a man who was totally involved in combat. Now he was coming home from the fighting, and there she was, looking at him with love and fear in her eyes, cheerfully serving him a sumptuous meal, yet at the same time realizing that when he walked out the door he might never return.

Every evening that he came home was like the triumphant return of the warrior with his family gathered around him. Each of his daughters—I, when I wasn't at school, Bonnie, and later my youngest sister, Francine—dressed up to greet him and eat with him. After dinner he would dutifully spend a few moments with us, then go to his room, shower, change his clothes, kiss Mother, and leave—to spend the wee hours of the nights in the criminal field of combat, directing the operation of bookies, loan sharks, vice rackets, garbage and jukebox rackets, and in endless meetings with other leaders in the mob.

In the period shortly after the birth of Francine, Sam would spend extra time with her. Francine was very special. Like me, she had been born prematurely and weighed less than three pounds. She was very frail and her eyesight was very bad . . . so bad, in fact, that she had to have special education. I found it rather amusing when reading FBI surveillance documents to find that the FBI reported that Francine was a retarded child. Nothing could have been further from the truth. Francine simply had bad eyesight requiring special training that average parochial and public schools were unable to provide.

Because of this handicap and because of the fear in her early years that she might die, Francine was babied and coddled by Sam. Yet even the time he spent with her was limited. Running a mob was never an eight-hour day; it was less his business than his life.

For most of my parents' married life there was never another woman for Sam. I say for most of their married life because in later years, just before her death, Momma told me she knew Sam was having an affair with another woman, a blonde whom she never identified and whose identity I was never able to discover. But that took place only toward the very end of their married life, and the blonde probably represented Sam's need as a mafioso to have a girl friend just as his peers did.

For members of the Chicago Mafia, having girl friends was a mark of manliness, a badge of honor. Those who didn't were considered strange, men who couldn't be trusted. Very few of Sam's associates didn't have girl friends on the side. But I must say that the ones whom I knew had them were very discreet for the most part. They didn't flaunt their relationships; they made an effort not to embarrass their wives and children. Sam was like that. Momma discovered the relationship only by accident when she overheard the wives of several of his mob friends talking about it at a charity affair.

Momma never said a word to me about it until the day she died in West Palm Beach, Florida, on April 23, 1954, and then she said it in anger because I had talked about bleaching my hair to blond.

"Only tramps have blond hair," she shouted, "like that woman your father's running around with."

A year earlier Mother had had to enter a hospital in Chicago for a hysterectomy. Sam was beside himself with worry about her.

From the moment she entered the hospital, he went to extraordinary lengths to be by her side, to comfort her. As often as possible, he sat with her for hours at a time, holding her hand, speaking words of endearment, kissing her forehead, puffing up her pillows to ensure her comfort. In those moments he showed a deeper love and concern than I had ever seen.

Sam stayed with her day and night, and woe unto the nurse or doctor who suggested that he was there past visiting hours. Her room was always filled with fresh roses at the hospital and when she returned home. He went to Saks Fifth Avenue and instead of buying one or two lovely negligees, he brought back three huge boxes of the most expensive and beautiful negligees and peignoirs I had ever seen. For weeks afterward he showered her with all kinds of gifts . . . beautiful clothes, gorgeous jewels, religious artifacts. It was as if he had become transformed.

Before she entered surgery he was very comforting, very supportive, and for the first time I could remember, he prayed aloud for her safety in surgery. After the surgery he was extraordinarily attentive and sympathetic over her slightest sign of discomfort.

Sam had a terrible fear that Mother would die during surgery. It was then he realized and expressed openly just how much he cared for her and needed her. For months afterward he stayed home with Momma more than he had in ages, and then as quickly as his attention to her began, it faded as he returned to the pressing needs of the mob he directed and to his girl friend.

As I look back on that period, I think what a hypocrite he was, and yet I am just as certain that he loved my mother as he loved no other woman, and he suffered deeply over her death for a long, long time.

6

Sam and the Church

For most Mafia families, growing up in the Catholic Church is part of a tradition that began in the Old Country, in Sicily, and was brought to Chicago and other regions of America during the great migration of Italians in the late 1800s. However, it wasn't that way for me and my sisters. Tradition had nothing to do with it. Sam, even though a feared criminal, wanted religious training, discipline, and values for all of us . . . and at times he even practiced some of those values himself for the sake of my mother. But it wasn't done out of any sense of tradition.

Catholicism wasn't something that Sam grew up with. It was something he grew into, and that in itself is strange. Almost every so-called mafioso I ever met—from Paul (The Waiter) Ricca to Jackie (The Lackey) Cerone—grew up in families that practiced Catholicism, had a sense of religion and faith. That the sons had strayed to become criminals and mafiosi was not so strange in a poverty-stricken environment. This was to some degree traditional. The Church had kept its silence about the Mafia in Sicily for centuries until Pope John Paul II called on Sicilians to "isolate and destroy" the Mafia, while the Archbishop of Palermo, Salvatore Cardinal Pappalardo, threatened to withhold absolution and other sacraments from suspected mafiosi.

In Sam's case his father, Antonio, never attended church nor did he require his sons to. It wasn't that Grandpa Giancana was against religion. He simply didn't make time for it. He was too busy trying to hustle a buck with his pushcarts seven days a week, and when he wasn't working, he was romancing women, both those he married and those he didn't.

So the values of the Church and of God were lost on Sam until he met my mother, a deeply religious woman from a deeply religious family. Even as a child, Mother went to church, to Mass, daily to pray. She prayed for a lot of things . . . for her own forgiveness and whatever sins she thought she might have committed, for her mother and father and her brothers and sisters. And when she married Sam, she went to Mass daily to pray for him, for his deliverance, for his safety, for forgiveness for him and for her children. That is not untypical of the wives of the older mafiosi. For centuries they have been in church praying for their sinning husbands.

It was because of Mother that Sam showed more than just a tolerance of religion. He showed, however silently, within the confines of his family and his home a sense of religious values that he wanted his daughters to learn and to follow. Some of us tried. In the end I failed.

When courting my mother, Sam was smart enough to realize that the DeTolves would not permit their daughter to marry a heathen. She had been schooled all her young life as a Catholic, and it was a certainty that Angeline DeTolve was not going to be married or bear children outside the Church. If Sam wanted Angeline badly enough, he would have to conform, or at least compromise. And he did. My father and mother were married in a traditional Roman Catholic ceremony and for a time Sam went to Mass with her. For a time.

By the time I was old enough to attend church with Mother, Sam had long since changed his attendance habits. He was down to going to church twice a year, at Christmas and at Easter. There were exceptions—funerals of mob friends and relatives, or weddings—but that was pretty much it. But when he did go, he looked elegant!

I remember particularly his attending Mass with mother and Bonnie and me in Florida, at St. Patrick's in Miami Beach, where Bonnie was later married. Whenever he went, he looked like someone in a *Fortune* 500 executive photograph. A hat, always a hat, perhaps a fedora, sometimes a fashionable and expensive straw hat. Tailored suits and white shirts with carefully selected ties. And cuff links, solid gold, or with star sapphires or black onyx, and, later, as the money flowed more easily, cuff links with his initials in diamonds. Then there were his shoes, beautiful, expensive shoes, brightly polished so that you could see your reflection in them unless they were white and then they were spotlessly white. He could have been mistaken for the president of General Motors. Funny. The corporation he headed probably had bigger annual profits than General Motors and they were tax-free . . . at least no one paid taxes on them.

Inside the church he was flawless in following the Mass, as if he had done it every day of his life. He would kneel and pray at the proper moments, reciting the "Our Father" prayer, the Apostles' Creed, and Latin verses, and I remember wondering how he did it.

I think my father believed in God. He violated all the rules of the Church and of God. He ordered murders, he lied, he cheated, he jumped into bed with more women than I can count, but still I know he believed.

Two incidents come to mind. The first was when my mother went into the hospital for a hysterectomy. While she was in surgery I vividly remember seeing him on his knees in a chapel, tears streaming down his face, hands clasped together, praying for her safety.

The second incident involved my sister Francine, who from the moment of her birth had been courted by death. She was so small when she was born that her eyes were damaged, and there was a time that we all thought, the doctors thought, that she would become legally blind.

In 1954, not long after my mother's death, I had been making novenas at St. Jude's on Ashland Avenue in Chicago. The church was also a Dominican Fathers' shrine to Saint Jude, the patron saint of lost causes, and at a special time of the year, relics of Saint Jude were taken out of the sacristy and placed on the afflicted portion of a believer's body.

Sam, though distraught over my mother's death, knew I was

making novenas for her at St. Jude's. I told him about the special power of the relics.

Sam's eyes were misty as he looked at me and listened. "The relics . . . they bring them out this week," I said. "Maybe . . . if I bring Frannie . . . maybe the power of Saint Jude will help restore her sight."

To my complete surprise, Sam nodded in agreement. "Maybe. Maybe you're right," he said. "Go ahead and take her."

And I did. Sam stood in the back of the church watching the ceremony, watching them place the relics on Francine's closed eyes, praying over her. Then it was over, and Francine returned home, and though her eyes remained slightly crossed, her vision improved gradually from that point on. Now she no longer requires thick eyeglasses or lives with the threat of an eye operation that might leave her blind. She sees through contact lenses. Was it a miracle, a spiritual cure? I like to think so, and I know Sam was convinced it helped.

Publicly Sam rarely showed an interest in the Church. That might have been construed as a sign of weakness by his underlings, the men whom he ordered to eliminate others. Yet there were other signs of his belief, signs that I grew up with as a child and knew even as Mother did, a strange paradox.

From the time I was old enough to kneel and say my prayers at bedside, I can remember my father coming home at night, when he wasn't in prison, sitting at the table, bowing his head, and clasping his hands in prayer as my mother said grace over each meal. It was not something that only my mother did; Sam wanted her to do it and he participated. Why, as head of the household, he did not say grace himself, I can only surmise. Perhaps it was because of embarrassment. Perhaps he knew his criminal acts defiled God. But he did require that grace be said before anyone touched a morsel of food. He also followed other Church traditions. No meat was to be eaten on Fridays, or on Christmas Eve, or on Good Friday. And each of his daughters was to get the best possible training in Catholic parochial schools that was available, whether we liked it or not. I'm not certain whether that was simply to shelter us from recurrent press reports of his criminal activity or to provide us with the religious background and education that he lacked. Dad had never had the luxury of attending a parochial school.

I know that in my early, formative years, I was difficult for my mother to handle. But I think now that was only part of the reason for sending me off to a Catholic boarding school, first as a child of five and later as a teenager. It became apparent later that Sam wanted a nun in his family. If there could be no priest, a nun would be just fine. And I was to be that nun.

My first inkling that Catholic boarding school was to become a way of life for me came in September, 1940, while Sam was serving time in federal prison for bootlegging. One Sunday afternoon I walked into my room and saw my mother sewing name tapes on my clothes, my towels, my linen, everything I owned, and packing them into a suitcase on the top of my bed.

"What are you doing, Momma?" I asked.

"I'm getting your things ready for school," she answered softly.

I looked at the clothes she was packing and they looked so strange. I remember thinking, Those aren't my clothes; I don't wear clothes like that. Instead of gay, frilly dresses, there were blue dresses with crisp white collars, the uniforms of the parochial school and convent where I was being sent.

I remember stepping from the car belonging to my uncle Michael DeTolve and looking up at an ominous, massive building and a convent with a chapel. Suddenly I was frightened, overwhelmed by the size of it all. The school was of course very neat. The grounds were well kept, with pretty flowers and shrubs and green, manicured lawns, but the school was frightening nonetheless, and even more so when I saw Mother hand my suitcase to a nun as we stood in the huge reception room.

Mother knelt to hug and kiss me good-bye. At that moment, I went berserk. I screamed and cried. I ranted and raved. I stamped my feet on the floor in a rage and screamed out at the top of my lungs.

"I won't stay here . . . you can't make me stay here!" I shouted. "I won't . . . I won't! You can't make me!" Then I kicked the nun, hard, in the shins. Startled, she cried out in pain and released my hand, and I ran toward my mother who was walking toward the front door.

"Momma . . . Momma . . . please don't leave me! Please," I cried, holding onto her skirt.

Firmly she pulled my hand away, shaking her head. "It's for the best, Annette," she said. "You'll be home again soon, you'll see. Be a good girl . . . be a good girl for Momma."

I had a difficult time at Resurrection Academy. In the beginning I hated it. I hated my mother for leaving me. I hated my father for encouraging her to send me there while he was away at "college." I hated the nuns, and I hated the discipline and regimen they forced us to live by.

I lived in a bare, drab dormitory that might have qualified as an army barracks were it not for the crosses with the Christ image hanging over each of the fifteen beds.

The beds were small, not big, soft, roomy beds with headboards like those at home. They were more like cots lined up neatly in a row. Next to each bed was a very small bureau, and outside in the hall was a little locker-type closet where we hung our clothes. Each day we were required to wear blue uniforms with stiff white collars and white cuffs, long white stockings, and black shoes that we had to shine each day. Sunday the dress routine changed only slightly. We wore spotless white uniforms because it was a day we all had to look pure, like little angels for the Lord.

School began very early in the morning with a 7:00 A.M. Mass. To be ready for that service, we were awakened at six. We had to wash, dress carefully, make our beds, and put away our nightclothes neatly. Just before marching off to Mass, we were required to stand in sections outside our room while the nuns walked slowly around us and inspected us, checking our hands, our faces, behind and inside our ears. Sometimes a student would have a little dirt behind her ears or on her hand. The nun would order the offending girl to hold out her hand and down came the ruler. We would all wince even before the sound of the ruler cracking down on her knuckles echoed in the hallway.

After Mass in chapel, we were marched to the academy's dining hall for a rather sparse and always hurried breakfast. Classes began promptly at 9:00 A.M., where we remained, except for a short luncheon break, until 5:00 P.M.

I did not adjust at all well to the routine. Having been thoroughly spoiled at home, I had no idea what discipline really was. I was lonely and I was afraid, and except for rare weekends once each month, I never saw my mother or sisters.

From the beginning, I had a problem: I wet my bed. I had never done that at home, but now at school I did. The nuns had a quick solution for such nonsense. Every night, while other children watched, I would have to take off my sheet, carry it to the laundry room, wash it by hand in a tub, and rinse it out while one of the nuns watched sternly. I would then have to hang it up to dry over the radiator. Later in the night, a nun would return, wake me up again, take me back to the laundry to get my sheet, and then make me make my bed.

Everyone in the dormitory made fun of me, taunting me. If it weren't for one particularly compassionate nun, Sister Roberta, I'm not sure I would have made it through those early years. Sister Roberta had soft brown eyes, a soothing voice, and a profound compassion for others, and there was a silent, almost telepathic communication between us that enabled her to sense when I was in trouble.

She would often help me with my sheets, and she made sure that I ate properly, that I wore my glasses; and as I was frequently ill, she would always be there by my side in the infirmary, holding my hand, wiping my fevered brow, softly saying, "Sleep, my little Anetka . . . sleep. God loves you as I do."

That almost telepathic sense she had of my danger was demonstrated when, on one occasion, she undoubtedly saved my life.

I was in the dormitory hallway, alone, not far from my room, when I began hemorrhaging from my nose. It wasn't a normal nosebleed because I was choking on my own blood, unable to cry out for help.

Sister Roberta was in chapel, praying. She recalled later that a strange feeling came over her and that all at once she had a "vision" of what was happening to me. She jumped up, asked for God's help, and ran from the chapel to the hallway where I was choking, crying out her special nickname for me: "Anetka . . . my Anetka . . . where are you?"

When she found me, I was covered with blood, gasping for breath, and terribly frightened. She scooped me up and ran with me to the infirmary where doctors were able to stop the bleeding. I did require transfusions, and later I was told that had she not found me, I very likely would have choked to death in the hallway.

It was my closeness to Sister Roberta that convinced me at a very early age that I wanted to become a nun, and after the bleeding incident, religion became a part of me. Up to that point I had been a terrible student, the first in the memory of the Resurrection nuns to flunk the first grade. Then suddenly I began appearing daily in chapel on my own, making the stations of the cross, reciting the prayers of the rosary, not once but twice, even three times a day.

There were several small grottoes at the academy, but I favored one called the "Dark Grotto" and visited it frequently. There I would pray as hard as I could that God would help me become a nun like Sister Roberta.

On May 10, 1942, with my father still away, I finally qualified to make my first holy communion. My mother, my aunts and uncles, my sister Bonnie, and Sister Roberta were there smiling at me as I walked down the aisle of the chapel and knelt in front of the priest to receive communion.

For me it was a theatrical event. For Sam, who was still away in prison, it was a moment he made certain I would always remember. Fat Leonard had been dispatched to our home with a special envelope weeks earlier so that I could have the finest of everything that day . . . a day he would see only in photographs sent to him.

My hair was carefully curled and combed. My communion dress was of the best quality with lace, flowered sleeves, mother-of-pearl buttons; I also wore a solid-gold medal and sterling silver and pearl, real pearl, rosaries. My hair was covered by a delicate soft veil with a fern design on the lace headdress. I was the picture of purity . . . a little angel of God.

After the ceremony, relatives, close friends, nuns, religious leaders, politicians my family knew, all gathered at our home to present me with expensive gifts of cash and jewelry and to congratulate me. The tables groaned with food and wine and delicacies, and my purse was filled with envelopes, all of them containing money, several thousands of dollars, which my mother kept.

The religious education that began in those early years at my father's orders was to continue as I progressed in age and aptitude, and Sam was not the least bit reluctant to use his money to get me accepted by the finest religious academies, including Ladywood, a finishing school for girls in Indianapolis. (It was here, ironically, that I finally turned away from the Church.) His direction was always toward preparing me to become a nun, perhaps to atone for his sins in some way.

Although Sam attended church rarely, he did like to spend hours examining old churches, not necessarily Catholic ones. In New York City, for example, I was with him when he sought out and attended Mass at St. Patrick's Cathedral. But there were other churches he made a point of visiting: St. Bartholomew's, the Cathedral of St. John the Divine, St. John the Baptist, and other smaller ones, all steeped in historical significance. He loved to visit them all.

Sam was also exceedingly generous to the Church. When he did attend Mass, he always put several hundred dollars in the envelope, whether we were in Florida or at our regular parish, St. Bernardine's Catholic Church in Forest Park, Illinois. At St. Bernardine's he also had very close personal relationships with a monsignor and a parish priest, visiting them often or having them to his home for long, private talks before and after Mother's death.

From the time that Francine went to school with a cousin, Andrea Perno, at St. Bernardine's, Sam was an especially generous contributor to that parish, and he gave heavily also to St. Francis of Rome in Cicero, donations that were made primarily through my mother.

Even the FBI took note of one of Sam's donations in one of its communications to J. Edgar Hoover from the Chicago office. The airtel (air telegram) to "the Director," dated September 25, 1961, was the daily summary of my father's activities. Apparently the FBI had interviewed someone at St. Bernardine's. The name of the person interviewed was blanked out.

"Daily Summary. [Blanked-out line] Subject [Giancana] is parishioner belonging to St. Bernardine Church, however, never attends Sunday masses. Claims subject, upon death of wife, ANGELINE, during April, 1954, donated communion rail for church in wife's memory at cost of thirteen thousand dollars. Later donated six stained glass windows at cost of $150." The communiqué ended with the notation "GIANCANA, Armed and Dangerous," a cautionary phrase the FBI used in all its memorandums about my father, although in all the time I was with Sam, I never saw him carry a weapon of any kind.

The donated communion rail the FBI referred to is now gone. The railing was made of exquisite marble. After its removal it was cut in sections and placed in front of statues of saints throughout the church. The memorial plaque was removed after Sam was assassinated. The final irony was supplied by the late Cardinal Cody. When my family wanted to have services for Sam in his parish and donate money in his memory, they were turned down on orders of Cardinal Cody in the chancery. He was, however, buried in holy ground in Mount Carmel Cemetery, but only because the family mausoleum was there.

When the FBI listed the items found in our home after Sam's assassination, among the most treasured items that had been locked in his desk was a photograph of a private audience he had had with Pope Pius XII, a scroll commemorating that audience at the Vatican, a bottle of water from the river Jordan, two solid-gold rosaries, and a plain rosary, like the ones he had had made for each of his daughters. These rosaries had been fashioned from the roses at my mother's funeral and preserved.

There were other artifacts: statues of the infant Jesus, of St. Anthony (his favorite saint), of Christ, of the Holy Family—he had them all. They were the spiritual reminders he kept about him that only his family knew about, not his friends.

There were also sometimes anonymous contributions of huge sums of money. I remember a private school, the Providence School for Retarded Children, to which Sam donated a huge stained-glass window as well as cash in the name of my mother's mother. And there was an entire room, as well as stained-glass windows, given to Columbus Hospital in memory of Grandpa De-Tolve. There were many, many others.

It wasn't that Sam was trying to buy his way into heaven. He knew better than that. He was showing respect for my mother, and without broadcasting it to his peers in the underworld, acknowledging that he had grown to believe in something besides violence and death and the ugliness of the Mafia.

7

Speak Softly

I began to notice the trappings of my father's growing power in 1945 when we moved from our home on West Lexington to a more luxurious two-flat at 1028 South Monitor.

It was an older home, very much like the much-sought-after brownstones that are now being restored and sold at astronomical prices in some sections of New York City.

That is not to say that the house on South Monitor was elaborate or ostentatious. Quite the contrary. Plain but comfortable, it was typical of all the homes Sam was to own or rent, with the exception of the estate he used in Cuernavaca. The house had been selected carefully with one thought in mind—blend into the community, do not attract attention. Still, it was a clear signal that Sam was moving up in the ranks of Chicago's underworld. He had "graduated" from being a bootlegger and low-level enforcer to being the boss of a gambling empire on Chicago's South Side, a lucrative empire that drew the attention of his elders in the Capone criminal syndicate.

While the exterior of our home was designed not to attract too much attention, particularly from the IRS, the interior was quite another matter. Here Sam could enjoy the luxury his money could buy and show it off only to those close to him, to people he trusted.

Sam and my mother liked the finer things in life and their tastes showed it. The rare oil paintings, delicate and exceedingly expensive Dresden china, Meissen porcelains, sterling silver flatware and tea services, Venetian mirrors, antique music boxes, objets d'art, all were prominently displayed, all paid for in cash. And the furniture wasn't the kind found in department store showrooms. Whether a French provincial bedroom set or a Louis XV mirrored display cabinet, every piece had been selected to suit my mother's tastes by an interior decorator who was paid top dollar in cash to make the house a showcase.

Even as we settled into the house on South Monitor, Sam was searching for something with more class, more permanence, something that would put more distance between his work arena and his home life. What he found was an attractive bungalow at 1147 South Wenonah Avenue in the suburb of Oak Park.

Once again this was one of Sam's cash transactions—$22,500, to be exact. But the tax man wasn't going to catch my father napping. Sam was never going to be caught the way Al Capone was caught, for showing a higher standard of living and assets than his income could account for. To prevent any such question arising, Sam had had the deed for the property made out in the name of his employer, my uncle Michael DeTolve.

Where was all the cash coming from?

Officially, since his release from federal prison in 1942, Sam had been employed as a forty-dollar-a-week sales representative for the Central Envelope and Lithograph Company, owned by Uncle Mike, on South Clinton Street in Chicago. While the business was profitable and Sam could show commissions in addition to his salary, it certainly didn't earn the kind of money Sam needed to live as he did.

When my father was released from federal prison, he looked up his fellow inmate, Edward Jones. Jones and his friends had made huge amounts of money in policy racketeering—from poor black people who bet their favorite numbers in the lingering hope they would win enough to lift themselves out of poverty with one big jackpot. They seldom did, and men like Jones and later my father and his cronies got rich off their dreams.

Anyhow, Sam remembered Jones and Jones remembered Sam when he was freed from prison. Both FBI documents and friends

who were close to Sam and talked to me about it later said that
Jones gave some financial backing to my father . . . enough so
that Sam could take over a black establishment known as the
Boogie Woogie nightclub and tavern and buy into some jukebox
businesses.

That wasn't enough for Sam. On May 11, 1946, Jones was kidnapped by four masked white men in two cars. Six days later,
Jones was released after paying a ransom of one hundred thousand dollars. That's what the newspapers said. And as a child I
heard whispers from children on the street, from the lowered
conversations of some adults that my father was part of that kidnapping. I remember asking my mother about some bad newspaper stories about Sam, and she told me quite angrily that they
were lies and I shouldn't be reading papers.

An FBI document dated July 16, 1957, puts the Jones kidnapping in sharper focus, by quoting a *Chicago Daily News* article
dated April 28, 1948. The document, which gives Sam's personal
background and a history of his activities up to 1957, states:
". . . the Chicago Police believe, but can't prove, that Giancana
was the brain in the $100,000 kidnapping of [Edward] Jones,
Negro policy king."

The document doesn't reflect why Jones didn't stay around to
talk much about his kidnapping to the police. Some friends of my
father's later explained it. They told me Sam had set up the kidnapping to convince Jones that he would remain healthy if he
retired in favor of my father. Which was exactly what Jones did,
and quite suddenly my father had a major foothold in the black
numbers racket, a foothold that would lead to the death of my
childhood Santa Claus, Fat Leonard Caifano, as well as of the
black policy racketeer Theodore Roe and a lot of other people in
between.

I guess Jones didn't protest too loudly because he knew what
everyone but Sam's own family knew, that Sam Giancana was
now a powerhouse in the Chicago crime syndicate. The FBI document strips away any doubt about Sam's stature with a few short
but succinct observations:

"Information was received that Sam Giancana and Tony Accardo left Chicago on October 11, 1946, for a visit to Miami, Florida. The nature of their visit or the extent of their stay was not

known." After noting that Accardo was the acting boss of the Chicago mob and that Dad was his "right-hand man," the document adds: "Information was received during 1948 that Sam 'Mooney' Giancana was one of the 'big shots' in gambling in the vicinity of Roosevelt Road and Halsted Street, Chicago." The area had been Jones's gambling territory and the Boogie Woogie nightclub and tavern was located on West Roosevelt Road, not too far from another business Sam had set up in Oak Park, the Utility Engineering Company, which was little more than a household-appliance store.

All this is important because it puts into perspective Sam's sudden prominence. It was certainly a far cry from the days after Christmas, 1942, when Sam, then on parole from federal prison, would sneak from our house on West Lexington, leaving by a back door, run down an alley, climb into a waiting car, and drive away with two other men. Late in the evening he would sneak back into the house the same way. The nightly clandestine meetings were, of course, violations of the terms of his parole. He was supposed to stay home at night. His meetings were with other criminals like the Caifano brothers, Sam (Teets) Battaglia, William (Willie Potatoes) Daddano, Joey Glimco, Dominic (Butch) Blasi, or Llewelyn (Murray the Camel) Humphreys. Even then Sam was building his organization, blending in with the older Capone members, preparing for the day when he would move up and stand above the likes of Accardo.

But for the time being, my father was content to stay in the shadows and work on building the confidence of others in him. Fat Leonard Caifano was very instrumental in those days in helping Sam. In the early 1940s there had been a lot of violence in Chicago, a lot of gangland murders, and Fat Leonard convinced his bosses, including Accardo, that they needed protection. One of those assigned to help in that protection was my father, and he was assigned to protect Charlotte Campagna, wife of Louis (Little New York) Campagna, one of the bosses who was in prison for intimidating the movie industry. Charlotte and my mother became very, very close, and she was at my mother's bedside when she died.

By 1945 Sam was off parole and was chauffeuring Accardo

around. In fact, the FBI notes that in February, 1945, Accardo and Sam were arrested together in Chicago's Loop and questioned about the kidnapping of one of my father's gambling friends, a Polish Jew named Jake (Greasy Thumb) Guzik. The FBI states that Guzik was kidnapped in April, 1944, and later released in a dazed state on West Roosevelt Road in Chicago. Sam and Accardo weren't responsible; in fact, Guzik supervised the finances of a lot of their gambling operations, but to the FBI, Sam's being with Accardo then was significant. It wasn't. He and Sam had been together secretly many times before, but the police and the FBI were only aware of the new public status of Sam Giancana.

It was really from 1945 on that I became aware of the frequent comings and goings of Sam's "business associates," men whose names engendered fear in Chicago's underworld for decades.

Some, like Rocco Fischetti, Willie Potatoes Daddano, or Chuckie English, were more than business associates, they were like members of the family. Even closer were men like Paul Ricca or Louis Campagna. Publicly their names had become synonymous with the crimes of Al Capone, but for me, they were second fathers—kindly, generous older gentlemen who treated me with affection.

In the mid- and late forties and early fifties while my mother was alive, visits by Sam's so-called business associates were a regular occurrence. Mother never knew how many people Sam was bringing home, but two to three times a week there were guests, and they would arrive promptly for dinner.

Somehow Mother was always prepared. She was an incredible baker, and each night there would be fresh homemade French or Italian pastries and cakes. The breads, also fresh, she would buy daily from an Italian bakery. She believed, rightly or wrongly, that only the impoverished baked their own bread, so she never did.

Since Mother knew Sam would more than likely surprise her with as many as five or six dinner guests, she always prepared stews with wine and Italian sauces, stews with veal, with beef, or meatballs and sausages. She preferred those types of meals because they were easy to add to, expand, and extend to accommodate any number of guests. It wasn't until my later years in high school that I learned there were other enjoyable foods besides Italian dishes.

This discovery doesn't detract from the excellence of Momma's cooking. Her scope was limited by two factors: the guests, who liked traditional Italian meals, and the number of people. Everyone had to be made to feel as though she had prepared the dinner especially for them on that night.

Every meal was an experience. Mother was quite flamboyant no matter where we were living at the time. The table had to be covered with linen tablecloths, and linen napkins were folded neatly at each table setting. Our finest china, delicate crystal, polished silverware were all featured. You just knew when you walked into the house that you were going to be served as if dining out at the Pump Room or at the Ambassador West or at the Waldorf-Astoria. Mother was a stickler for service to Sam's guests. The only two things she left for him to do were pour the wine and make the espresso.

When guests arrived, I was required to stand by the door next to my mother and greet them: "Hello, how are you, Mr. Moretti . . . Mr. Fischetti?" Never would I address them by their first names even though I had known many of them from the time I was old enough to recognize my father. If I was introduced to an unfamiliar visitor, it was always: "Annette, this is Mr. Humphreys." The rest of the world might know him as Murray the Camel or Murray the Hump or Curly Humphreys, but not Sam's kids.

There were others who were Uncle So-and-so and Aunt So-and-so. I had more aunts and uncles than England's royal family. It was all a matter of respect that my father demanded be shown his friends and associates. Everyone had to show respect to the people who flocked around Sam even though most of them were thugs.

Occasionally a political flunkey of my father's would slip through the cracks and show up for a special conference or, on rare occasions, for dinner. One I remember particularly was James J. Adduci, a Republican who was the Illinois state representative from Chicago's West Side for years.

FBI documents identify Adduci as having had a business relationship with my father in a company known as Windy City

Sports Enterprises. The company had been set up ostensibly to operate softball games, but it was really a front for some of Sam's gambling activities, and at the same time it provided him with a declarable source of income that he could use to keep the tax agents from his doorstep.

Adduci was more than just a business partner. Sam used him to get special legislation passed that would benefit the Outfit. Of course, Adduci couldn't do such things alone. He had plenty of help from other politicians whom Sam and the Outfit controlled. Adduci is dead now but he and Sam were quite close, and I will always remember his most notable achievement, helping Sam get Chicago Stadium for a charity affair my mother ran that turned the Windy City on its ear.

All of Sam's visitors, particularly those in the mob, would greet him with great warmth. Most greetings were limited to a clasp of the hands and a firm handshake, but there were some who were particularly close or high in stature in the mob, and in those instances there was a warm embrace, sometimes even a kiss on the cheek. Embracing among Italians is not uncommon, particularly among old-school Italians, but these embraces were meant to express special respect.

Of all those who frequented our house and sat at our dinner table, only one, Salvatore Moretti, sent chills of fear up my spine. There was something devious about the man, something about the way he looked at you and yet didn't look right into your eyes as the others did. I always felt a sense of mistrust when I was around him, but of course I never dared say anything to either my mother or my father.

Moretti arrived at our home, on South Monitor and later in Oak Park, usually with Willie Potatoes for whom he drove. Later he drove my father around for a short time.

Moretti was one of six children who had grown up on Chicago's West Side and become very influential in politics. Sal was one of the more violent members of the family, and on April 12, 1957, like so many of my father's former friends, he was found murdered. I had to go to his wake with Sam, but it wasn't until years later that I learned from FBI documents that Moretti had been murdered on my father's orders. Moretti had apparently com-

mitted a terrible blunder when he carried out an order from Sam
to kill a banker-land developer named Leon Marcus on March 31,
1957. The FBI reports disclosed that Moretti had left a document
on Marcus's body which identified Sam as having made a hun-
dred-thousand-dollar cash payment for a motel which Sam secretly owned with Willie Potatoes.

The FBI documents implied that Moretti was murdered because he had made the grievous error of leaving that document on
the banker's body. Maybe. Certainly the discovery of the document on Marcus's body caused my father considerable embarrassment and harassment by the police and the newspapers. They
said publicly that Moretti didn't die easily. They said my father's
hired killers had tortured Moretti before they shot him and
stuffed him into a dry-cleaning bag, which they left in the locked
trunk of an abandoned car.

If anyone knew Sam was responsible for Moretti's murder, they
certainly didn't show it at the wake. My father showed the proper
remorse at the loss of a friend. All I knew then was that a friend of
the family had been murdered, and I had an obligation to pay my
last respects at his wake with my father.

As I look back now, I can't help but feel there was something
grotesque about attending the wake of someone you were responsible for having murdered. My stomach would have been jumping
and I would have been sweating heavily from fear of being caught
or, worse, being killed by a member of Moretti's immediate family. But not Sam. He didn't show a trace of real emotion; he just
presented an envelope for the family, and spoke his regrets, and
donated flowers for the departed Moretti.

I attended many wakes of my father's so-called friends. Now I
wonder how many of those deaths he was responsible for.

Unlike with Moretti, I felt comfortable around Rocco Fischetti,
who, with his brother Joe, was very friendly with entertainer
Frank Sinatra, as was my father.

Rocco was the rigid, formal, and respectful type when he was
around Mother and me, but he was very nice and at times could
be very warm. He wasn't a particularly handsome man, but he
was always neat and he treated me with kindness and respect. He
had a way of making me feel that my father was really something
special and that I was also something very special.

The FBI records show that in Sam's mob, Rocco had a side that I never knew, a reputation for brutality that made men and women quake with fear. He, like his brothers Joe and Charlie, were related to Al Capone. They also chased women, many of them Chicago's glamour queens, and when they got tired of the women, they tossed them aside, sometimes beating them. One of the women Rocco was supposed to have tired of and beaten was a former Miss Chicago, according to published reports by newsmen Jack Lait and Lee Mortimer. That was the Mr. Hyde side of Rocco Fischetti. The Dr. Jekyll personality was the man I knew— generous, respectful, gentle, and an absolute railroad freak!

Every Christmas, after we had moved to South Monitor, Rocco would invite my father, mother, sisters, and me to visit his home. After the proper respectful greeting and hugging of Sam, he would lead us all into a huge room in his home where he had set up one of the most remarkable model railroads imaginable.

It had cost thousands of dollars to build and thousands more to equip. Rocco had designed most of it himself, and he had built every inch of landscape—from the valleys and mountains, to the towns and villages, to the tunnels, railroad stations, bridges, and loading platforms. There were even coal mines with small chips of real coal. There were freight elevators to unload grain, water tanks to fill the steam engines of the locomotives, animated conductors and railroad workers. Everything was set up with meticulous attention paid to detail. And the trains were of every conceivable type—passenger, freight, military, steam, electric. It was remarkable!

I still marvel at the ingenuity and creativity of this man, this racketeer cousin of Al Capone. Here was a man with a reputation for hobnobbing with the high and mighty of the entertainment world and the Mafia. With Louis Campagna and Paul Ricca and Frank Nitti and others, he and the Chicago mob had sought to control the movie industry through its unions. He was seen with Frank Sinatra, and his brother, Joseph Fischetti, was a constant companion of Sinatra's. There were reports in the press that Rocco Fischetti had personally delivered two million dollars in cash to Charles (Lucky) Luciano in Havana. He wintered in Florida, and he ran a huge gambling complex for Sam in Chicago. Where had he found the time to build such an intricate model railroad complex? Had he come home from beating up straying models or torturing an informer or worse, to spend hours "relaxing," building a train station or a model mountain?

Once we entered his "game room," we would all sit down and the show would begin and last for hours. Rocco was like an overgrown kid, playing with his train sets, showing them off to all who would watch. When he had shown us all the tricks, he would take Bonnie or me, put an engineer's cap on our heads, and let us run his railroads under his careful direction. Even Sam would take a turn at donning the cap and running the trains while Rocco smiled broadly.

Once the show was over, the family, led by Rocco, would retire to the dining room, where he would have a delicious lunch waiting for us and presents to hand out. He was in his glory entertaining Sam and pleasing us, and for our part, we never tired of the visits or the show. Until he died in 1964, those model railroads and the show he put on for the children of his mob peers were his greatest and most secret pleasure. It was a side of Rocco Fischetti that the public and law-enforcement officials never knew about.

Another of the more frequent visitors to our home was Willie Potatoes Daddano. Willie was only five feet five, but he was a human dynamo. He was an engine in high gear that never seemed to run down. He reminded me of the cartoon character Mighty Mouse . . . small, powerful, always darting here and darting there.

Willie is dead now. He died of a heart attack in a federal prison in 1975, and I was told that when he heard of my father's murder, Willie actually broke down and cried. Sam's assassination was very traumatic for Willie who had spent a good part of his life as one of my father's closest friends, protectors, and business associates.

When Willie Potatoes was alive, the press, FBI reports, and the Chicago Crime Commission described him as a ruthless and heartless killer. They pointed to his long history as a criminal and to a federal trial of a bank robbery conspiracy that resulted in the theft of $43,097 by four masked men on September 23, 1963, in Franklin Park, Illinois.

The Chicago Crime Commission stated in its annual report dated August 27, 1969:

"The federal trial of William Daddano, Rocco Montagna, Richard Cain [Scalzetti, a former Chicago cop and chief investigator for the Cook County Sheriff's office from November, 1962, to December, 1964], Frank DeLegge, Sr., and Frank DeLegge, Jr., provided an insight into the operation of organized crime in the Chicago area. It revealed the alliances that frequently exist between racket leaders and officialdom—alliances that are essential for organized crime to exist and to flourish. It furnished a dramatic example of the discipline that is maintained by crime syndicate bosses over underlings—discipline that is inexorable, certain, and unappealable. Had any of the gunmen [in robberies] been approached by duly constituted officials and asked to take a polygraph test there would have been a flat refusal and a hiding behind the Fifth Amendment. Yet, when William [Willie Potatoes] Daddano issued orders for the gunmen to submit to lie detector tests on two occasions, they meekly complied even though they realized that failure to pass the tests meant summary execution. And, according to one witness, the men had to pay a fee of $25 for the 'privilege' of submitting to the tests."

So reported the crime commission. The newspapers were also filled with the details and reports of the murder of at least one gang member who had failed the test. I have to admit that for many years I didn't believe Willie Potatoes was capable of such cruelty. He got fifteen years on the case and died in prison, but accounts of Willie's brutality, like those of so many of my father's friends, bore no relation to the Willie Potatoes who ate at my parents' table and whom I grew to love as a child and as an older woman.

Like Sam, Willie had to go away to "college" in 1945. He had been charged and convicted of burglary and sentenced to up to fourteen years, but he was back on the streets within a year doing his thing for Sam. And like my father, he had been a suspect in homicides, seven in all, according to FBI records.

An FBI weekly summary airtel to Director J. Edgar Hoover from the Chicago office of the Bureau described Willie Potatoes' relationship with Sam rather succinctly on January 6, 1961. It read in part:

"It is noted that William 'Potatoes' Daddano is considered as the top lieutenant for Giancana and in this capacity controls Will, Kane and DuPage Counties, Illinois, in gambling and vice."

A month later, in a February 15, 1961, updated summary of my father's activities for the period November 23, 1960, through January 27, 1961, the FBI said that Willie was the brains behind the infiltration and planned takeover of Chicago's "scavenger" (garbage) industry with my father and Chuckie English.

Most of what I know about all these men I learned by reading the government files on my father. Criminal activities just weren't discussed in front of children or family. When the men wanted to talk about "business" among themselves, wives and children went to the kitchen to mind their business. Except once.

It was in the mid-forties, sometime after I had made my confirmation. Sam hadn't been there for that very important moment in my life, just as he hadn't been at my first holy communion. He didn't know how much I had learned and I desperately wanted him to be proud of me.

Sam was standing in a group of men in our living room. Willie Potatoes was there. So were Fat Leonard Caifano and Sal Moretti.

Anyhow, this was a party of sorts and instead of staying in the kitchen with Momma, I walked into the living room where Sam and his friends were talking. I remember hearing just a few phrases. The discussion was apparently about the trouble they were having with the black policy rackets king Theodore Roe, who was later killed.

"Goddam that nigger . . ." Fat Leonard was saying. "We just gotta make a move . . ."

"Yeah . . . he's the only one . . ." said Willie Potatoes, and then he noticed me.

I smiled brightly, grabbed a chair and stood on it in front of them, and began to recite all the prayers and the Ten Commandments and the Apostles' Creed that I had memorized at school and St. Patrick's Church. I saw it as a golden opportunity to show Sam and his friends how smart I was.

As I look back now, I understand the startled looks on their faces, how uncomfortable and embarrassed they and Sam were. There I was, standing in front of all these mobsters, reciting the Ten Commandments: Thou shalt not steal. . . . Thou shalt not kill. . . . Thou shalt not . . . And I must have done it just after they were discussing ways to get rid of Roe.

Before Sam could act, Mother saw what I was doing and recognized the danger I was in. Sam's facial color was almost beet red. She moved swiftly, grabbed me by the hand, lifted me from the chair, and rushed me off to my room. Nothing more was said. I was told to play with toys I had just received for Christmas and to stay in my room. Somehow Mother calmed Sam down, and I learned later that Willie made light of it and even made a point of telling Sam how well I had learned my prayers in school.

That, to me, was typical of Willie Potatoes. Despite his reputation for violence, Willie was a pussycat at home. He was, in every sense of the word, a family man. In fact, Sam used to go to Willie's home on North Riverside quite often because Willie's wife, Mary, was always pregnant, and Sam would bring things for her and for all their kids.

Willie was terribly jealous. Mary was very special to him, and while he trusted her, he didn't trust other men around her. He didn't want anyone to so much as look cross-eyed at Mary. If there was a hint of a look that Willie thought was out of the ordinary, he would take Mary out of the room. He even went so far as to make her stop wearing makeup because he thought that attracted men's glances.

There was one occasion when Willie almost went too far with his jealousy. Sam, who adored Mary because she was such a loyal wife, decided to give her a special treat. He took her to the Fontainebleau Hotel in Miami and introduced her to Frank Sinatra, who autographed a picture for her. Mary was thrilled beyond words, but Willie was so upset and angry that he not only berated her but turned on Sam. That didn't go over very well with my father, and I understand that for weeks Willie was afraid that he had alienated Sam, a mistake that could have been fatal.

I remember talking to Mary about the incident years later and asking her why Willie had gotten so upset at her being greeted by Sinatra as so many of us had at Sam's behest. Mary said it was because Willie believed she belonged at home taking care of their kids, not out on the town meeting celebrities. Willie was really from the old school, a man who believed a wife belonged at home, barefoot and pregnant and minding the kids and getting the dinner on the table for her man.

Until he went away to jail, Sam or my mother and I went frequently to Willie's home for visits, so frequently, in fact, that Sam never questioned me when I said I was going to Willie's house to see Mary. He never suspected in later years, when I was a teenager and older, that I was lying to him, that I was using Mary's house as an alibi to cover secret dates I was having I didn't want him to know about.

There are times I miss Willie and Mary and their kids. They were good to me. They were like family. I don't care what the rest of the world thought.

8

That's Entertainment—
Part I

In the witness chair in Manhattan's Federal Court sat bland, wily Willie Bioff (pronounced Buy-off), blackmailer, panderer, labor leader, and now star Government witness against eight ex-pals, who are charged with shaking down $1 million from the movie industry (Time, October 18). From wily Willie's reminiscences U.S. citizens learned much.

Question: Was it true that Bioff once had a five-year plan for taking over 20% of Hollywood's profits—and eventually 50% interest in the studios themselves?

Bioff (wistfully): "If we'd lasted that long, we would have."

Question: Did you ever say you were boss of Hollywood and could make producers do whatever you wanted?

Bioff: "Yes—and I could make them dance to my tune."

—Time *magazine, November 1, 1943*

It required considerable influence in 1949 to prod a major Hollywood producer into squiring a skinny, fourteen-year-old kid from Chicago around the huge studio facilities of Metro-Goldwyn-Mayer (MGM). It took even more influence to induce such a starmaker into dining with that same teenager at the MGM commissary and introduce her to studio superstars of the era, people like Greer Garson, Jimmy Stewart, Walter Pidgeon, and Spencer Tracy.

In June of that year I found out my father had that kind of clout when movie producer Joseph Pasternak spent an entire day taking me on a guided tour of the MGM studio facilities, introducing me to stars, and placing much of the glamour and glitter of Hollywood at my fingertips.

All that and more was part of my reward for finally graduating from grammar school after so many years of failure and frustration. I had graduated from Lincoln School, Oak Park, where I finally made the grade after so many failures at Resurrection Academy, at St. Patrick's Academy, and at St. Francis of Rome Catholic School in Cicero. I think my success at Lincoln School was largely because I was no longer boarding out. I was able to commute by bus from our new home in Oak Park.

Oak Park was a rather sedate, respectable, suburban, upper-middle-class community adjoining the western boundary of Chicago's city limits. It had elected to remain a "dry" community where liquor was not available to "keep the bad elements out," and it prided itself on its reputation as a quiet, law-abiding suburb whose residents kept to themselves for the most part. When we moved into the area, my father was to change all that, and I doubt that Oak Park will ever be the same again.

It wasn't long before quiet suburbia became what amounted to a combat zone as police and federal agents turned the quiet streets into something out of a Grade B gangster film.

Cars of all shapes, types, colors, and makes patrolled the streets or parked in the vicinity of our home as their occupants with their long-lensed cameras photographed Sam, the family, and everyone who came to visit us. What wasn't photographed was jotted down on notepads and recorded on memorandums to FBI Director J. Edgar Hoover, the Chicago Crime Commission, the Chicago police, and just about every other law-enforcement agency that had any interest in Sam.

Sam lived with it; we all did, sometimes not very gracefully.

I clearly remember that on many an evening in Oak Park, Sam would climb into his car and suddenly roar out of the driveway with the lights of his vehicle off. The lights would stay off as he sped down first one block, then another, tires squealing, often at incredible rates of speed. Within minutes he had shaken whatever police or federal surveillance cars had been following him. He knew every side street, every alleyway, like the back of his hand, and he enjoyed those moments of victory when he lost his law-enforcement tails.

Yet there were other times, generally in the daylight hours, when he would walk up to an unmarked police surveillance car and tell the surprised detectives:

"Look, I'm going to the Armory Lounge." Or, "I'll meet you at Celano's [Tailor Shop in Chicago]. Why don't you just take your time? Enjoy the weather and drive carefully. We wouldn't want to upset the neighbors or hurt some kid, would we?" Then, with a smirk on his face, he would walk back to his car, climb in, and drive off slowly with a parade of vehicles following behind him. It was crazy and I know that this constant flurry of activity drove some of our neighbors wild, but they never openly complained to Sam or to Oak Park authorities to my knowledge. I suspect that those who were upset believed that for them discretion was the better part of valor. They didn't want added trouble.

The FBI, in a number of its reports to Washington, took note of its agents' problems in watching my father. There was one fifty-five page summary of Sam's surveillance over a six-month period in which the Bureau's Chicago office tried to explain some of its problems watching him:

> It is virtually impossible to physically surveil the subject [Giancana] as he is very adept at noting he is being surveilled and then takes evasive tactics to elude the surveillances. Other obstacles to physical surveillance of the subject . . . are that the neighborhood in which the subject resides is residential and does not lend itself to physical surveillance and a local ordinance in Oak Park prohibits the parking of cars on the streets during the night so that a car that is parked on the street becomes conspicuous.

The FBI also noted that Sam "always drives a 'souped up' car [and] has had a propensity for fast cars for many years and acted as a 'wheel man' for leading hoodlums when he himself was known as a small-time punk years ago."

Oak Park had other advantages for Sam. It was very close to the Utility Engineering Company, which Sam and Tony Accardo owned, and it was not very distant from the Boogie Woogie nightclub, the seat of Sam's power in the black policy rackets and a place where he later let me accompany him when I was older.

Oak Park's principal advantage, however, was its close proximity to Cicero, a community which achieved national notoriety as the headquarters and playground for Al Capone and his men during the days of Prohibition. Cicero was an area where Sam had operated for years, where he had many, many business and gambling interests, and where many of his associates lived and worked. It was a place ideally situated for meetings of the Outfit because it had been the underworld's backyard for decades, and outsiders, particularly those in law enforcement, were quickly spotted. It was here also, I was to learn later, that many of my father's friends and associates, like Paul Ricca, Rocco Fischetti, Louis Campagna, and Capone's famous trusted lieutenant, Frank Nitti, plotted and executed the takeover of the movie industry in the 1930s.

It all began when Willie Bioff and a friend, George E. Browne, president of the International Alliance of Theatrical Stage Employees, tangled with some friends of my father's from Cicero. It wasn't long before the men from Cicero convinced Bioff and Browne that they should do what they were told and that included collecting protection money from Chicago movie exhibitors and, finally, from major Hollywood studios that were anxious to prevent labor trouble at all costs. The whole plot was spelled out at a trial in Manhattan, where Bioff, after serving two years in prison following his conviction, decided to testify against the upper crust of Chicago's underworld, as did Browne.

During the trial, Bioff recalled that at one time he considered retiring from the union because he disliked taking orders from the men from Cicero.

Under the bland, long-lashed stare of roly-poly defendant Louis Compagna, wily Willie Bioff testified: "Compagna came to me and said he heard what I said about resigning. 'Anybody resigns from us resigns feet first, understand?' he tells me. So I didn't resign."

Then the court got an eyewitness account of Willie's business with one Jack Miller, labor representative for a group of Chicago movie exhibitors.

Bioff: "I told Miller the exhibitors . . . would have to have two operators in each booth. Miller said: 'My God! That will close up all my shows.'"

Prosecutor: "And what did you say?"

Bioff: "I said: 'If that will kill grandma—then grandma must die.' Miller said that two men in each booth would cost about $500,000-a-year. So I said, well, why don't you make a deal? And we finally agreed on $60,000."

Judge John Bright: "What was this $60,000 paid for?"

Bioff (beaming): "Why, Your Honor, to keep the booth costs down . . . You see, Judge, if they wouldn't pay we'd give them lots of trouble. We'd put them out of business and I mean out."

—Time *magazine, October 18, 1943*

The men Bioff had accused of extorting more than a million dollars from studios like Loew's Inc., Twentieth Century-Fox, and Warner Brothers, as well as from the union, were all men my father knew, men I had met, some of whom came regularly to our home. They were all men who, with one exception, my father had hustled with on the street or taken orders from. The exception was Frank Nitti, for years portrayed on TV's *The Untouchables* as a fearsome killer and the right arm of Al Capone. Nitti was probably all that and more, but he was also a coward who feared the confines of a federal prison more than he feared some of his underworld enemies.

Nitti, along with the eight who were placed on trial in New York, had been indicted for the same crimes based on the testimony of Bioff and Browne. But rather than face the trial and the consequences, Nitti committed suicide and so never stood trial. My father had worked for him briefly at one point, I learned from some of his friends, but he had never come to our home and he wasn't someone Sam showed much respect for.

Among those convicted in that famous 1943 trial and ordered to serve ten-year sentences in federal prison were Paul Ricca, Louis

Campagna, Charles (Cherry Nose) Gioe, Phil D'Andrea, Frank Maritote, John Roselli, and Newark labor leader Louis Kaufman. Ricca, Campagna, Gioe, and Roselli all paid us visits, had dinner with us, and were very close to Sam. Campagna, in fact, had made a special point of coming to pay his respects to Sam in 1948 shortly after he, Ricca, and Gioe were freed on parole.

Then in 1955 my father's friend Marshall Caifano found that Bioff, who was using the name of William Nelson, was handling entertainment at the Riviera Casino-Hotel in Las Vegas, an establishment that Sam and Accardo and the Chicago Outfit controlled. On November 4, 1955, outside his home in Phoenix, Arizona, Bioff was blown sky-high when a bomb exploded in his truck as he turned on the ignition switch. The case was never solved, and of course my father and his friends never discussed what had happened. Not even FBI documents provide an answer to who put the bomb there. But there is no doubt in my mind that Willie Bioff was repaid for being a traitor and an informer on my father's friends.

But in 1949, long before Bioff's murder became a national example, the movie colony was aware of the power of the Chicago underworld. They still, as Bioff had put it, danced to the tune my father and his friends Ricca, Campagna, Fischetti, or Accardo wanted to play. They were still dependent on the theatrical stage employees' union the Chicago underworld controlled and they must have been even more impressed by the underworld's power when Ricca, Campagna, and Gioe obtained paroles after only three years in prison despite protestations by prosecutors, judges, congressional committees, and the press.

So if Sam Giancana wanted to send his little girl to Hollywood, or if he wanted a friend to play a movie role, or if he just wanted to see the studio sights and meet some stars, he got what he wanted and he got it with red-carpet treatment.

I think my father went into shock when he learned I had successfully finished grammar school. He even attended my graduation, a first in my life as a student. And he showed a sense of pride in my achieving that plateau, something he had never accomplished as a boy.

Certainly my eventual success in school, however difficult the past had been, contributed to Sam's pliability when my mother suggested that as a reward I should be allowed to spend the summer in California, studying drama, public speaking, and theater makeup with drama coach Wally Stark.

Stark was the brother-in-law of my mother's friend and dress designer Georgianna Jordan, a wonderful lady who reminded me of Ethel Merman. She was a highly successful Chicago dressmaker and designer who not only supervised and designed my mother's wardrobe, but designed clothes for many of Chicago's elite and for film and stage stars performing at local theaters. I know at one time she was an actress and wrote books on fashion.

Georgianna and my mother were close, even though her husband was an ex-traffic cop and Sam hated cops of all sizes and shapes, active or not. She knew of my great desire to study acting, as did my mother, and after many discussions with me, she convinced Mother that I would learn a great deal by making such a trip and I would mature. She assured her that I would be safe and carefully supervised, and that she and her sister, Estrellita, would act as my chaperones.

Wally Stark was a professional teacher who taught drama at a college in beautiful downtown Burbank and provided special coaching for aspiring young actresses whose parents had lots and lots of money to squander on such instruction. I wanted to become one of those aspiring actresses.

It took a lot of coaxing by Mother, unaccustomed sweet talk from me, and promises of close supervision from Georgianna before Sam agreed to the trip. There was, of course, a quid pro quo. He said that if he allowed me to make the trip, I would have to agree to attend, without fuss, an exclusive, private, all-girl college-preparatory school in Indianapolis.

The school of course was Ladywood, run by the Sisters of Providence. It had been carefully selected by Sam and my mother following intensive consultation with a priest to whom I shall refer only as Father Joe. I have decided not to identify Father Joe further because of a rather special relationship that developed later between us after I began attending Ladywood.

Father Joe was not the family priest. He had been introduced to my father by one of Sam's close friends. Sam, as I said before, was not a regular churchgoer, and he had an inherent mistrust of

priests in general. Yet there were exceptions . . . and Father Joe
was one of them. For some reason they hit it off together, so
much so that at one point they exchanged Christmas gifts, something Sam had never done before with anyone from the Church.
There seemed to be a special quality about Father Joe that encouraged trust and that quality affected Sam. For a time he
trusted Father Joe as much as he trusted any man, although he
never fully trusted anyone in his life.

Sam put Father Joe to the test early on while I was in grammar
school. He asked him to counsel me, help calm me down, act as a
sort of religious psychiatrist. That in itself was quite amazing. Sam
hated and mistrusted psychiatrists, who he believed would sell
out for a price. He viewed anyone who required psychiatric treatment as a person who couldn't be trusted, and God help anyone
in the mob who dared see a shrink. His life wouldn't have been
worth a plugged nickel.

Sam's feelings about psychiatrists stemmed, I think, from his
early years in prison when he registered for Selective Service. An
FBI report dated July 16, 1957, and an interview Sam gave to
Chicago Tribune reporter Sandy Smith on April 4, 1959, at my
wedding reception give some insight into the contempt Sam had
for psychiatrists.

The FBI report took note that my father registered for the draft
on December 14, 1942, while he was an inmate at the Terre
Haute federal prison. Then the FBI reported: "A report of Giancana's physical examination dated February 12, 1944, reveals that
he was rejected for military service because of a constitutional
psychopathic state and inadequate personality, manifested by
strong anti-social trends."

In an interview with Sandy Smith, published in the *Chicago
Tribune* in April, 1959, my father gave his explanation: "'Who
wouldn't pretend he was nuts to stay out of the army. When they
called me to the [draft] board they asked me what kind of work I
did. I told them I steal for a living.' He chuckled over the board's
reaction to the statement. 'They thought I was crazy, but I wasn't.
I was telling them the truth.'"

So Sam had avoided the draft, avoided fighting in a war, and
returned to build his empire.

While Sam considered psychiatrists on the whole to be untrustworthy, he felt priests lived by different standards. He knew they would never violate the secrets of the confessional. One of his closest friends, advisers, and former bosses Paul Ricca apparently believed as Sam did. When Paul died on October 12, 1972, of heart disease, a Catholic priest appeared at the funeral home to deliver a brief message of condolence, which was reported in the *Chicago Tribune*.

Explained the priest: "Paul DeLucia received the last rites of the Church upon his death. What greater consolation can there be for a family than to know that their loved one died in the grace of God."

Paul had made his peace with God and to do that, he had trusted a priest with secrets of his criminal life, of his violations of the laws of God and man that no one in the world knew about except God . . . and the priest to whom he had confessed.

Sam treated Father Joe in much the same manner, although I'm certain Sam confessed none of his own sins. What he did was reveal secrets of his personal family life and the problems that were generated by his children, particularly by me. Father Joe treated that knowledge as though it had come to him from the confessional.

In retrospect, I have to admit that Father Joe was of considerable help to me. We talked frequently about my problems at school and how they related to my home, to my frustrations at failing to please my father. At first our conversations were quite superficial. I didn't trust him any more than I had trusted the nuns, whom I felt had sold out to my mother and father years before when I was boarded out. But Father Joe had patience and understanding and slowly he gained my confidence and cautiously approached the subject of a college-preparatory school.

Almost immediately my reaction was rebellion and rejection. Once again I was to be farmed out, uprooted from my home, and sent off to another Siberia so Sam wouldn't have to be bothered with me.

Father Joe convinced me that wasn't the case. He explained that he, my father, and my mother were looking for a school that would prepare me not just for college, but for life, for the role of being a lady, of engaging in social contacts, of rising above my background. Sam wanted only the best for me, not to get rid of me. He wanted me to succeed where he had failed, and he was willing to spend great sums of money to help me accomplish it. Then Father Joe added the clincher. He said my father had promised that any school they selected would include the necessary courses in drama and public speaking to enable me to further my acting skills. So when they settled on Ladywood, I decided to put up no more fuss, since Sam had also agreed to my California excursion.

If there was one thing the trip was to fulfill for me, it was the final realization of my fantasies of going to Hollywood and mingling with the stars.

From my early days at Resurrection Academy, I had wanted desperately to be an actress. I wanted to wear gorgeous clothes, I wanted to have my picture on the screen and in magazines, and I even wanted to leave my footprints embedded in Hollywood's sidewalks with those of the great stars. It was a foolish dream, but it was my dream.

Of course, the last thing Sam would have wanted was for his eldest daughter to be in the movies or on the stage. That may seem somewhat contradictory, particularly since he was frequently in the company of some of the world's most famous entertainers. The truth is Sam had little respect for them as a group. He used them to further his own interests, to make money for him, and to provide him with an entrée into a world of semi-respectability. But for his daughter, he wanted something different. He wanted me to be married to the right person, and that person would be someone who would promote Sam's interests by cementing the blood ties of the Mafia or by his political influence. And if that failed, there was always a nunnery.

Mother knew but never really let on to Sam that I was deadly serious about becoming involved in the field of entertainment, whether through Hollywood, the theater, or modeling. Secretly she had encouraged my efforts largely in hopes that it would improve my attitude at school. At each of the schools I attended she arranged for me to receive special training at extra cost to Sam. Sam never understood what the additional study costs were; he just paid the bills as they came in.

I had a modicum of success in some school plays. Of course, I was far from a star performer in any of them because I was such a poor reader and had difficulty memorizing lines. But I could do mime, and I could do it very well. So I was included in many plays, some of which Sam even attended.

To Sam's credit, once he had decided to let me go to California, he made sure I went in a manner that would befit the daughter of Sam Giancana. European royalty wouldn't have fared better than this Mafia princess.

Everything about the trip was triple-A in luxury, from the limousines that took me and my chaperones to the train station, to the accommodations on the train itself. My wardrobe, much of it designed by Georgianna Jordan, would have matched that of any Hollywood star my age. And there were the finest in perfumes and cosmetics as well as expensive new luggage.

I had a luxurious stateroom, as did my chaperones, on a super-deluxe streamliner. For a fourteen-year-old who had never traveled much farther than Wisconsin, the sights and sounds of this royal treatment were very exciting.

There was more than just the magnificence of the Rocky Mountains and the beauty of the endless fields of greenery of the Midwest farms. There was a young midshipman from the U.S. Naval Academy at Annapolis, Maryland.

We met in the dining car; and later in the observation car, we talked about his Navy career and about my drama studies while my two chaperones kept an ever-watchful eye.

His name was Bob, and he was an engaging, charming young man, extremely self-confident yet not overbearing. He was tall and tan and handsome in his uniform, and I became infatuated almost from the moment we met. He even impressed Georgianna, who, on the second day of our trip, invited him to join us at an informal celebration of my fifteenth birthday.

I didn't know it then, but Bob was to have a profound effect on my life many years later and we were to have a tempestuous, if clandestine, romance that could never be legitimized by marriage but still would span more than twenty years. I also didn't know it then, but Bob was secretly married in violation of naval academy rules.

From the moment I stepped off the train, I loved California. It was everything I had dreamed of and more.

We were met at the train by Wally Stark and his wife, and for the next three months I was to live in their apartment just three blocks from the 135-acre Warner Brothers studios, where some of my father's houseguests had exercised their special form of intimidation to extort hundreds of thousands of dollars and to exert influence on the careers of favored actors and entertainers. Of course, at fourteen I knew nothing of this, and my interest in Warner Brothers was much like that of a starstruck girl who spent much of her free time sitting in a drugstore across the street from the studio, sipping sodas, reading *Variety*, and waiting to be "discovered."

The Starks' apartment was lovely if modest, and quite comfortable. The Starks were wonderful hosts but very demanding as tutors. They set up a training schedule of six days a week, and all I knew was work . . . work . . . work.

Mornings were spent with Wally on public speaking and drama. Afternoons were spent reading scripts. Sandwiched between were lessons in theatrical makeup—how to simulate blood, gashes, and wounds, how to make myself age—tricks of makeup essential to the theater and even to modeling.

Occasionally Sam would phone me to hear how I was doing, and there were other calls to the Starks and to Georgianna to check on my progress and on my behavior.

Mother, God bless her, was much more excited about what I was doing than Sam was. She secretly thought it was an opportunity for her daughter to have a career, and she encouraged me because it was something she had never dared dream of when she was a child. The entertainment world titillated her, and through Sam she had acquired some close show-business friends, one of whom was Jimmy Durante.

Durante was one of many entertainers Sam introduced to Mother. She had met Frank Sinatra, Dale Robertson, Sammy Davis, Jr., and a long list of both rising and established stars, but Durante was her favorite, and she his.

Durante treated Mom like a queen. He truly loved her. He had been introduced to her at a Chicago nightclub by Sam. After that, no matter where we were, if Durante was in the house, he would come to our table to pay his respects to my mother and ask how she was doing. And wherever he was in the world, he would have roses sent to her. Sam never took offense. He was rather proud of the attention that Durante paid to Mother and to him. When Durante died, the world lost a great performer and I lost a great friend.

While I was at the Starks', Mother would phone me and spend what seemed like hours getting the latest gossip, or talking about the sights I'd seen, or discussing my studies and how I was doing with them. I think that through me she was living a life that was forbidden to her.

My first real introduction to the glamour that was Hollywood in those days was a trip Sam arranged for me to visit the Metro-Goldwyn-Mayer studios. I'm not sure exactly how he did it, but with the influence he and his friends had over studios and entertainers throughout Hollywood, a trip of this magnitude was probably rather simple, more on the order of asking a favor than making a demand.

One would never have found Sam at a studio in those years, nor would anyone have dared talk about his influence in Hollywood. There are many who would never have known or believed it. His power was unseen, unspoken, but very real—and it was awesome. Its long reach extended not just to MGM, but to Paramount, to Twentieth Century-Fox, to Warner Brothers, to the largest, most lavish casinos of Las Vegas. FBI documents are filled with descriptions of his influence with people in the entertainment world.

Whether or not Sam's power, the influence of his friends, or the history of the Chicago crime syndicate in the movie industry made a difference I'll never know, but when I was ushered into the office of Joseph Pasternak, I was treated with as much respect as if I had been one of the studio's superstars. I do know that I was very nervous and quite starstruck when I was introduced to him and shook his somewhat sweaty hand.

Pasternak was a rather short man, about five and a half feet tall, with deep-blue eyes, thinning sandy hair, a quick mind, and a reputation as a starmaker. He had worked at Paramount and Universal studios before joining MGM, and he had produced films with such stars as Marlene Dietrich, Jimmy Stewart, Frank Sinatra, and Vic Damone. His discoveries read like a *Who's Who* of filmdom during the 1940s and 1950s, performers like José Iturbi,

Deanna Durbin, Jane Powell, and Kathryn Grayson. He wasn't the boss of MGM, but he was one of their biggest moneymakers and a man of considerable influence and popularity. He was also someone I had heard about from the Starks and from Jimmy Durante, who had been in Pasternak-produced films since 1944, including two with swimming star Esther Williams in 1947 (*This Time for Keeps*) and in 1948 (*On an Island with You*). In short, Pasternak was a very busy and successful man, but not too busy or successful to take time out to play escort to the fourteen-year-old daughter of Sam Giancana.

For an entire day, Pasternak squired me around the MGM lot, taking me to studios to watch movies being filmed, introducing me to dozens of actors and actresses, and lunching with me at the then famous MGM commissary where all the studio's major stars and executives gathered. He was a wonderful host, infinitely courteous, kind, and generous, and for me, it was the most exciting day of my life. When we parted, he kissed me lightly on the cheek, told me to call him whenever I came to town again, and helped me into a waiting limousine that whisked me swiftly back to the home of the Starks and out of the Land of Oz.

That day at MGM was only a small demonstration of Sam's enormous influence and power in the entertainment world. In later years I became more aware of his ability to make or break entertainers, to influence producers in their choice of actresses in a film, or to boost the popularity of a singer through his organization's control of jukeboxes, nightclubs, and gambling casinos from Chicago to Los Angeles. It rather amuses me that some of those entertainers, like Frank Sinatra, try to put distance between themselves and my father in terms of their relationship now that they are once again in demand at the White House or when they seek casino licenses. Sam never denied them when they needed him.

No matter where I went in California, whether to a restaurant, a nightclub, or a show, I was treated as though I were royalty. It seemed as if Sam's reach stretched everywhere in California. Whether I was in Burbank with the Starks or alone, the red carpet was always rolled out.

About midway through my study-vacation, Sam and Momma came to California for a visit. They stayed at the Beverly Wilshire while I remained at the Starks'. One evening Sam was in an expansive mood and quite proud of the way I looked, acted, and dressed, and he announced that he was taking all of us out for a celebration at Ciro's.

His mood changed markedly when actor John Ireland came to our table, introduced himself, and asked me to join him at his table for a drink. Of course, I was thrilled, speechless that a handsome star of Ireland's stature would even notice me, let alone invite me to his table. Mother was somewhat amused and her eyes twinkled with a secret delight when she looked at me. But my.father . . . ah, that was another matter.

Sam's eyes narrowed and he stared coldly at Ireland as he talked. I could feel the chill of that steely, snake-eyed look that Sam took on when he was angry. He didn't say a word. He knew that with that look I would give the right answer to Ireland and politely refuse, and that one of our guests would quietly explain to Ireland the serious error of his ways. I did as expected and so did one of Sam's friends. Ireland turned chalk-white as he reached his table and never looked back at me again.

John Ireland wasn't the only Hollywood star to come to our table that day. Robert Mitchum, who was then almost every woman's heartthrob, introduced himself, complimented me on my appearance, and paid his respects to my father and my mother as well as to the Starks. He was the perfect gentleman, and Sam smiled rather proudly when he paid me a compliment.

California, Hollywood, the studios and the stars . . . it was all grand while it lasted, but all too soon it ended.

It was, however, just a preview of things to come.

9

That's Entertainment— Part II

In 1945 a charitable organization known as the Italian Welfare Council of Chicago was established by a group of wealthy and well-meaning citizens of Italian descent. Its purpose was noble enough: to help both the aging and the impoverished children among the city's more than 400,000 Italian American residents. Of course, a great many of these poor inhabitants came from territories controlled by the old Capone mob, most particularly those who lived in Chicago's First Ward, a political subdivision that for decades had been dominated and run by Capone and his successors, including Anthony Accardo and that rising star, my father, Sam Giancana.

I suppose it was natural for an organization like the Italian Welfare Council to have among its members many of my father and mother's closest friends as well as a substantial representation of associates of other Capone mob figures like Paul Ricca. What is surprising is that neither the FBI nor the media recognized many of the relationships within the organization or understood the political power it held. Nor did they recognize the connection between the council, the world of entertainment, and the mob.

The council's founders, directors, and officers were a classic cross-section of Chicago's Italo-American society. Judges and physicians hobnobbed with society matrons and politicians. And there were the inevitable groupings of attorneys and labor leaders, many of whom had connections to the Capone organization. And out of the limelight was my mother.

Mother had always been active in charities, particularly those connected with the Catholic Church, but she became involved with the Italian Welfare Council at the urging of two people in particular . . . Dr. Eugene J. Chesrow, the family physician who had delivered and saved me when I was born prematurely, and Anthony V. Champagne, my father's personal attorney and a man who also arranged many of Sam's secret business investments. Both wanted Mother on the council, originally to serve as its president, a proposal my father flatly rejected. They compromised with Sam, and Mother became the organizing force behind the council's fund-raising efforts.

By 1948 the council had opened a thirty-room residence on a seven-and-a-half-acre estate it had bought on Pistakee Bay in McHenry County, Illinois. The residence served as a home for the elderly who were not bedridden, while the estate itself was turned into the Jolly Boys and Girls Summer School Camp. On the site, purchased for $37,500 were fourteen cabins and a girls' dormitory, which had been built at a cost of more than $50,000. Each year, for ten days at a time, 150 of Chicago's underprivileged Italian American children were sent to the camp in seven contingents, with all expenses paid, to enjoy a country vacation complete with boating, swimming, fishing, nature study, and camping.

The year-to-year operation of such a facility for over one thousand kids annually, however, was a very expensive proposition, and the council and my mother found that local fund-raising efforts weren't enough even if the mob was putting the arm on some people behind the scenes to get extra money for the camp.

I remember times when Mother used to come home almost heartbroken because it didn't seem as if they were going to reach their goals and raise enough funds to continue the camp. She loved helping poor kids and, surprisingly, so did Sam. I remember taking trips to the camp on several occasions with Momma and Sam, and watching him hoist youngsters into the air, playing with them, making sure they were getting the kind of vacation they had dreamed of having. Several times I saw him reach into his pocket when he learned that the camp was short on funds for some equipment, and give camp officials cash on the spot to go and buy what they needed.

Still, the program was just barely making it from year to year, hobbling along with fund-raising dinners and cocktail parties, door-to-door collections, and similar events. For the most part, monies were raised primarily by the ladies of the council, many of them wives of other mobsters or business associates of the mob. They looked to Momma because she had a talent for organization. She was very precise and meticulous in developing the fund-raising events. It was as if she was driven by a need to make the organization succeed. And in that drive, there was growing frustration as the council was having more and more difficulty in raising money until Momma came up with an idea for a very special event. She called it the "Night of Stars" benefit show.

Now, it's one thing to have an idea, it's another to translate that idea into action. Mother knew entertainment stars like Jimmy Durante, Tommy Leonetti, and Frank Sinatra through Sam and through Joe and Rocco Fischetti and Paul Ricca. But she wouldn't have dared call on them herself; even if she had, she knew of no place to hold a big enough crowd for such acts.

It all came to a head one night when I was home from Ladywood. Mother began coaxing Sam, appealing to him for help.

Sitting on an ottoman in front of him, her chin resting in the palms of her hands, her eyes twinkling, looking up into Sam's eyes, she said:

"Sam, darling, I need you desperately."

Sam always melted when Momma turned it on, and she was really fine-tuning him that evening.

"I want to run a 'Night of Stars' benefit . . . the biggest, the best, the most important Chicago's ever seen to raise the money we need for those kids . . . but I can't do it without you."

Sam protested, weakly, I think. "Angie . . . the publicity . . . we can't get involved publicly. The papers, they'll . . ."

Momma cut him off.

"Nobody will know, Sam . . . just you and me and one or two of our closest friends. But think of all the good we can do for all those poor children . . ."

Sam never really could resist giving Momma something she really wanted, and the "Night of Stars" was no exception.

What was needed was a location large enough to draw the crowds that were necessary for the "Night of Stars" to be a financial success. What better place than Chicago Stadium?

Now Sam Giancana, even if he owned all the politicians in Illinois (and he didn't), couldn't have his name or his wife's name connected to the use of the Chicago Stadium. Such a blatant display of raw power and influence would have created a tremendous scandal. And things were even touchier considering the fact that Senator Estes Kefauver and his Special Committee to Investigate Organized Crime in Interstate Commerce was having a field day holding hearings and summoning some of Sam's associates—Accardo, Ricca, Charles Gioe, Louis Campagna and his wife, Charlotte, and others—to testify about the circumstances leading to Ricca's, Gioe's, and Campagna's unexpected and scandalous paroles.

So my father, after getting Accardo's and Ricca's permissions, sought a rather obscure route to pave the way for the "Night of Stars" in Chicago Stadium.

To understand how he could swing this, it's necessary to understand something about Chicago politics, particularly the politics of the First Ward. It's also necessary to realize that members of the Italian Welfare Council included several people with strong ties to my father's political associates, men like John D'Arco, currently First Ward committeeman, a post that dispenses a great deal of political patronage. D'Arco and my father were close friends, and quite often as a child and as a grown woman, I spent time with my father at D'Arco's summer home or his winter vacation home in Florida.

Close to both D'Arco and Sam was Frank Esposito, a council director and the union boss of thousands of city and county workers. The FBI said Esposito was responsible for putting many of my father's criminal associates on city payrolls, often in sensitive positions, to ensure the election of people like D'Arco or the late state senator James Adducci, both of whom had the necessary influence to make a stadium available for a charity affair.

An FBI report dated December 29, 1962, entitled "Influence of Samuel Giancana and His Organization in Activities of the First

Ward Political Organization of Chicago" gives a better perspective on the forces that my father could set in motion politically and the history behind them.

The report explains in part:

"The First Ward of the City of Chicago has been said to contain the best of everything—and the worst. The reason for this is that it contains the Loop, the business center of the country's second largest city, but also the teeming slums which crowd in on the Loop.

"Inside and on the fringe of the Loop are some of the largest and most luxurious building structures in the world, such as the Merchandise Mart, the Board of Trade Building, McCormick Place, the Civic Opera Building, the Prudential Building, City Hall, and the County Building, the Chicago Public Library, the Art Museum, Marina Towers Apartment Building, and Marshall Field's Department Store, along with the finest of hotels, theaters, and restaurants.

"Outside the Loop, but remaining inside the First Ward, to the south and southwest of the Loop, is a two-square-mile section of low-income housing, blending the best and worst of many groups, but mainly Italians, Orientals, Negroes, and Puerto Ricans. For the First Ward extends from the Chicago River on the north to as far as 31st Street in some areas on the south, and from Lake Michigan on the east, to as far west in some locations as Damen Avenue.

"During the heyday of AL CAPONE, the First Ward was 'bossed' by the infamous alderman, MICHAEL 'HINKY DINK' KENNA, and by Democratic Ward Committeeman JOHN 'BATH HOUSE' COUGHLIN. They were followed briefly by FRED MORELLI, until 1947, when the old First Ward merged with the 'bloody 20ths,' the scene of many a vicious struggle for power, to become what is today known as the First Ward. At that time, PETER FOSCO of the 20th became Democratic Ward Committeeman of the First, and ANTHONY PISTILLI, also of the 20th, became alderman of the First. FOSCO, also a Chicago labor leader, who now [1962] represents the Hod Carriers, in Washington, held power until one of his henchmen was named as one of those who handled the money spent to obtain paroles for CAPONE mobsters, PAUL RICCA [DeLucia], LOUIS CAM-

PAGNA, CHARLES GIOE, and PHIL D'ANDREA. FOSCO was then dumped, and a man with an unblemished record, FRANK ANNUNZIO, was given the title of Acting Democratic Ward Committeeman, and was appointed State Director of Labor by Governor ADLAI STEVENSON. In the early 1950s, JOHN D'ARCO, former secretary of PISTILLI, left his post as state representative, and was elected alderman of the First Ward. Shortly thereafter, D'ARCO was also elected Democratic Ward Committeeman of the First Ward."

The FBI report went on to note that United States Congressman Roland V. Libonati, and my cousin, State Senator Anthony J. DeTolve, were also First Ward political graduates who were later described as taking their orders from Sam. The most damning description of First Ward political machinations, however, was detailed in that same report when the FBI interviewed Benjamin "Buddy" Jacobson, executive secretary of the First Ward after he, my father, and D'Arco were observed meeting on November 29, 1962, at the Czech Lodge, a popular restaurant.

Bragged Jacobson: "I am the fixer in the First Ward, and I've been the fixer in the First Ward for 44 years. I take care of everybody, including policemen, politicians and judges. Everybody who needs anything comes to me for favors in my ward. That is my function."

It was that combination of political "friends" inside the Italian Welfare Council and the First Ward and the old Twentieth Ward that enabled Sam to arrange quietly for the use of the stadium. No one so much as raised a question about the propriety of such a use, but then no one knew that my father or my mother had anything to do with the council, let alone be the major driving forces behind its success.

For three years, beginning in May, 1951, the council sponsored the "Night of Stars" at Chicago Stadium, and for three years Sam and his friends reached from one side of the country to the other to bring in the nation's biggest entertainment stars to perform.

They were really glittering affairs. Dean Martin and Jerry Lewis, Frankie Lane, Tony Martin, Tony Bennett, Jack E. Leonard, Jerri Southern, Bob Hope, Frank Sinatra, Johnny Desmond, and Jimmy Durante . . . all turned out to help Chicago's impoverished Italian American kids. Arm twisting wasn't necessary. The power my father and his organization had over the movie, record, and jukebox industries, over nightclubs and Las Vegas casinos, that was enough of a drawing card. It was like a "command performance" for royalty, Chicago mob royalty, and everyone had to pay their dues.

Some weren't there just to pay dues, some came because they were true friends of Sam's. Like Durante. That wonderful man loved my mother, and he adored Sam. They had met at the Chez Paree, an extremely popular nightclub that Sam and his friends frequented. Sam would often take Momma there when she was feeling well, and occasionally he would bring me. I remember when Durante was doing commercials for Sheaffer Pens, at the Desert Inn, Las Vegas, they gave him a special pen for his television work. Durante turned around and gave it to my father, saying, "Here . . . it may not be much, but it's from the first commercial I have done." That so impressed Sam that he never forgot it, and he and Durante remained close friends until their deaths. I still have that pen.

Johnny Desmond was very much like Durante, down to earth, totally unaffected, and like Jimmy, there was nothing phony about him. He not only performed at the "Night of Stars" on two occasions, but he came to our home for dinner, and he remained not only Sam's friend but mine to this very day. But then Durante and Desmond were cut from different cloth. They would no more have dreamed of denying that they knew Sam or Momma or me, as Sinatra did, than they would have refused to spare us time in their dressing rooms at the Chez Paree, in Las Vegas, in Hollywood, or anyplace else.

For me and for Momma, those "Night of Stars" events in 1951, 1952, and 1953 were memorable events. I was brought in from Ladywood School to help Momma with her cocktail parties and fund raisers before the affairs because I had learned, or so she believed, how to carry myself like a cultured young lady. My reward was to be brought backstage by Sam after the performances to be introduced to the stars who had packed the stadium and raised hundreds of thousands of dollars for my mother's favorite charity. This, like my trip to California, was one glittering reward of being a Mafia princess.

The events were enormously successful. I can't recall ever

seeing such a gathering of stars during that decade, or such a turnout by the people of Chicago for an event of that nature.

Financially it put the Italian Welfare Council on easy street. Its summer camp at Pistakee Bay flourished, and thousands of kids got a taste of a life in the fresh country air that their parents would never have been able to provide them. Hundreds of other children won scholarships enabling them to study to become doctors and lawyers and nurses . . . useful and productive members of society. And a lot of elderly people obtained help that they otherwise might not have received.

The council wasn't at all like the Italian American Civil Rights League that Joseph Colombo, the Mafia boss of Brooklyn, created and used as a publicity tool to rally unwitting people to fight the FBI and the government in their pursuit of the Cosa Nostra. Colombo took money from Italian Americans and got a lot of publicity, but in the end he got shot and later died because of it. They raised some two million dollars, but where it went has never been accounted for. I always felt it was a terrible misuse of Italian American pride and did more to hurt our cause as an ethnic group than it helped.

Mother would have hated such a misuse. The council she struggled so hard to make a success had given the Italo-American community of Chicago a different sense of pride, a feeling of really doing something to help its own people.

Then on April 23, 1954, Mother died from a cerebral hemorrhage in West Palm Beach, Florida. Her death appeared to signal the end of the Italian Welfare Council. Sam was morose, disconsolate, no longer interested in what happened around him, least of all in the council. Mother was gone and there was no one left for him to please. And without Mother, the council lost its driving force and its inside track with the entertainment world. On June 15, 1954, after disclosing that it had been unable to gather the necessary entertainers to organize another "Night of Stars," the council agreed to dissolve, and it turned over its assets of more than $400,000 to the Damon Runyon Memorial Fund for Cancer Research.

It was rare that my father sought out the services of entertainers for such "noble causes" as the Italian Welfare Council.

What he had done for the council was done primarily to please my mother, to guarantee her success. And I suspect Sam also realized it wouldn't hurt the image of his organization if the street people knew that the mob was the behind-the-scenes power that sent poor kids from Chicago's West Side to the country for a vacation.

The usual reason Sam wanted entertainers to appear in Chicago or to be with him was to further his personal interests or those of his friends. Take, for example, Dean Martin. For some reason Sam didn't like Martin. It had to do with his splitting with Jerry Lewis. Sam thought Martin was a prima donna, that he'd forgotten where his roots were in the days when he was hustling to earn a living back in Steubenville, Ohio. But Dean Martin was a great entertainer and a big name and drawing card, so when Sam wanted to use him, he did.

FBI documents put to rest any doubts about my father's attitude toward Dean Martin, through a conversation recorded on December 6, 1961, at the Armory Lounge, a favorite meeting place of Sam's that the FBI had bugged illegally.

The discussion was between my father and an underling of his, Johnny Formosa. Sam used Formosa to carry messages back and forth to Las Vegas and the West Coast when there were problems with entertainers or casinos that Sam wanted solved without his having to make a personal appearance.

The discussion between Sam and Formosa centered on Martin, Frank Sinatra, and Paul (Skinny) D'Amato, who was from New Jersey and who, Sam told me, took care of things for him, looked after his interests at a Lake Tahoe casino called the Cal-Neva Lodge. Sam had told me that he and Sinatra had an interest in the casino together, and FBI documents make the same conclusion, but Sinatra has denied that mutual interest in testimony before the Nevada State Gaming Control Board. At one point in this recorded discussion, Sam and Formosa talk about Dean Martin, and Sam gives Formosa marching orders for Dean:

GIANCANA: You see Dean. You tell him I want ten days out of him.
FORMOSA: Ten days?
GIANCANA: In other words, you get two weekends in.

FORMOSA: Where? At the lake [Tahoe]?

GIANCANA: No, no. For a friend of mine.

FORMOSA: What if he says he's booked?

GIANCANA: Find out when he ain't booked.

FORMOSA: All right.

GIANCANA: Right after, ah, January, about the tenth.

FORMOSA: In other words, you want ten days, three days a week.

GIANCANA: January, February, March, and April.

FORMOSA: Ten days, three days each week.

GIANCANA: Yeah. You start on a Friday, Saturday, Sunday, Monday, Tuesday, Wednesday, Thursday, Friday, Saturday, and Sunday.

FORMOSA: Oh, that way?

GIANCANA: Yeah. In other words, you get two weekends.

FORMOSA: Oh, I get it.

GIANCANA: January, February, March, around there. That'll give you a long time.

FORMOSA: . . . I'll tell him this is a must, right? Tell him you said it. Tell him, hey, Dean, this is a must. Sam wants you for ten days.

GIANCANA: Just put it to him for a couple weeks.

FORMOSA: Couple weeks. And if he says where, I'll say in Chicago. He'll give me that date and then I'll get ahold of you. You'll give me more on it?

GIANCANA: Yeah.

FORMOSA: Well, I better go west then. After Sunday, I'm free.

GIANCANA: Don't make a special trip. Call him.

FORMOSA: That ——— prima donna. You can't call him. I gotta go there and lay the law down to him, so he knows I mean business.

GIANCANA: It seems like they don't believe us. . . . Well, we'll give them a little headache, you know?

FORMOSA: We gotta get this worked up and get it over with. Maybe none of them gotta get hurt. Maybe they'll come to their senses.

The Dean Martin episode was typical of Sam. Whatever he wanted, he got when it came to people in the entertainment world, and if it upset the schedules and routines of other people or establishments, well, that was too bad. Whatever Sam wanted, particularly when there was money to be made, he got. Like the Villa Venice episode. Now there was a demonstration, a classic example of Sam's ability to get who he wanted, when he wanted them, and where he wanted them. He drove that point home to me one day when he told me he had arranged to have the nation's top entertainers of that time—Sinatra, Martin, Sammy Davis, Jr., Eddie Fisher, and Debbie Reynolds—open up his new club, the Villa Venice in Wheeling, Illinois.

The Villa Venice was a deteriorating, rundown restaurant-nightspot until Sam took it over from Alfred (Papa) Bouchay. It was located on Milwaukee Avenue in a somewhat rural community northwest of Chicago. But as rundown as the place was, my father saw a lot of potential in it. With the right redecorating, the right boost, it could become a popular nightspot—and a prime location for his men to set up a shuttle service to a planned gambling casino that could operate nearby unmolested by the Chicago police or federal agents. At least that's what he thought.

FBI documents show that the owners of record were Alfred and James Meo, both friends of my father's. The Meo brothers had run the Norwood House, a very popular restaurant and hangout for Paul Ricca, my father, and other people in the Outfit. When I was a child attending Resurrection Academy, one of my rewards for being good for a week or two at the boarding school was having Sunday dinner with Sam and my mother at the Norwood House in Norridge. On occasion, I had seen Anthony Accardo and his family having dinner there too, and sometimes Sam and Accardo would leave their respective tables to hold private meetings away from the dining room. I resented that, particularly then, because as a child I had so little time with my father.

In 1960 Sam put the Meo brothers in charge of the Villa Venice to handle the private parties and weddings. I even had one of my bridal luncheons there, complete with ice sculptures on each table. It was really an elegant place, but it wasn't making money and Sam wanted to upgrade it and turn it into a showcase nightspot.

So in 1961, according to FBI records, another paper transaction took place and Leonard A. (Leo) Olsen became the new owner and president along with a Richard Bernas who Sam really put in charge of the remodeling. Bernas had remodeled and decorated a place that my mother and father had owned in Florida.

An FBI report dated December 14, 1962, states bluntly what I had known all along from Sam. Blanking out the source of its information, the report states:

"[Blank] that Sam Giancana is definitely the owner of the Villa Venice, and has spent many hours overseeing the remodeling operation of the Villa Venice during the past several weeks. Giancana is referred to at the Villa Venice as 'Mr. Flood.'"

The remodeling job was wonderful, and it cost a fortune. There was elegance everywhere, and incoming guests got a taste of that elegance when they climbed into restaurant gondolas that were steered back and forth along a river by appropriately costumed gondola rowers, complete with music from the Old Country—all on the house, part of the ambience. The seating capacity had been increased to eight hundred. The interior renovation was absolutely exquisite. It was a romantic place to take your girl or your wife . . . the food was perfection and the table dinnerware was the finest that could be found in the Chicago area. And for those who wanted excitement, Sam and his underlings had thought ahead. They arranged what amounted to a bus service to a nearby mob casino known as the "Quonset Hut," a structure located two blocks north of the Villa Venice near the Flamingo Motel on River Road and Milwaukee Avenue. Boy, did that place get headlines!

Sam knew that the only way he could boost trade at the Villa Venice and turn it into a top nightspot was to bring in the best entertainment, the best acts the country had to offer, that normally only Las Vegas casinos could afford. To get the Villa Venice off to a flying start, Sam pulled out all the stops. The FBI takes special note of how much clout my father was using in a report dated October 11, 1962. This report, which mentioned meetings my father was having with singer Phyllis McGuire in Palm Springs, California, Las Vegas, Nevada, and in Hot Springs, Arkansas, specifically talks about the preparations under way for the Villa Venice. It says in part:

"Public source information reflects that the Villa Venice has been undergoing extensive remodeling during the past several months and is scheduled for a gala reopening on or about October 31, 1962, and the new Villa Venice will feature as its opening star attraction, Eddie Fisher. Following Fisher will be such notables as Frank Sinatra, Dean Martin, Sammy Davis, Jr., Jimmy Durante, and others of equal stature in the entertainment field.

"[Identity censored] advised in September, 1962, that the Villa Venice is definitely an operation of the Chicago criminal organization headed by Samuel Giancana. . . . Sinatra made the arrangements for Giancana concerning the appearance of Eddie Fisher for the opening act commencing with October 31, 1962. This presented a problem for the Desert Inn casino in Las Vegas, Nevada, in that the scheduled appearance of Fisher [at the Villa Venice] conflicts with his appearance at the Desert Inn during the same period. Upon the insistence of the Giancana group, however, Fisher is being brought to Chicago for the Villa Venice opening rather than stay on at the Desert Inn."

While the identity of the source of that information was not disclosed in the above document, it became evident in another FBI document dated September 13, 1962. This recorded a conversation between my father and another unidentified person at the Armory Lounge in Chicago, where the FBI was engaged in some illegal eavesdropping with the approval of then United States Attorney General Robert Kennedy.

GIANCANA:	We'll open up the 31st and then . . . you'll [identity not disclosed] work a weekend then . . .
[IDENTITY CENSORED]:	Frank [Sinatra] and Dean [Martin] and, uh, Sammy [Davis] . . . Frank, uh, Debbie Reynolds . . .
GIANCANA:	. . . Eddie Fisher comes in first. And that's all taken care of . . . I mean the livin' quarters. . . . You know that Eddie Fisher? There's a guy with a broken heart. He can leave the 7th, or whenever his week is up. All you got to do is call Eddie and tell him to come in. Get Frank . . . Then we're gonna do a show around Debbie Reynolds. There's nothing yet.

(Later Giancana complains about Sinatra):

> That Frank, he wants more money, he
> wants this, he wants that, he wants
> more girls, he wants . . . I don't need
> that or him. I broke my ———— when I
> was talking to him in New York.

At that point my father was obviously considering providing
gambling facilities in conjunction with the Villa Venice, and had
contemplated having gambling inside the nightclub itself. In a
conversation also recorded at the Armory Lounge between Sam
and another unidentified person on October 29, 1962, the FBI
quotes the following conversation:

UNKNOWN: The old man [Papa Bouchay] was quite a dancer,
           wasn't he, Moe [Giancana]?
GIANCANA: He looked like an idiot.
UNKNOWN: He must be eighty years old.
GIANCANA: He brought over some beautiful broads. He never
           gambled, though, except on the horses. He never
           used our crap tables up in Deerfield. Say, you
           know, we can make a gambling room out of that Ve-
           netian Room [a cocktail lounge off the main room at
           the Villa Venice].
UNKNOWN: No, it would never go.
GIANCANA: Sure. It would make a hell of a place. We can push
           one or two walls out.
UNKNOWN: That would be a hell of a spot. We could put the
           wheels and crap tables right outside, in tents.
           [Laughter]
UNKNOWN: Wait until you see that place. Everything is beauti-
           ful. As you walk in, it's great. Fireplaces, foun-
           tains . . .

I found those FBI reports, as well as others about my father
and Frank Sinatra, particularly interesting after I read Sinatra's
sworn testimony before the Nevada State Gaming Control Board.
This testimony was given on February 11, 1981, after a parade

of witnesses from a former Los Angeles sheriff to Attorney General William French Smith to President Ronald Reagan had assured everyone on the board that Sinatra was an "honorable person."

Frank flatly denied in his testimony that he and Sam had interests together in the Cal-Neva Lodge, a statement that conflicts with what my father and Roselli were overheard saying in conversations recorded by the FBI. He also said that he had only known my father since early 1960 and had met him for the first time in a hotel in Miami. And when it came to the Villa Venice, Sinatra testified that he was unaware of Sam's interests in the nightclub, and while he spent six days there entertaining at the club, he wasn't sure if he had seen my father there. The sworn testimony reflects the following:

CHAIRMAN [RICHARD] BUNKER:	Did you see Mr. Giancana while you were entertaining at the Villa Venice?
SINATRA:	I might have.
BUNKER:	You don't recall?
SINATRA:	No, but I might have. Just possible.

Just possible! I couldn't believe my eyes when I read that any more than I could believe the other things that he said about my father.

I myself first met Sinatra with Sam years before the Villa Venice engagement at the Fontainebleau in Miami. I remember going to watch his show and then going backstage to his dressing room with Sam to meet him. And there were other meetings in his private suite at the Fontainebleau, and each time he greeted Sam with an embrace of respect and friendship.

We were at the Villa, almost every night that Sinatra and his Rat Pack were there. Sam took us—friends, family members—to the dressing rooms of Sammy Davis, Jr., and Sinatra, which were upstairs. Sinatra and his group would be eating some bagels or some Italian food, and Sammy Davis and his group had these barbecued ribs that looked and smelled so good! "Ol' Pickleface" would give my father a hug, and so would Sammy Davis whenever Sam entered their rooms, and pictures were taken. Unfortunately, the photographs were confiscated by my sisters when my father died, so I no longer have copies of pictures taken of Sinatra and Sam and me.

I realize that Sinatra wanted to get a license as an entertainment consultant for Caesar's Palace in Las Vegas and that he wanted to invest in a casino again. But to deny that he knew Sam owned the Villa Venice, to say that he and Sammy Davis, Jr., and Eddie Fisher and Dean Martin and other entertainment stars came to a nightclub in a place called Wheeling, Illinois, only because Sinatra knew Leo Olsen is just incredible to me. Interestingly enough, he didn't testify that he went to the Villa out of friendship for Olsen, a story he told the FBI in 1962; he said he did it because his agent arranged it for a fee of fifteen thousand dollars over seven days of appearances.

I was so upset over Sinatra's testimony that I called the Nevada State Gaming Control Board to tell them what I knew, that there were FBI documents that showed a different relationship than that pictured by Sinatra. The board people I talked with weren't very interested. They never bothered to come to see me to examine what documents I had.

And the Villa Venice? It folded and burned to the ground after my father sold it. It had made a big splash and played to packed houses while Sam brought in all the entertainers and threw expensive parties in a Villa suite attended by his mob friends and by the entertainers, including Sinatra.

Before the Villa's end came, my father and his underworld friends literally coined money at the gambling operation they had set up for patrons two blocks away in the Quonset Hut.

A *Chicago Daily News* article on November 30, 1962, spelled out the gambling operation, which of course Sam never let me get near. The article stated in part:

"During the last 20 days since singer Eddie Fisher started off the new star policy at the Villa, a heavy toll has been levied at the hut on the [Villa] patrons. Individual losses of as much as $25,000 have been reported.

"A shuttle service has been provided for some of the customers who want to leave their cars at the Villa. The hut is camouflaged with old trucks and pieces of road machinery."

The article reported that at least two dice tables, blackjack tables, and roulette wheels were in operation at the Quonset Hut.

A day later, on December 1, 1962, the *Chicago Tribune* said that the illegal casino was set up "by the syndicate chief, Momo Salvatore (Moe) Giancana, to tap the bankrolls of patrons drawn to the Villa Venice by the nightclub act of Frank Sinatra, Sammy Davis, Jr., and Dean Martin.

"The betting den began full blast operations when Sinatra and his group opened at the Villa Venice, it was learned.

"A host of gangsters were on hand for Sinatra's first night, investigators said. Among them were Giancana, Willie (Potatoes) Daddano, Marshall Caifano, Jimmy (the Monk) Allegretti, and Felix (Milwaukee Phil) Alderiso.

"Sinatra's gangland fans from other cities appeared too, authorities disclosed. The Florida contingent was led by Joe Fischetti, from Miami. A delegation of Wisconsin gangsters, including Jim DeGeorge, occupied a ringside table."

Before it was all over, friends of my father's told me that the casino had brought in several million dollars. An FBI estimate, based on overheard conversations, apparently placed the figure at over three million dollars.

Sam always did know how to use entertainers.

10

Sex and the
Mafia Princess

When I returned from California and the movie colony in late August, 1949, Sam was still busy organizing the Chicago mob's takeover of the black policy rackets. He and his friends were moving into restaurants, and the record distribution and jukebox businesses, all enterprises that were to make millions for Chicago's underworld.

With Sam's growth in the organization came an increase in violence as he and his men carved out new territories for the mob. The violence and pervasiveness of the political corruption the Chicago mob was behind would attract not only the attention of the press, but the microphones and attendant national publicity that accompanied United States Senator Estes Kefauver's special committee in its investigation of organized crime, which included special public hearings in Chicago in 1950 and 1951.

Mother was equally busy in her own way, being knee-deep in fund-raising activities for the Italian Welfare Council.

Sam's decision to make her keep a low profile in this Italo-American group turned out to be a very wise one. Had she been more publicly active in the group—acting as its president, for example—most certainly the council and Sam would have drawn the unwanted attention of the Kefauver committee, particularly when they were questioning Paul Ricca about his relationship with an attorney who served on the council with Momma.

Mother was also spending a great deal of her time helping Francine who, with her sight problems, needed special attention. Bonnie, my other sister, was also in school, but she posed no special problem. She was a relatively quick study. She learned fast in school and adhered to the disciplines required by Sam and Momma. That left me. I had a learning problem that had begun at an early age and had not improved with time.

The solution, according to Sam, Momma, and Father Joe, lay in sending me to a very special school with very special surroundings—Ladywood.

Sam had first met Father Joe through the Moretti family. At that time Salvatore Moretti worked for Sam, and the entire family, including Sal's five brothers, were politically very important on Chicago's West Side, which was controlled by Sam and the mob. The one who introduced Sam to Father Joe, however, was Michael Moretti, a cop who had been convicted in 1951 after shooting three teenage boys in a car, two of whom died. The third boy lived to testify against him. The case became a major scandal, and the gun used in the shooting was brought to Moretti by an investigator from the state attorney's office. Salvatore, of course, was later found murdered in the trunk of a car.

Father Joe was very active in a West Side Catholic church as a fund raiser, and during major charity affairs the Moretti brothers would escort him to and from the bank to make sure no one would rob him.

As I said before, Sam and Father Joe became close. My father gave him an envelope filled with money whenever he was running a charity affair, and at Christmas he would stuff a special envelope with money for Father Joe's personal use.

By 1949 Father Joe had in effect become Sam's personal private priest. Not that that was unusual in the Chicago mob. Tony Accardo, Ross Prio, Rocco Fischetti, and others all had priests from their parishes to whom they gave special consideration and from whom they received special treatment. Many of the priests in Chicago catered to the families of crime figures when I was young. What the mob did was done to help their parishes, and their own and their family's position in those parishes, or in the diocese, or in the chancery of the cardinal where Sam and his friends had strong, influential friends. It wasn't venal . . . it was practical.

I suppose some of Sam's friends must have thought they were buying their way into a place in heaven, or a plot in a church cemetery, or a special remembrance. There may even have been a few who did it for altruistic reasons, but I suspect the principal purposes behind their strong support of the Church was first of all, tradition and second of all, to keep their kids in parochial schools and win favors for their families when they needed them.

I discovered recently that Sam was and still is almost revered by many of the Resurrection Academy nuns who went on to work at the Catholic hospitals. They revered him principally because he treated them with such deep respect and because he was always generous and helpful in causes they espoused. I have had some nuns tell me they never believed what the newspapers, television, or law-enforcement agencies had to say about Sam. Some have told me they considered him almost saintlike and that I should be proud of him. Others have told me how they prayed for Sam when he was murdered and have done so ever since. So there was a strong relationship between men like my father and clergymen like Father Joe, and that was usually based on having been raised in the traditional Italian reverence for the Church and God.

Almost all the daughters of Sam's mob friends went to schools near their homes. I was the exception to the rule. Sam would always arrange for me to go to school away from home. I suppose he thought I'd learn more and be better equipped to live in the world outside the Outfit. To that end he spent a lot of money to get me into schools like Resurrection Academy and Ladywood.

It was 1949. I had returned from California and Sam was still busy taking over the black policy rackets of Chicago while moving into the restaurant, record, and jukebox industries, and other enterprises.

Since Father Joe, Sam, and Momma all agreed that I required special training to correct my shortcomings, and after talking to Father Joe, I had agreed once again to leave home to be educated in a strange place.

I must admit Sam and Momma did everything possible to make it easier for me to attend. I had a completely new wardrobe that cost thousands of dollars. There were new and expensive sheets and blankets for the bed I would be using, a plush carpet for the bathroom, curtains for the window, and two beautiful new bedspreads, one for myself, and the other for whoever I might have as a roommate so our beds would match.

In the fall of 1949, we left for Indianapolis and Ladywood School, the way paved by Father Joe's sponsorship and padded by the long green Sam was willing to spend. And make no mistake, Father Joe had spent months, at Sam's expense, shuttling back and forth to Ladywood to convince school officials that I should be accepted in spite of my poor scholastic record.

One look at the long, winding roadway leading up to Ladywood School and I was ready to return home.

The school was isolated (it was twenty minutes by car from thriving downtown Indianapolis), and its main administrative building and dormitory were situated high atop a hill, the upper-floor turrets and dormers protruding menacingly into the sky, permitting the winds to scream eerily around their many corners day and night. And there were nights that would follow when, as I stared up at the multitiered staircase, at the long hallways and archways and the carved wooden gargoyles, I would tremble with fear as the winds howled and I would wonder if the old mansion were haunted. I was frightened by the immensity and the coldness of everything. If there was a beauty to this Tudor-style mansion, it was lost on me.

To reach the entrance, we had to scale twenty broad and seemingly ancient stone steps before reaching the huge latticed entrance doors of what was then called Laurel Hall.

As we entered the building, my eyes flicked up and down, from side to side, and with my mouth open I tried to cope with everything: the polished, hand-hewn walnut paneling, the multifloor, winding stairway leading to long, magnificent, and dark arched hallways with gargoyles, and with priceless Oriental rugs covering their gleaming wooden floors.

Ladywood was a very fashionable, very expensive college-preparatory high school as well as a finishing school. It had been established in 1926 by the Sisters of Providence who had maintained and operated St. Mary-of-the-Woods College in Indiana since 1840. The nuns had simply moved the college-preparatory and finishing-school sections of the campus to what had been a private estate. Twenty years later, in 1970, it would merge with St. Agnes Academy, another Sisters of Providence school, and it closed as a boarding school in 1974 when Laurel Hall and nearly one hundred acres of the property were sold.

The school attracted the cream of society in Indiana as well as from outside the state. Most of the girls' fathers were politicians, or doctors, or lawyers, all wealthy people from professional families. I was the exception and it was an exception that I suppose haunted them later when the Kefauver committee hearings identified my father in Chicago.

Among my roommates and close friends at Ladywood were Mary Antonia Hulman, whose family still owns the Indianapolis 500 Speedway; Mary Brown, whose father was a judge; and Claire McKinney, whose father, Frank, was the Democratic Party's former national chairman and the owner of a professional athletic team. I doubt that the parents of any of my friends, nor those of other students, would have appreciated knowing that the daughter of one of Chicago's top mobsters was a member of Ladywood's student body.

I remember quite vividly, right after there had been a storm of publicity over the Kefauver hearings in Chicago, Sam was called to Ladywood for a conference and advised that the school did not feel it would be in its best interests to retain me as a student because my grades were low and I was having particular difficulty with Spanish.

That Sam showed up at the school at all was really remarkable. Investigators of the Kefauver committee had been trying to find him for months to slap a subpoena on him, and he had managed to avoid service.

At the same time, Sam's mentor, Paul Ricca, had appeared before the committee, at which time he was questioned about the special treatment he got in federal prison. He was also questioned about his sudden release from prison with Louis Campagna after someone had mysteriously donated $120,000 to pay back taxes and fines Ricca owed. The influence of the two men in the movie industry, their friendship and relationship with Al Capone and

Frank Costello, and the visits paid them by Anthony Accardo—all these things came out.

What I remember most, however, was that the timing of that conference at the school seemed to be more than coincidental. It came within a day or two after my father had been briefly identified at the hearings as "Momo Giancana," the driver of Chicago mob boss Accardo and a rising star of that organization.

Mentioned in much more sensational detail was the West Side Bloc, "the Italian bloc . . . of the bloody Twentieth Ward," led by the old Capone mob's handpicked political hack, Roland Libonati. It was the same group of politicians that had been so helpful to my mother in organizing the "Night of Stars" and other fund raisers of the Italian Welfare Council.

By 1958 the Kefauver revelations notwithstanding, Libonati became the Chicago mob and Sam's personal congressman—a launching pad for legislation to help crime figures like my father while opposing the anticrime measures of such groups as the Chicago Crime Commission. One of the more famous pieces of legislation Libonati attempted to have passed was a law that would have made it a federal crime to keep criminals under surveillance. At the time, the FBI was keeping my father under what the Bureau likes to call "lockstep surveillance."

I was in the administrative office when one of the school's staff members demonstrated in a circumspect way that coercion and extortion weren't only the tools of organized crime, as suggested by Kefauver. She showed me that there were times when so-called educators and religious figures are not above such tactics to achieve their goals.

As I sat silently and watched, she made it plain without saying it directly that she knew exactly who and what my father was. She reminded him of the long and unblemished history of Ladywood, of what a proper school it was, of how much its reputation meant, and of what could happen to the school if it "received the wrong kind of publicity."

Never once did she say, "I know you are a hoodlum and I think your daughter should leave because you and your reputation could become an embarrassment to the school." But Sam knew what she was driving at, and he could be just as circumspect as she was. He might have had only a sixth-grade education, but he hadn't gotten to his position in the Mafia by being a fool.

"Annette's been having a difficult time, hasn't she?" he asked.
The educator nodded with a frown. Hadn't my father heard
what she had said?

"What do you think we should do about it?" he continued.
"You know I want the best for my Annette. . . . I am willing to
pay . . . whatever it takes to see that she improves . . ."

The educator lost no time moving into the opening Sam had
deliberately provided her, and I watched the traces of a slight
smirk cross the edges of his mouth as she made the pitch Sam
knew was inevitable. He was always a superb judge of character.
He could always read a person better than any man I ever knew,
and he knew every person had a price, a need. It was just a question of finding out what that need was.

Quickly she suggested that what I needed was "very special
tutoring" in geometry and Spanish. Ladywood lacked the teaching
resources for such a requirement, she said, but she knew someone
who might fill the bill—a bright, articulate young Costa Rican girl
who wanted to study in the United States and who spoke English
well enough to tutor me in the subjects in which I was deficient.
There was just one problem. The young girl was from a very poor
family and she was still in Costa Rica. Now if there was some way she
could be brought to this country, if her tuition and her expenses
could be paid by some benefactor while she was tutoring me at
Ladywood, well then, maybe, just maybe, I might be able to bring
my grades up sufficiently to remain at Ladywood.

Even at fifteen I knew what was going on. I realized that this
official was in effect shaking down Sam. As she spoke, she tapped
incessantly with her pen on the front page of a newspaper that
had a story referring to the Kefauver hearings and Chicago's
crime syndicate. Sam's name wasn't in that particular story, but
the meaning she wished to impart was clear enough.

So to keep me in Ladywood, Sam sponsored the educator's
Costa Rican ward, paid all her travel expenses, her tuition,
bought her new clothes, and provided her with a weekly allow-
ance while she tutored me in math and Spanish for less than a
year. And I remained at Ladywood until I was a senior, finally
returning home to Oak Park to finish school in the Oak Park-
River Forest High School in 1952.

*   *   *

As a freshman I couldn't stay at Ladywood's main manorhouse, Laurel Hall. Like all the freshmen and sophomores, I was assigned to a nearby dormitory facility with classrooms on the first floor, student bedrooms on the second floor, and two students to each room with walk-in closets and a bathroom.

The sisters ran the school with militarylike discipline. Each morning before meals and class we were required to line up and walk to church in supervised groups with veils draped carefully over our hair and faces as was the custom in those days. There were regular room and clothing inspections, and students received demerits if something was out of order. Girls who received three demerits by the end of the week were not allowed to go to town on Saturday . . . they couldn't even call home. Those who did qualify for trips were transported to and from Indianapolis in a small, white, six-passenger school limousine and were allowed to stay just two hours for shopping or whatever else they wanted to do as long as it was ladylike. All letters, except those from parents, were carefully monitored and censored. There was an exception to this rule for me. I did get permission to write to Father Joe, and I could receive mail from him that was not censored. But the mail I received from Tony Tisci was read by the nuns before I received it.

Tony was a college law student and really a very bright young man. His father was a hardworking railroad construction worker who had laid railway tracks to make his way in life. He was a simple man, an honest old Italian who worked like a dog to put Tony through college and who was very close to my father.

As far as I know, Tony's father had nothing to do with the rackets. Sam simply liked him and he liked Tony even more. I think from the beginning he wanted Tony as a son-in-law, and since I was the eldest and most eligible daughter he virtually threw us together.

Tony was quiet, reserved, and a very, very handsome young man. He was desirable, intellectual, and intelligent. He was also intensely jealous, but he was a fun person to be with.

Until Sam introduced me to Tony, I had never been allowed to go out on a date with a boy, and whenever I came home from school for a holiday or a vacation, Tony would be there and we would go out . . . that is, when I wasn't seeing Father Joe.

Momma had also taken an interest in furthering our relationship, waiting up at night until I returned home from a date and then sitting with me over hot cocoa to talk about where I had been and what our date had been like. Tony was always a perfect gentleman, and beyond the usual teenage necking, nothing ever happened in the three years we went out with each other.

For a time, I suppose I was in love with Tony. But there were many years of intellect, education, maturity, and experience that separated us. He was a difficult man to be with, too prim and proper and unreasonably jealous. If I so much as looked at another male, it brought an angry outburst from him. My dress was also of his concern—nothing must be cut too low.

I finally exploded when he criticized me for talking to a young man while I was in a hospital in Chicago recuperating from facial surgery after leaving Ladywood in late June, 1952. We made up for a while after that, but it was never the same. Later he married my sister Bonnie, and my father, as he had planned to do, groomed him for big things in Chicago politics. When Libonati went to Washington in 1958, Tony went with him as his administrative assistant. Sam's plan was to replace Libonati with Tony and then push him to the heights—to governor, United States senator, who knows how far and how high. With the Chicago political machine dancing to the tune of the Outfit then, anything was possible.

It was a dream that Sam could never fulfill. Tony, for a long time his regular companion and one of his trusted legal advisers, developed a severe heart condition and had to leave the rigors of the political arena.

That first year at Ladywood was hell for me. I was constantly in trouble. I almost always had too many demerits at the end of a week to be able to go to town. I couldn't get candy, soda, cosmetics, all those things a young girl loves when she is in school away from home. Momma, God bless her, knew I had a problem, and since she required that I send all my laundry home each week to be cleaned to prevent my blouses from being ruined at the school laundry, she would use the return packages of clothing to smuggle candy and cosmetics to me.

It wasn't until my sophomore year in 1950 that something nice happened to me at school—after Sam agreed to finance the Costa Rican girl's trip to America to be my tutor.

First, I had qualified for training in horsemanship as a sophomore. During the summer prior to my return, Sam had taken me shopping for a complete English riding outfit. I think he was almost as excited as I was. He took me to Bailey's, a very expensive Chicago store, and had me outfitted from head to toe: black, shiny leather boots, riding pants, jackets, blouses, hats, ties, and a riding whip. He spent well over two thousand dollars on that little spree, seeing to it that I had nothing but the best. I didn't know how to ride yet, but I sure looked great.

By then—it was June, 1950—I was about to celebrate my fifteenth birthday, an event that was not celebrated at home but at Father Joe's rectory.

In my parents' household, sex was never discussed with children. I certainly would never have dared ask Sam about it. Not only would I have been too embarrassed but, worse, Sam might have thought I was doing something wrong. That was the way his mind worked.

And Momma? Sex was something she was too embarrassed to discuss at any time. Until the day she died, she never once talked to me about the facts of life. The closest she ever came to discussing sex in any fashion with me was before her death, when she made the crack about her suspicions that Sam had a blond girl friend.

So in June, 1950, just before my birthday, I called Father Joe and asked him if when school ended I could come to see him for counseling and advice on the subject of sex. What I got was more than advice, it was a primer.

Sam and Momma, of course, had no way of knowing what I was going to see Father Joe about. It was not unusual for me when I was home and not dating Tony to seek out Father Joe's advice and have him hear my confessions.

Without my knowledge, Father Joe, after I called, had told my parents that he planned a little prebirthday celebration for me at the rectory—a dinner, a cake, presents, and some extensive discussions about my studies and problems at Ladywood. Because of their close relationship, Sam saw nothing wrong in such a party. In fact, he encouraged it.

My chauffeur to the rectory was Joe DiPersio, who dropped me off and returned later when I called him.

The evening began innocently enough. There were before-dinner drinks to toast my birthday—Manhattans, as I recall—then some sweets and a lovely dinner topped off with a small but very sweet birthday cake and a glass of wine.

At dinner the discussion was casual: about school, problems I was having with some subjects, the discipline exercised by the nuns, and how lonely I felt so far away from home and family. After dinner Father Joe brought me to his suite in the rectory, where we had often talked privately in the past whenever the pastor of the church was out. Nothing improper had ever taken place before.

I was feeling warm and strangely excited as we sat down in his suite. Father Joe wasn't a particularly handsome man, but he was attractive and he was gentle and soft-spoken. His eyes were soft and understanding, even behind his glasses, and he was trim for a man in his forties and not particularly athletic.

Maybe it was the wine, maybe it was the occasion, maybe it was the subject, but I was physically attracted to Father Joe in a way I had never thought possible. I sat on an ottoman at his feet while he looked down at me from a large easy chair. Haltingly, I began asking him what happened between a man and woman when they were married? What was this I had heard from girls in the school about sex between a man and a woman?

At first, he began to explain things to me and then he began demonstrating—first with light kisses, then with fondling—how passions were stirred. Before long things got out of hand. We were undressing, we were in his bed, and I was having my first experience in sex. At no time during that evening or during subsequent evenings did Father Joe ever say that what we were doing was wrong, yet I knew it was and I think I realized what the consequences would be for us both should Sam ever discover what had happened.

Our relationship, however, continued to grow, and each time I returned home for a vacation or a holiday, we had new and more torrid meetings at the rectory. Finally, one of our liaisons took place at our house. Sam and Momma were out for the evening.

When we had finished, I forgot to straighten up my bed, and as Father Joe left, my cousin Marie Perno drove up.

While I was in the kitchen, Marie went upstairs and for some reason went into my bedroom. Suddenly she was downstairs, standing in the kitchen doorway, staring at me.

"Have you been doing something with that priest?" she asked sharply.

I looked at her in shock. "My God, Marie . . . how can you even think something like that?" I answered. "With Father Joe . . . with a priest? Are you crazy?"

She didn't press it, but she didn't appear to believe me completely either. I don't know what she told Sam but after that, the relationship between Sam and Father Joe cooled, and he and Momma restricted my meetings with the priest. Obviously Marie had not told Sam everything she suspected. If she had, he most certainly would have had the priest eliminated . . . and possibly me along with him. He didn't, but things were never the same between my father and Father Joe after that. The priest was no longer invited to our house, and Sam and Father Joe no longer exchanged gifts.

Nevertheless, my special relationship with Father Joe continued for many years after. But he had let a genie out of the bottle, and after him would come a long line of men, many of them honest love affairs, others just quick flings to satisfy my need for sex and excitement. A new door to life had been opened for me that would never close again.

11

Farewell, Sweet Angeline

In June, 1952, Sam arranged for two of Chicago's best plastic surgeons to operate on me at Michael Reese Hospital. Their assignment: cosmetic surgery that would change a rather large, unattractive nose into a delicate and functional breathing device that would be compatible with a theater-arts career.

For years I had had problems with my nose. Bonnie had hit it with a ball, nearly breaking it, and Francine banged it accidentally when she swung a club at a ball. And I had fallen on it going up flights of stairs. The net result was damage, including a deviated septum and a crooked, somewhat flattened noseline.

Momma knew it caused breathing problems and took me to a doctor to see if the difficulty could be corrected. His recommendation was an operation to correct the breathing problem and cosmetic surgery to improve the outward appearance.

At first, Sam resisted the idea of surgery as unnecessary, particularly because of my often expressed desire to get into modeling and show business. But in the end he relented, admittedly under heavy pressure from Momma and my somewhat childish histrionics—an overreaction to the fact that I would be going to a new school in the fall. I was about to enter Oak Park-River Forest High School after failing to measure up to the standards of Ladywood, and I absolutely refused to go to a new school looking like an anteater with a swollen sniffer. When Sam did agree, he made certain I had the best of surgeons and hospital accommodations at the Kaplan Pavilion.

The state of the art in cosmetic surgery then was primitive by today's standards, and it was a terrifying experience. I was given a general anaesthesia, and while I experienced no pain, I was awake throughout the operation, watching the surgeons as they used every hammer and saw and whatever other surgical tool they required to cut away the tissues and cartilage necessary to re-form my nose structure. I imagined pain that was really nonexistent at that moment, and while I had private nurses and very comfortable surroundings, I imagined that I surely was going to die.

My entrance and exit from the hospital went unnoticed by the press, and Sam's visits were infrequent and often at odd hours, primarily to avoid Kefauver committee investigators and their subpoenas as well as the press, and to organize the Chicago mob's control of what had been the black policy rackets. But he did come to visit me and console me, and to be certain I had the attention I needed, as did my mother.

At the end of ten days, I returned home to spend the summer recuperating and healing so I could enter the new high school without feeling like the class ugly duckling.

During this period of change and following the Kefauver committee's public disclosures Sam and our family seemed to spend more and more time with Accardo and with Paul Ricca. Both men knew how to live and I had the feeling at times that Dad was like a peon to them; yet it was during these years that they both gave Sam more and more responsibility in running Chicago's underworld.

There were frequent visits to the palatial Accardo home with its carriage and coach houses, glittering indoor swimming pool, and high vaulted ceilings.

All around Accardo were the trappings of opulence: the magnificent polished-wood spiral staircase, the inlaid mosaics, the Italian marble, and the bathrooms with their shiny gold-plated fixtures. It was almost obscene the way he flaunted his wealth. He reminded me of some medieval Sicilian godfather dispensing baronial favors from his stately, wood-paneled library filled with valuable and classical gems that I bet he never bothered to open, let alone read. But he was nonetheless impressive, and his manner was designed to awe those who worked under him, to remind them of his station in mob life and of theirs.

The greetings were always warm, very warm. A half hug, a firm handshake, a pat on the back, and the two men would retire to a room off the library to talk privately while mother and I talked quietly with other members of the family. Accardo, I recall, had one son, his namesake, who was very attractive and whom I thought at one time I might like to date. Tony Accardo was nice, pleasant, and polite, but it was a fleeting fancy, nothing more.

Sam had become even closer to Paul Ricca, a very shrewd move on his part, I always thought. Ricca was the elder statesman of the Chicago mob, a man who never spoke a vulgar word in my presence or that of my mother, who was the very essence of the Mafia godfather. He just exuded propriety, respect, dignity— name a superlative and he had it. He was the don of dons and regardless of his terrible history of criminality, a history that included the cruelties of the old Capone mob and two murders in Italy plus countless other crimes, according to law-enforcement agents, I can speak of him only in terms of respect and love. I worshiped the ground he walked on, and in later years I wished that he had been my father. When you were in his presence, he was very European, very courteous, and always respectful no matter who you were, and he professed a deep sense of honor and tradition.

Paul Ricca told me on many occasions when I was older about the impoverished conditions his family had had to live under back in Naples, Italy, and how proud he was to be an American. It wasn't until the Kefauver hearings and the deportation proceedings that followed that I learned he had murdered the boyfriend of a sister, a man named Emilio Parillo, because the man had dishonored his sister.

Ricca had been tried and convicted of that murder—based on the testimony of a Vincenzo Capasso, according to federal records—and served a prison sentence at the age of nineteen. When he was freed from prison, he killed Capasso and then came to the United States using false credentials. To Paul the murders he had committed in Italy were matters of honor and he freely acknowledged them, but he never discussed them or his much publicized record with the Capone criminal organization or his associations with the movie colony with me or with anyone else that I knew. Such matters were private, and I would never have dared offend him by asking about his past, although we often talked about his days of poverty in Naples.

Paul treated me like a daughter, but he also loved my father, honestly and truly, as though Sam were a younger brother. Each time we visited his River Forest estate, he greeted Sam with open arms, with a true camaraderie that I have never seen or felt with any other man my father associated with.

I know that it was Paul who guided Sam along, who sponsored his elevation to boss of Chicago, and it was he who was most disappointed and hurt when my father deviated from the ways of the Old Country, became involved with women in the entertainment world, and focused attention on himself and the Chicago mob. I'm grateful Paul did not live long enough to see my father murdered.

The year 1952 also marked a period in my life when I became closer than ever to my mother. She was ill more frequently now, constantly under treatment for her heart condition. Still, she continued with her personalized touch at housework, often getting on her hands and knees to scrub the floors of my father's private den and conference room or the kitchen, despite protests from Sam and from all of us. She also saw how unhappy I was and understood my need to do things she knew Sam would disapprove of even if they weren't wrong. One of those forbidden activities was modeling.

Mother had many friends and she used them to help me get minor modeling jobs under a variety of names, aliases such as "Antoinette Jordan," "Toni Jordan," and "Toni Wanette." The one I used most frequently was Toni Jordan, but I gravitated toward French-sounding names, hoping they would spark bigger things for my career—all while I was attending school in Oak Park.

Most of my modeling was done for photographers and fashion shops, and when I would receive an assignment, Mother would cover for me, telling Sam I was visiting some girl friend or the home of a relative. Momma liked my modeling, just as she had liked my short-lived dramatic training in Hollywood. She had always arranged for special dramatic, posture, and ballet classes, no matter what school I attended, to help further my theatrical ambitions.

Finally, however, Sam discovered what was happening. My pictures began appearing in photography studios and in the newspapers, first locally and then in the *Chicago Sun-Times* and the *Chicago Daily News,* always under an alias, never under the name of Giancana.

I'm quite certain that the newspapers never knew whose picture they were featuring in fashion shows or other modeling events. Had they known, they most surely would have given Sam and me notoriety that he did not want for his family or himself.

I recall one day in particular when Sam came home in a fury, waving a copy of a newspaper at me and shouting at the top of his lungs.

"What the hell is goin' on?" he yelled. "What are you doin' in this damn rag . . . and where did you get this name . . . this Toni Jordan crap?"

Momma entered the room from the kitchen and, sick as she was, put her arms around Sam to quiet him down.

"Now, Sam, Annette's done nothing wrong . . . really," she said softly.

His voice came down a few decibles, but he was still upset.

"I don't want you modeling," he snapped. "Only whores and tramps go into modeling. I don't give a damn what she's modeling," he said, turning away from Momma. "I don't care if she's showin' off at the Saddle and Cycle Club [a very elegant club where society's upper crust met for fashion shows] for a lot of ritzy broads. I don't want her in any of those places . . . you hear me?" he said, raising his voice again.

And once again Mother spoke soothingly to him, gently turning down his temper until he was just shaking his head.

"Sam . . . Sam . . . your daughter is born of good stock," she said. "She's a very moral person . . . she has all this religious training. I trust her . . . you must trust her."

Inwardly I cringed as she said that. I knew that her faith in me, in the Church, and in the priests she trusted so much would be shattered if she knew about my affair with Father Joe.

Her argument worked. Sam lowered his voice, threw up his hands in despair and frustration. But he had the last word.

"Angie . . . I'm warning you," he said, "this modeling can only lead to bad things, I tell you. It can't go on . . ."

In the long run, Sam put an end to my fledgling modeling career without further arguments at home. He simply reached out and through his muscleheaded henchmen, warned whoever was taking pictures of me, providing assignments for me, that they had better stop if they cared to continue breathing.

There were exceptions and for a time I was able to keep Sam from knowing, but they were rare. One of those exceptions was provided by Morrie Mages, the owner of a Chicago sporting goods store who did live radio and television commercials. Mages didn't know who I was, he just knew I had credentials as a model, had heard about me through a popular sportscaster who was a mutual friend. He hired me and used me on some of his advertising assignments. Of course, it wasn't long before Sam discovered that and put an end to it.

The same thing happened later at the Desert Inn in Las Vegas where my picture appeared under the name of Toni Flood on a billboard advertising a casino event. Sam was enraged when he discovered what I had done, and he put an immediate end to it by coming down hard on people who had to answer to him at the casino.

Both events happened after Momma died and Sam laced into me about that.

"Your mother, God rest her soul, didn't know . . . wouldn't listen to me!" he shouted. "I warned her . . . I warned you. You're going to end up in the gutter. You're going to be a whore because that's what models are . . . nothing but goddam dressed-up whores. Now you stay away from it . . . you stay away from photographers . . . you hear me?"

I heard but I wasn't listening. Why should I? By that time he was making a fool of himself running around with half a dozen other women, many of them models and entertainers.

While I modeled and went to senior high in Oak Park, I convinced Momma that it would be nice if I could do something to help others, just as she had done at the Italian Welfare Council. The vehicle I chose was the United Service Organization, the USO, where some friends of mine were already working as volunteers.

The Korean War was nearing an end, at least there were cease-fire negotiations under way, but Chicago was a town filled with servicemen, many of them Navy recruits at the Great Lakes Naval Training Station.

"I'd like to help out at the USO center, Mom," I explained. "A lot of my friends are helping and they feel good about what they're doing, but Dad will have a fit if I do . . . I just know it."

Momma promised to talk to him and see if something could be worked out. To my surprise, Sam came to me one night after dinner and said he had talked to Momma and told her I could work at the USO as long as I kept my grades under control.

"I think it's good you wanna work as a volunteer . . . helpin' out those boys, Annette," he said. "It's the patriotic thing to do. I approve . . . but you be home at a decent hour and you work on your grades at school."

I threw my arms around him, gave him a hug and a kiss on the cheek, and watched him grin broadly as I said, "Thank you" over and over again. That was in November, 1952. A few weeks later, as I helped out in an art class at the center, I met Alan W. Sulwk of Kingston, Pennsylvania.

Alan was a young sailor, not a very tall or impressive young man, with a lonely, faraway look in his eyes. I was attracted to him almost immediately. Alan's family owned and managed a rather large potato farm, and he was the very antithesis of the macho Italian stallions I'd been surrounded by all my life. The Alan Sulwks of the world treat women as equals, as people, not things to be used in bed or showcased at parties and shunted off to kitchens while the men go off into their own little world, a world that doesn't consider the intelligence or capabilities of women. That was the world I had always lived with, grown up with. That was the world of my father, of Tony Tisci, of the Accardos, and of the Riccas. Alan showed me the other world that I had never seen.

There was a hard-and-fast rule at the USO, a code of ethics that all volunteers had to live by: We were not allowed to date or bring home any of the servicemen we met. On the first night I broke that rule with Alan. I gave him the keys to my flashy new chartreuse Ford convertible to drive another couple to their home. Then we drove to the Great Lakes Naval Training Station where Alan was quartered, and I dropped him off. It wasn't long after that that I brought Alan home to meet Sam and Momma.

Alan was a hit right from the start. He was clean-cut, all-American, and a gentleman, and he catered to my mother more than anyone I had ever seen. I think it was because of his attention to Momma that Sam overlooked the fact that Alan wasn't Italian.

Tony Tisci, despite all the things Sam and Momma did for him, would never have gotten down on his hands and knees to wash floors, but when Alan first saw my mother scrubbing, he lifted her up from the floor very gently and in gentlemanly fashion, while she protested mildly. Then he placed her in a chair and scrubbed the floors himself until they were spotless. From that moment on, Mother loved Alan and Alan loved her.

Alan was always doing things to help her, to make her life at home easier when he was there. And when she became so ill in 1954 that she was confined to bed, Alan would cry openly about her state of health and would yell at me for not doing more for her, for not staying home with her when I wasn't in high school or college.

Equally as strange was the attraction that Alan and Sam developed for each other. Sam actually appeared to like him more than he did Tisci, possibly because of the way Alan treated Momma but also because they seemed to communicate, to relate to each other on different subjects. They often spent hours talking about communications techniques and electronics, a field that Alan knew a good deal about in the Navy. Sam was particularly interested in the methods used in wiretapping. I'm sure Alan didn't realize it, but my father's interest was designed to provide himself with a better background on the use of wiretaps and electronic bugs so he could employ defensive tactics against police and federal agents, or perhaps listen in on people who worked for him whom he didn't trust.

If Alan knew what and who Sam really was, he never let on. He would just show up at the house before a date and either just talk electronics with Sam or, when the weather permitted, help my father cut and manicure his precious putting green.

Meanwhile, I was falling head over heels in love with Alan, and to my surprise, Sam approved as did Momma. When Alan was transferred to Norfolk, Virginia, I was desolate, so much so that Sam and Momma arranged to fly him home for weekends, paying not only for his travel expenses but for his room at the Oak Park Arms Hotel.

Our biggest evening together was the night of my senior-class dance, a promlike affair for which all the senior girls dressed up in white formal evening gowns. The dance was held in the grand ballroom of the posh Edgewater Beach Hotel. Not only had my parents flown Alan back to Chicago for the affair, but Sam and Momma actually attended. It was the first time my father had ever seen me in a formal gown, but he was on hand for another reason.

That night, as both of them watched proudly, Alan gave me my first engagement ring, a lovely alexandrite birthstone, set in 14-karat gold with two white-gold hearts on either side which he promised to replace with diamonds as soon as he could afford them. It was a night worthy of a princess, even if her seat of royalty was the Mafia.

The dream ended abruptly just before Momma's death when I flew to Norfolk to spend a weekend with Alan. He had changed, and while we retained a strong affection for each other, he wasn't ready for marriage. I left Norfolk in anguish, certain I would never fall in love again. Of course, I was wrong.

April 9, 1954, is a day I shall remember and regret all the days of my life. It was on that date that Momma and I had a violent argument at our summer home in West Palm Beach. An hour later she had a cerebral hemorrhage, and two weeks later, on April 23, she died.

Momma had been constantly ill that year and every day she looked worse, like walking death. The truth was her illness had gotten progressively worse. Even Alan had remarked about how seriously ill she looked each time he saw her.

Instead of accompanying us to Florida, Sam had remained in Chicago to tend to the problems of mob leadership, problems which had multiplied and were keeping him away from home more and more. Sometimes, embarrassing newspaper stories and headlines resulted from these trips, for example, the stories coming out of Los Angeles in January, 1953. An incident had occurred that not only embarrassed Sam but also Anthony Accardo, the Italian Welfare Council, and Momma.

It all happened when Sam, Accardo, and Dr. Eugene J. Chesrow, the family physician and a past president of the Italian Welfare Council, took a trip to Los Angeles en route to planned stopovers in Las Vegas and Arizona. I suppose the police had been alerted to the fact that Accardo was coming because they were at the Los Angeles airport watching and waiting when Sam, Accardo, and Dr. Chesrow were met by two other Chicago mobsters, Frank Ferraro and Anthony Pinelli.

Everybody apparently was using a phony name, and when the Los Angeles police closed in, Sam and Accardo gave names that were plainly false. I guess the police knew what was happening because they decided to make a big splash in the newspapers. Accardo and Dr. Chesrow were identified by their real names; but for some reason—I suppose because they weren't sure—police identified the third man as "Michael Mancuso." Mancuso, of course, was my father.

The press quickly zeroed in on the weakest link in the chain, Dr. Chesrow, who was identified not only as the surgical superintendent for the Oak Forest Infirmary, but also as Accardo's personal physician.

It was all very embarrassing . . . and revealing. Dr. Chesrow, the council's fund raiser and my mother's close friend, was unmasked as Accardo's physician and associate. Everybody was released without charges being filed, but Dr. Chesrow, poor man, was hounded by reporters in California, and in Nevada and Chicago, all the while denying he was Accardo's doctor or that he was traveling with Accardo. In a sense he was right. He was our physician and he was with Sam, not Accardo, but nobody knew except the police and the FBI that Mancuso was really Sam Giancana and I suspect no one was saying anything because they weren't absolutely certain of the identification then.

The disclosures were extremely upsetting for Momma as well as for Dr. Chesrow. She was afraid that reporters would connect

the council and its charitable work to Sam and his cronies through
Dr. Chesrow. She was wrong, fortunately. The press barely noticed the council connection, and that organization folded gracefully after Momma's death before more bad publicity could
surface to destroy its image.

Still, the trip was typical of Sam's accelerated activities in those
days. More and more he was away from home, meeting with
Murray (The Camel) Humphreys and Jake Guzik—whose nickname was "Greasy Thumb" because of his flair for counting bills
rapidly—and Accardo.

Sam was building, strengthening the Chicago syndicate's principal source of money, gambling, through the stalwarts of the Capone days, through men like Guzik, while training and preparing
his old 42s gang members not only to follow in Guzik's footsteps
but to take over whole industries, associations, and unions that
would be useful to his organization's profit-making activities.

By being away from home so much, Sam saw less and less of
the family, and particularly Momma who was almost always ill, so
when it came time to vacation in Florida and enjoy a family
Easter, he was too busy. On April 9, I was on a special quick-
weight-loss diet of grapefruit and eggs, trying to trim my figure so
that I could return to some modeling assignments that I knew
Sam wouldn't know about. It was then I announced to Momma
that I had decided to change the color of my hair. I was going to
become a blonde. Not only do blondes have more fun, they get
more modeling jobs—at least that's what I flippantly said to her.

What happened next was totally unexpected!

"Over my dead body!" Momma shouted. "Never . . . do you
understand . . . never will you cheapen yourself like that and
have blond hair."

I was in a state of shock. I had never seen my mother react so
violently to anything and this remark seemed so innocuous. I
found it hard to believe what I was hearing—and seeing.

She threw a pillow across the room. Then one of my father's
prized figurines followed, crashing against the wall, splintering
into small pieces.

"I won't have a floozy for a daughter!" she yelled. "Blondes are
cheap. They look cheap . . . they are cheap . . . like that little
bitch your father's been running around with."

I was stunned by her outburst. The last time I had seen her even approach this level of anger was when she and Sam had had a battle over his coming home late and missing the dinner that she had set out for him.

"Where were you . . . out with some tramp?" she shouted as he sat down at the dinner table.

Without warning, she suddenly picked up the first thing she could find, a homemade blueberry muffin, and threw it at Sam. My God, what a battle that was. There were blueberries all over the house. There were blueberry stains on the walls in every room . . . all over Sam's five-hundred-dollar suit, his face, everywhere. From that day until her death, blueberry muffins and pies were forbidden fruits. Sam hated the sight of them.

When Momma jumped all over me about changing the color of my hair, I was slow to react, but the more I thought about it, the madder I got. I was being verbally abused because of what my father was doing. I was being compared to a blonde he was running around with, a woman I didn't know then and still don't know.

"I'm not a child anymore, Momma," I snapped. "I don't give a damn about Poppa's blonde. I don't even know her. I just want to be a model . . . to be myself and be a success on my own."

"Never!" she screamed, throwing another figurine at the wall. "I'll see you in hell first before I let you be a blonde . . . be a tramp."

"You can't stop me!" I shouted back angrily, storming out the door. "I'll damn sure do what I want." As I slammed the door, I said to myself, Damn you, I wish you were dead! God help me, I didn't wish any such thing, really. It was momentary anger lashing out. If only I could wipe away the memory of that thought . . .

I jumped into the car, carrying my towel and swimsuit, and headed for the home of Aunt Rose Eulo, my Catholic confirmation godmother, whose husband, Frank, worked for my father. Rose had been one of those who had originally arranged the secret meetings between my mother and Sam when her family opposed their dating.

As I drove off, I found myself cursing my father for not having built a pool next to our house, for having a girl friend on the side, and wishing I hadn't said anything to my mother.

I hadn't had a chance to change into my swimsuit or talk to Aunt Rose about my fight with Momma when the phone rang. It was my mother's sister, Anna Tuminello. Aunt Rose looked up at me, cupping the mouthpiece of the phone. "Your mother just collapsed," she said.

I was in an absolute panic as we rushed to Good Samaritan Hospital in West Palm Beach where Momma had been taken. By the time we arrived, half the family was on hand, and Sam had been notified in Chicago. She was in intensive care and her condition was listed as very critical.

The next two weeks were an absolute hell for me. Aunt Anna told the family about the argument that Mother and I had had just before she collapsed, and their eyes told me what they thought: They blamed me for what had happened.

I tried to stay at the hospital to be near Momma, but my aunts wouldn't let me. I had to give all kinds of excuses about going to the grocery store, or seeing a girl friend, to sneak past the royal guard at my house, get to the hospital, and wait outside the intensive-care-unit door. Seeing her in that oxygen tent, lying there motionless with all those tubes in her arms, I wanted to die for her. Occasionally, when I was allowed in the room, her eyes would open, but there was no sign of life or recognition.

On the day she died, Charlotte Campagna was there watching over her, watching over all of us. She camped in the room and wouldn't let me in to see her. I guess she wanted to spare me the agony of seeing my mother's pain, but I remember feeling how unfair it was that I couldn't be by my mother's side in those last moments, that it was the wife of a hood like Louis Campagna who had taken charge and was dictating who could and couldn't see Momma. Of course, I realize now that she was just following Sam's wishes and trying to spare us unpleasant memories, but for years it left a bitter taste in my mouth.

While no one said anything to me about the fight, or openly blamed me for my mother's condition, I felt as if I were being looked at with accusing eyes, particularly by Sam, who avoided me as if I were carrying the plague. Finally, one evening before she died and before I left for the hospital, I confronted him.

"Please, Dad . . . talk to me . . . hold me!" I cried.

There was a coldness in his eyes as he looked into mine. "Your mother's lying in there because of you and your mouth," he said sharply. "We've got nothing to say."

I wanted to scream out at him, hurt him as I was hurting, let him share the guilt, let him understand that it was because of his girl friend that Momma had lost her temper with me. Instead I said nothing. I turned from him, went to my room, and cried myself to sleep.

When Momma died, Sam walked around as if in a trance, tears welling in his eyes as he stared at her lying there in the casket, dressed in a beautiful pink Spanish dress with new shoes and a diamond collar necklace that he placed around her neck each day before family and friends arrived and removed each evening when he was the last to leave for home at night.

It seemed as if the whole world inside and outside Chicago turned out to pay its respects. Politicians from every corner of the city—Congressman Roland Libonati, James D'Arco, James Adducci, representatives of Mayor Daley's office—came en masse to pass by her bier. The mobsters came whom I had known since a child—Paul Ricca, Anthony Accardo, Jackie (The Lackey) Cerone, Sam DeStefano, Murray Humphreys, Ross Prio. If they were anybody in the mob, they came to pay their last respects. And there were scores, hundreds of people I had never seen before, many of them from out of town. When they placed Momma in the family mausoleum, it was as if a door had slammed shut on Sam's life.

He could not bring himself to get rid of anything that was hers. Her clothes remained in the dressers and closets for months. Then one day he gathered Bonnie and Francine and me in the front room of his basement apartment and laid out all my mother's jewelry. And to prevent any bickering between us he had made sure that there were three of every item, as near to being identical as possible.

By then, the wounds we shared had healed somewhat, and he took me aside as the eldest daughter and told me to choose the jewelry I wanted first. I took those things that Momma had worn most of her life, and I also took the diamond collar necklace that Sam had placed around her neck while she lay in the casket. I desperately needed that jewelry to ease my pain. My sisters weren't suffering the way I was for having hurt her that last day. I would wear her jewelry in the years that followed, and Sam glowed when I did. Perhaps in some small way I was atoning for my sin.

For Sam, however, the transition was difficult, if not dangerous. He was constantly morose. He traveled frequently back and forth to Florida because that was where Momma died and the house held memories he did not want to shake. For a time I really feared for him, feared his peers in the Mafia would react to his lack of leadership, to what they perceived as his inability to make decisions and meet regularly as he had in the past with the people who ran Chicago's rackets for him.

Then in July, 1954, Grandpa Giancana died of a heart attack. The trauma of it all came back for me, but Sam handled this death better. While most of us, wives, relatives, and friends gathered at the Cermak Funeral Home in Cicero to pay our final respects, Sam's associates met elsewhere, at Joe Corngold's cocktail lounge, to pay their respects to Sam out of sight of inquisitive police binoculars and pushing and shoving news photographers.

It took the FBI three years to learn the identity of those who had come to pay homage to my father at that funeral, and to put a new perspective on his power and role in the crime family.

Sam was in fact the new boss by then, for not only did Paul Ricca and other elder statesmen of the mob show up, but the upper echelons of the Outfit also came out en masse and in public.

In an FBI report dated December 26, 1957, the long list of attendees, including such notables as Anthony Accardo, Milwaukee Phil Alderiso, Jake Guzik, Joey Glimco, Obie Frabotta, and Ross Prio, were duly noted as having been at Joe Corngold's cocktail lounge with Sam on July 29, 1954.

With Grandpa's death, Sam's star had reached the heights. For him, it was the adrenaline shot that he needed to lead him to new underworld roles, those of international traveler, headline-grabbing lover of entertainer Phyllis McGuire, and crime boss of such awesome power that he would eventually also play a part not only in the candidacy but the presidency of John F. Kennedy and that never-never land of Camelot.

And for me, there would be an emotional breakdown, followed by a roller-coaster love life that would reach the heights of excitement and the depths of degradation.

12

The Trojan Horse

Clickety-clack . . . clickety-clack, the sound from the wheels of a small cart with a gray metallic box covered with dials, switches, wires, and electrical connections was slowly making its way down the hall. Clickety-clack . . . clickety-clack, there was something familiar about the sound, and suddenly I began to tremble.

Why? Why was I shaking? I slowly opened my eyes and looked around. I was in a bed with high metal tubing on either side, like a crib side designed to prevent a child from falling out of bed. The room was white and sterile except for a small bureaulike table next to my bed covered with flowers and a small stand across the room, also covered with flowers.

Clickety-clack, CLICKETY-CLACK, the sound was getting louder now. It was close to my door. My mind seemed to be moving in slow motion. The smell of the flowers made me sick. They had that sickly sweet odor so familiar to the funeral parlors I had been in so many times for Sam's friends, for Mother, for Grandpa.

CLICKETY-CLACK . . . CLICKETY-CLACK. That noise— that familiar noise had stopped outside my door! I was shaking uncontrollably now. Suddenly the door to my room swung open, and a very short, very stocky, pleasant-faced little Italian man in a white doctor's jacket stood there. Next to him was a stern, middle-aged nun and a hard-featured nurse of about thirty with cold blue eyes. Between them was the cart, the gray, metallic cart with all those dials and electrical cords, and suddenly I knew why I was trembling. Suddenly, I remembered . . .

It was October, 1954. Mother and Grandpa were dead and Alan was gone. Sam was never home, and when I did see him, his manner was cold and his eyes seemed always to scan me with suspicion, with accusations. I felt desperately alone and trapped.

I began drinking—at first, with students I knew at Northwestern University where I was studying drama and public speaking, then at bars in various parts of Chicago and its suburbs. When I came home, and it was often late, invariably there were long and bitter arguments with Sam. I had difficulty sleeping, so for help I turned to a physician I knew who provided me with prescriptions for sleeping pills and tranquilizers.

The pills didn't help but I still used them, and often, when Sam had taken the keys to my car away from me or I had no money for gas, I would call the local liquor store and have them send over a bottle of vodka to the house and I would drink. The more I drank, the more remorse I felt, and the greater my guilt. In October it became too much for me to deal with. I was only nineteen, but I was convinced that I had nothing to live for. The car, the mink coat, the expensive clothes, the jewelry—they meant nothing if I was unloved and unwanted by Sam. My solution came late one evening after a long round of drinking. I called Tony Tisci, whom I hadn't seen in months.

I'll never be certain how I managed to dial his number. My condition was such that I'm not sure I could see the dial. I suppose it was second nature, and I suppose the call was my subconscious way of crying out for help.

When I called Tisci, I was rambling, crying, in a deep depression. I suggested that life wasn't worth living. Then I hung up and started to drink some more until I had finished the whole bottle. It was then I took the bottle of sleeping pills and downed them.

I guess somebody was watching over me that night because before the pills could take effect, I began throwing up violently. By then Sam had arrived, alerted by Tisci, who suspected I was drunk enough to try something stupid. As I stood there alternately crying and vomiting, I looked at my father and screamed: "I want to die . . . do you understand? I want to die . . . for God's sake, let me die." I fell to the floor and in my stupor I remember vaguely hearing Sam talk on the phone to Dr. Carl Champagne, a physician he knew and trusted, and saying, "It's got to be handled quietly, Carl. Nobody's going to hear about this. I don't want any ———— reporters nosing around . . . you get it?"

Dr. Champagne got it, and he got Dr. William Parrilli, a psychiatrist who could be trusted. He also arranged for me to be in a private room in the psychiatric ward of Columbus Memorial Hospital, and registered me under the name of DeTolve, which was designed to keep reporters off the scent.

I tried to cry out as Dr. Parrilli walked over to my bed and lowered the rail nearest him. All that came out was a low, slurred word.

Parrilli smiled. "Good morning, Annette," he said. "It's time for another treatment."

Oh, God, I wanted to scream and I couldn't. All I could do was watch. I felt paralyzed. I watched in a daze as they strapped my arms and legs to the bed, as the nurse began rubbing jelly on my temples. Then Dr. Parrilli put a bit in my mouth. He patted my cheek gently and began attaching the electrodes to my temples. I felt cold, so cold, and everything seemed to be moving in slow motion. Suddenly I felt a jolt, a surge of electrical current coursed through my body as I jumped, then convulsed on the bed. It was a horrible, terrifying feeling, and even as I was convulsing, I had a flashing hindsight of the weeks of treatment I had been through.

It got worse. There were twelve electric shock treatments in all. I would hear those wheels come clickety-clacking down the hall, and as the noise became louder I would begin shaking and then cry out:

"Please . . . dear God, please . . . I don't want the treatment. No more treatments! You're killing me . . . please, God, no more treatments."

I was so afraid, I became violent, and as a result I was put in restraints. My arms and legs were restrained by straps on the bed. At one point I was kept in a straitjacket because they were afraid I'd fall out of bed. How the hell do you fall out of bed with guardrails and straps?

The treatments were very primitive by today's standards and very painful. There were no injections to calm you as there are today. The treatments were supposed to take away the depression, but all they seemed to do was increase my fear.

At first, the only people I saw were my aunts. Then Sam showed up bearing gifts of flowers or cards. I'd beg him to take me out of there and sobbing uncontrollably, I'd ask him what I'd done to make him hate me so, to put me through such pain.

"Why, Daddy?" I would cry. "Why don't you love me anymore? Please, Daddy, they're killing me here . . ."

Sam would just shake his head, leave the room, and send up another of my aunts to take care of me. All I could say to anyone was how I wanted to die.

The treatments continued for six months, and each time I heard those wheels I knew it was a Monday, Wednesday, or Friday, and that the electrical jolt would be more severe than the one before. Finally it ended, and in all that time only once did Sam show any real compassion, any real feeling.

I had just come through one of my treatments and was semi-conscious when he came into the room and saw what I looked like. For the first time since I was a small child, I saw a softness in his eyes. He leaned over the bed to kiss me lightly on the forehead, and I heard him say softly, "I care, Annette. I care."

I didn't know it then, but Sam was having problems with the law. From 1950 to the end of 1951, he had made himself scarce because the Kefauver committee had subpoenas out to force him to appear before them.

They never did successfully serve him because he spent some of his time hiding in Bimini, in the Bahamas, where he and Accardo frequently went when they weren't hopping over to Cuba from vacations in Florida. Sam usually registered under a different name, his nickname, Sam Mooney, or Sam Flood, this last having been taken from a relative's. His favorite place in Bimini was the Compleat Angler Hotel, where FBI documents indicate many crime figures stayed.

Sam was also knee-deep in operating nightclubs and other Chicago mob hangouts, many of which were centers of gambling, according to the FBI. One such place was the Wagon Wheel, a restaurant and nightspot in Norwood Park Township where Sam had taken me many times to dinner. Because the Wagon Wheel was also a hub of gambling, according to authorities, Sam was indicted on sixty-seven counts of permitting a building he owned to be used for bookmaking purposes. However, the Wagon Wheel was more than just a bookmaker's betting palace. It was also a casino that Sam operated in somewhat the way he had used the Villa Venice except that it wasn't as classy nor was it used to draw name entertainers.

What did surprise many in Chicago and outside the city was that Sam not only was never brought to trial on the charges, he was never arrested. The excuse given by deputies of the Cook County Sheriff's office, when Sam appeared to face charges in another case six years after the Wagon Wheel indictment, was that they could never find him to serve an arrest warrant. Of course, this is like saying you can't find the mayor in city hall. The pure and simple fact was that Sam and the organization had so much political influence that they quashed the indictment in their own way outside the courtroom.

Toward the end of 1954, in January, 1955, and through June, 1955, my father's problems with the law multiplied. In January, when he should have been spending time comforting me, he was busy ducking the subpoenas of a grand jury investigating what the FBI describes as a twenty-million-dollar-a-year numbers racket. And on May 30, 1955, Louis Campagna died. Not only did Sam have to turn out for his funeral because they had been so close, but he had to make another of his quick trips to Florida with Accardo and other members of the family. At this meeting they apparently had to choose a successor to Campagna, one of the old bosses who had made it possible to infiltrate the movie industry.

That didn't leave Sam much time to be with me, and since everyone was looking for him and he wanted to keep my presence in Columbus Memorial Hospital a secret, I saw very little of him during this very traumatic period of my life.

One of the men who for years had played an important role in my father's life, both in the political arena and in gambling as well

as enforcement, was a rather dashing Greek hoodlum named Gus
Alex.

Gus gave the mob a touch of class. He dressed impeccably,
right out of Brooks Brothers, and he was an international traveler.
London, Geneva, Paris, Athens, the Caribbean, you name it,
Gussy went there and he went there in style. His clothes were all
extremely expensive, hand-tailored, and selected with care from
the best fabrics available. And wherever he went, beautiful
women abounded. Sometimes his reputation as a hoodlum caused
him problems, as for example in Switzerland where at one time
he was banned, but I think his style of living had a considerable
influence on my father after my mother died.

In addition to being a very loyal friend and business partner of
Sam's in many transactions involving gambling and politics, Gus
had a flair for fitting into the social world. He knew and patronized the finest restaurants worldwide, and he frequented
them often. Gus knew important people in important places, and
he and Sam met frequently in those places—London, Miami, Las
Vegas, New York. And when they met they partied with class.

I first saw Gus while I was on a trip to New York with Sam. I
had long since left the hospital and recovered from the electric
shock treatments and additional months of psychiatric therapy.
The trip was one of several Sam had taken me on to help me
recover from the long six months I had spent being treated.
Hawaii, Mexico, the Caribbean, I went with Sam to a number of
exotic places when it didn't conflict with his work.

Gus then was about forty-one, five feet eleven inches tall, with
salt-and-pepper hair; he was well built and had a bug about fit-
ness. I had heard lots of stories about his being a killer. In fact,
there were tales about some of his victims giving deathbed confessions, but Gus was never convicted of such crimes. He and
Sam were heavily involved in gambling, and he packed a lot of
influence politically in the Loop.

Gus was anything but the typical American hood. For one, he
was a Greek, a Greek god who somehow by his wits and his loy-
alty managed to survive very nicely with the Capone organization
and the largely Italian–Irish-dominated criminal underworld of
Chicago. He had come up in that underworld as the protégé of
Jake Guzik before Guzik died in 1952.

Gussy was a charmer. FBI Agent William Roemer, who kept tabs on him and my father, testified in 1983 before the U.S. Senate Permanent Subcommittee on Investigations that Gussy was the successor to Guzik and Murray Humphreys as the Chicago mob's corrupter. There's no doubt of that in my mind. Gussy could make politicians jump through hoops when he wanted to, and he did whenever Sam wanted him to.

Gussy was also the mob's man in charge of the Loop. He ran or controlled most of the nightclubs and the strip joints in the area. But with all of that, Gussy was a well-spoken, articulate man who, while very businesslike, was physically attractive to women.

While women loved him, they were intimidated by the constant presence of Gussy's tall fashion-model wife, Marianne Ryan, a beautiful woman with copper-colored hair, gray eyes, and an awareness of other women who might covet her husband.

Marianne was very straitlaced. She didn't like Gussy having anything to do with the rackets. She was a high-fashion model with Bernice Korshak, the wife of attorney Sidney Korshak whom I had met through Sam on several occasions on the West Coast and who had enormous influence in the movie colony. I never knew what other relationship Korshak had with Sam, but they were very friendly and he treated me with great deference and respect.

Gussy idolized Marianne. He even used the name Mike Ryan when they were married and living together to avoid newsmen and publicity. Later, although she was a devout and practicing Catholic, Marianne divorced Gussy because he wouldn't get out of the mob. She wound up working as a fashion adviser for entertainer Dinah Shore on her television show. And Gussy, heartbroken though he was, found someone else to fall in love with and marry. Gussy was unusual for a mobster: He was very loyal to the women he married. He never fooled around as far as I know.

In July, 1957, just four months before Sam and other crime leaders across the nation were to make headlines by attending a crime conclave in Apalachin, New York, at the home of Joseph Barbara, Sr., Sam brought me to New York City for some shopping and sightseeing while he attended the heavyweight championship fight between Floyd Patterson and Hurricane Jackson at Madison Square Garden.

Both Sam and Gus were avid fight followers and bettors. I remember my father attending bouts fought by Rocky Marciano, Sonny Liston, and others. The Patterson-Jackson fight was significant, though, because for a time it changed my life.

Over the years Gus and I had been very close because of Sam, so it wasn't so unusual when I received a call from him at my hotel room at the Waldorf-Astoria.

"Toni . . . it's Gus," the voice on the telephone said. "Put on your glad rags and come on down to the Twenty-one [Club] and join us."

About thirty minutes later, I was dressed to kill and in a cab on my way to the club. When I arrived I was led to Gus's table. There he was with his gorgeous wife, Marianne, and another handsome Greek god.

His name was Dr. William Nestos, and he and Gussy had been friends for a long time. It would be years before I would learn that Nestos, who had an office on the edge of what was Chicago's old skid row, on West Madison, was more than just a friend of Gus Alex's. He took care of women who developed unexpected pregnancy problems while working in Gussy's strip joints and nightclubs.

Gussy didn't promote prostitution as a business, but many of his girls would take up prostitution as a sideline on their own. When they became pregnant, as sometimes happened, they went to Gussy for help and he sent them to Nestos to have their abortions taken care of. I never knew the extent of that relationship until years later when it was too late.

Nestos was forty-four, strikingly good-looking, with great presence. He was a staff physician at Chicago Wesley Memorial Hospital, but his role as an abortionist for call girls and mob prostitutes was unknown to me, although I have since learned it was not unknown to FBI Agent Roemer, who attempted unsuccessfully to interview Nestos when he learned of his close relationship to Gus Alex.

While Nestos had never been convicted for performing an abortion, I learned later from Roemer that he had been arrested. I also learned that Nestos had handled an abortion for one of Sam's girl friends. This led to Sam's bitter opposition to my continued dating and subsequent plans to marry him. In fact, it was because of Nestos's operation on Sam's woman—Sam never disclosed her identity to me—that I learned how deep-seated my father's hatred and mistrust of Greeks had become. He said they couldn't be trusted, not even his friend Gus Alex, that they were all like "Trojan horses." His prophecy was somewhat fulfilled at one point during my relationship with Nestos when the doctor gave me a huge diamond ring as an engagement ring. After looking at the ring, Sam went wild and demanded I give it back to Nestos. It seems that the ring, a beautiful marquise with large rubies on the side, was stolen and Sam recognized it as such. I found his attitude rather hypocritical, particularly since he had given a five-thousand-dollar bauble to a woman who had found out later that it was stolen when she took it to a Chicago jeweler to have a diamond chip fixed. That little gift almost landed Sam in jail, but the FBI and the police couldn't prove that Sam had given her stolen property because she refused to testify against him.

"What did I tell you about Greeks," he shouted, "particularly that Greek? You can never trust them. Never."

Sam had said all along to remember the old saying "Beware of Greeks bearing gifts." He was right.

That first evening, however, I had no suspicions about Dr. Nestos, and I was greatly attracted to him. Sam also had no suspicions at the time or he would not have let Gussy arrange our meeting at Club 21.

I didn't think too much about the meeting after that evening until I returned to Chicago. Then one night I pulled out the business card Nestos had given me and I called him. It took about five days before I finally reached him. I learned later he was difficult to reach because frequently he was ducking from the law or was in hiding for periods of time in order to perform illegal abortions in the Madison Street area, a well-known center of prostitution in those days.

It wasn't long before the rather casual attraction turned into a full-blown romance and affair. It could have been a storybook relationship for me. I felt like I was dating an Onassis.

But at home, while Sam was the king of his castle, he could go just so far and I was a source of frustration because I defied him.

Sometimes the scenes, particularly when Sam decided I should no longer go out with Nestos, were crazy. Lamps would be thrown; knives, whatever we could lay our hands on, we would use against each other. He had guns, but they were put away and thank God they were, because there were nights when I really thought I would end up with a bullet in my head or in my mouth because I wouldn't shut up.

I can remember evenings when, after he learned I had defied him and gone out, Sam would wait up and then we would start yelling running up and down the stairs, around the dining room table, screaming and shouting at each other. It had been like that from the time Mother died, and each year it seemed to grow worse and worse.

I remember one night in particular when I came home at about four in the morning. Sam was sitting in a chair waiting for me. I had been out with Nestos after Sam had told me to stop dating him, and he was seething with fury.

"Goddam you, Annette!" he shouted. "Didn't I tell you to stop going out with that ——— butcher . . . that rotten bastard? I oughtta kick you the hell outta here."

"Go ahead!" I shouted back. "Just do it. I don't need you. Bill will give me whatever I want and he won't be so goddam cheap about it. He'll give me my own charge account. He doesn't have to be worried about the goddam IRS. Maybe I ought to tell the IRS what they want to know about you and all your goddam money."

At that his steam rose, his face darkened, and his eyes turned steely-cold and his lip . . . He had a peculiar curl to his lip that said more than words or his eyes, that made you feel he was cutting right through you. That night his lip curled into what was almost a snarl, and he came after me, belting me across the face. I ran from him to the kitchen and pulled out a huge butcher knife he used to chop garlic and parsley with. I dragged it out and lunged toward him. He jumped from the path of my swing or he most certainly would have been cut. Then I ran to the dining room table, downstairs to the basement, and then upstairs to my bedroom, still carrying the knife, with Sam in hot pursuit. I didn't have enough sense to put the knife down. I could have fallen while I ran, killed myself with that knife. At any rate, when I got to my room I slammed the door shut in his face. He was in such an enraged state that he kicked open the door, picked up a lamp, and almost hit me with it as he threw it at me. It shattered against the wall. Then he grabbed me and began slapping me back and forth across the face, whipping me against the wall, using my clothes as a sling to throw me into the wall. At that point Joe DiPersio and Jimmy Perno, who were awakened by the noise, came running up and pulled him off me and away from the room to calm him down.

It took a long time for Sam to reach that stage of hatred of Nestos. In the beginning it was different. In the beginning Sam seemed to be impressed with him, particularly because of the way he handled an incident in Florida.

The year I met Bill Nestos had been a particularly turbulent one for Sam, for the whole world of the Mafia in the United States for that matter.

It was the year that Senator John McClellan and his chief investigative counsel, Bobby Kennedy, began to hold hearings on organized-crime racketeering across the nation, an investigation that would lead to subpoenas not only for Sam but for me in an attempt to force him to appear before the U.S. Senate Select Committee on Improper Activities in the Labor or Management Field. The hearings began in February, 1957, but it would be years before they would finally track Sam down, hand him the subpoena, and listen to him invoke the Fifth Amendment every time they asked him a question. It was also the year that more than sixty of the top Mafia leaders were identified at the famous Apalachin meeting on November 14, 1957, at the estate of Joseph Barbara, Sr.

Sam was at that meeting and though he wasn't caught and identified positively as a participant until later, when he came home he was beside himself with anger over the stupidity that had led to the media exposure and charges against crime leaders from one end of the country to another. Sam particularly blamed a man called Stefano (Steve) Magaddino, the boss of Buffalo, and Joseph (Joe Bananas) Bonanno, who had insisted on the New York location of the meeting.

It was several years before I heard parts of the story from him, and then I overheard it during a conversation he had with one of his underlings in his basement apartment. Sam didn't realize I could hear what he was saying, or I'm sure he would have sent me upstairs or closed the conference room door. But he didn't, and I heard portions of what he was telling Johnny Roselli, a Las Vegas flunkey of his, who sometimes angered Dad but was important to his scheme of things in the control of various Las Vegas casinos.

Sam was laying the blame for the fiasco at Apalachin at the doorstep of Magaddino and Bonanno, for whom he had a particular dislike.

As best as I can recall, this is the way the conversation went:

SAM: I told that ——— jerk in Buffalo that we shouldn't
            have the meeting in the goddam place . . . that he
            could have the meeting here . . . in Chicago, and he'd
            never have to worry about cops with all the hotels and
            places we control . . . but he wouldn't listen. Him
            and Bananas . . . he thinks he's the big cheese and he
            tries to make out like he's better than the rest of us,
            that bastard . . . they pushed through that place . . .
            Apalachin.
ROSELLI: Christ, they were stupid . . .
SAM: Yeah. So while I'm in this Barbara's place, these cops
            close in and start grabbing everyone in sight. I took
            off like I was some sort of gazelle out the back door
            . . . I mean I ran like I was doing the hundred-yard
            dash in the Olympics. I made the woods in the back
            by going out the back door, and I stayed there and
            watched them pull everyone in. When it was all over
            . . . when it was dark and safe . . . I got the hell outta
            there.

I could barely contain myself when I heard his story. The mental picture of my father sprinting out the back door of a strange New York farmhouse and hiding in the woods like some kid out of Mark Twain still makes me chuckle.

There was nothing funny about it to Sam. He said the stupidity and stubbornness of Magaddino and Bonanno caused the problem, a problem he said could easily have been avoided by having the meeting in Chicago and some of the surrounding towns where he could control things and would never have had to worry about a raid. I guess he was right. A lot of meetings had been held in Chicago in the past, and Sam and his cronies in other cities around the country had had meetings in places like Miami and Havana without ever being caught.

Years later, while I was reading FBI documents of recorded conversations my father had had with other members of the Chicago mob, I learned how deep Sam's hatred of Bonanno went, and it all seemed to fit together when I recalled his conversation with Roselli at our home.

One of the discussions I partially overheard had involved Bonanno, the boss of a Mafia family in New York at the time, moving some of his people into Arizona and Nevada. Sam seemed to think that Bonanno was trying to move in on territory that had already been staked out by Chicago. As I recall, Sam thought Bonanno coveted some of the casinos that his organization dominated or some other casinos that Bonanno had no business getting involved in because everybody had agreed to the role that syndicate people played in Las Vegas. Bonanno somehow was violating that agreement.

One FBI document dated September 9, 1960, and covering a period between December 9, 1957, and September 6, 1960, included a conversation between my father and Tony Accardo that was recorded on September 8, 1959.

My father and Accardo were talking about problems Sam was running into while dealing with other members of the Mafia's commission, the ruling body of what the FBI likes to call La Cosa Nostra and what I call the Outfit or the Mafia or the mob. This commission is made up of varying numbers of crime bosses, all of Sicilian heritage, across the country. At the time, four of the bosses were from the New York-New Jersey metropolitan area: Thomas Lucchese, Vito Genovese, Giuseppe Profaci, and Joseph Bonanno. There was also a probationary commission member, Carlo Gambino, who was related to Lucchese by marriage and had replaced Albert (The Executioner) Anastasia following his murder in October, 1957, in a Manhattan hotel barber shop. It was because of his murder that the Apalachin meeting was called.

At that time Magaddino represented upstate New York, and Raymond Patriarca, New England, while Sebastian LaRocca represented Pittsburgh, Joseph Ida, Philadelphia, and Joseph Zerilli, Detroit. Sam had replaced Anthony Accardo as Chicago's representative, and he also had powerful friends with influence on the commission, including Santos Trafficante of Florida and Carlos Marcello of Louisiana.

What apparently was disturbing Sam was that Bonanno had arbitrarily decided to put his son, Salvatore, in a position of power in Tucson, Arizona, a state where Sam, Accardo, and the Chicago mob had a lot of power, influence, and investments.

In the following portion of the conversation, Sam has told Accardo that Bonanno has made his son, Salvatore, the boss in Tucson:

ACCARDO: Made him the boss in Tucson now, huh? He's in position.

GIANCANA: In position. Who's ever out for vacation or lives there, they gotta go to him now. Ask him.

ACCARDO: I'd like to go out there for a visit, I'd ask the ————, I'd ask him and his son—

GIANCANA: In other words, you gotta fugat [FBI notation: "Sounds like an Italian idiom"].

ACCARDO: Fugat. He's forfeited the fugat. He's already lookin' in advance. He figures New York's gettin' too ———— hot, now he brings his son over there, with his son, he's the power behind the throne. That ————.

GIANCANA: That used to be what's-his-name's territory.

ACCARDO: That's open territory.

GIANCANA: Yeah, that's open territory, but—

ACCARDO: Who the ———— is he to go and put him a ———— flag up there and claim squatters rights?

GIANCANA: I even talked to Tommy Brown [now-deceased crime boss Thomas (Three-Fingers Brown) Lucchese of Long Island], and he said you gotta make the bag for those two people that, uh, they're over in the Riviera [a casino]. [Blank] get over [blank] they found [blank]. And he says my son and this and that. The day it happened, that day he went to Vegas and they pinched him. The night before he made a call to Vegas and he was supposed to meet some people and when he got there, the meet was canceled. What happened out there?

ACCARDO: So what does he want? He put his son in position.

GIANCANA: Well, he figured it might take the heat off up here.

ACCARDO: Yeah, Vegas. Yeah, that's what the move is around there. He's figured in case anything happens around Tucson they already got the ——— flag staked over there. Well, that's a close contact there. [Blank] Tommy Brown and [blank]. That's the contact. Them are all paisans there . . .

In a later FBI document dated October 27, 1964, the FBI reported that they had learned that Sam had been meeting with other members of "the commission" concerning a dispute that involved Joseph Bonanno.

Bonanno had defied the commission when it ordered him to appear before it to answer charges that he had plotted the assassination of three of its members. Sam had tired of the waiting game played by Bonanno. Said the FBI report:

"It was further learned that Giancana apparently was strongly in favor of having Bonanno killed and saw no further reason to continue to invite him to come before the 'Commission' to explain his actions. It was further learned that certain New York hoodlums have ventured to Chicago within the past few months for the purpose of contacting Giancana and obtaining his views on this matter."

It was against this background of trouble—the publicity over Apalachin, the drumbeat of disclosures out of the McClellan committee in Washington with subpoenas being served on many of Sam's friends, the problems with Bonanno in Las Vegas, and investigators seeking Sam himself—that my father sent me to Florida.

At the time Dr. Nestos was not out of favor with Sam, so he had no objections to my going out with him as long as I conducted myself properly. Sam had no idea at this point that Nestos and I were having an affair.

In any event, Nestos and I had just had dinner at Maxim's in Miami. With us was his attorney, Andrew Cardaras. Suddenly, Cardaras asked us if we had noticed that Vice-President Richard Nixon was sitting at a table behind us. I turned around almost immediately to take a look, and as I recognized him, I noticed another man seated next to him, C. G. "Bebe" Rebozo. I stared at him for a moment and he stared back. I really felt as though we had met somewhere before, and later he asked me if we *had* met before. Quite suddenly we began to talk table to table, which isn't very polite in a place like Maxim's, but we did it anyway.

Rebozo began the conversation by introducing himself and Nixon. Then he introduced Nixon's wife, Patricia, and one of their children, I think it was Tricia, but I'm not certain now. The Nixons were charming, and the Vice-President made the evening for me by autographing a menu and later sending a bottle of wine from his table to ours.

It was a thoroughly lovely and exciting evening for me, and before it ended, Rebozo and I exchanged telephone numbers, names, and addresses. The name I gave him was a professional name, Toni Jordan.

I told Sam about meeting the Vice-President and Rebozo, and he chuckled, particularly when I told him the name I had used.

"That was smart, Annette, very smart," he said. "If they knew who you really were, it could have caused some problems. You used your head for a change."

That was the highest compliment Sam had paid me in ages. Of course, I hadn't told him about giving Rebozo my home address or writing a little note reminding him to let me know if he was coming to Chicago so we could have dinner. In fact, I really didn't think about it until June 16, 1958, when I received a typewritten letter from "C. G. Rebozo, Plaza Building, Miami 32, Florida." It was addressed to "Toni Jordan, 1147 So. Wenonah, Oak Park, Illinois."

Bebe's letter was short, polite, and to the point. He said he was coming to Chicago on June 28, and that he would be leaving on the second of July. During that time he was staying at the Hilton Hotel. Noting that Dr. Nestos and I would probably be busy with other matters, he said he didn't want to impose on our time, but asked if it would be possible to arrange a date for him because he wasn't acquainted with anyone in Chicago other than delegates to the convention he was attending. He also wrote he had tried to call me at my home unsuccessfully. The letter was signed "Yours truly, Bebe Rebozo."

I wrote a short answer to his letter and received a handwritten reply postmarked June 24 from International Airport in Miami. In that letter he said he was arriving early on the afternoon of June 28 and that he would like to see me that evening unless I had something else planned. He promised to phone as soon as he learned what the schedule of convention events was, and if I wasn't going to be home to call him at the hotel between four and five that evening. In that letter, "Yours truly" had changed to "Best regards," and again it was signed Bebe Rebozo but without the formality of a printed C. G. Rebozo underneath.

Nestos couldn't make it, but I could and did, and instead of providing Bebe Rebozo with a date, I WAS HIS DATE. We had a few drinks, something to eat, and then it was up to his suite in the hotel.

At the time I remember feeling a strange excitement about the entire evening that transpired, an unexplainable thrill, a sense of intrigue. I knew that Bebe hadn't the faintest idea of who the hell I was, and I was intrigued about becoming involved with a man who was not only very wealthy, but a man who had the ear of the Vice-President of the United States, and close to the highest seats of power.

I remember thinking, Here I am, the daughter of a Mafia boss, going to the private suite of a man who might one day influence the man in the Oval Office. How was I to know that a few short years later Sam, introduced to a woman by Frank Sinatra, would have a coast-to-coast affair with that woman, Judith Exner, while she was secretly having an affair with President John F. Kennedy. It is really a very strange and intriguing world!

Rebozo was a very appealing man, exciting, a typical romantic Latin, and quite attractive. It was a rather interesting moment in my life. The next day I met him again and drove him and his crew to the International Amphitheater, and that was the last I saw of Bebe Rebozo. When and if he reads this, he will realize probably for the first time that the girl he dated in Chicago in June, 1958, was the daughter of the Midwest's most powerful and dangerous crime boss.

In the late summer of 1958 I became pregnant. My God, the fear that went through my mind, the chill of possible discovery! I couldn't have a child and live, I wouldn't survive! Sam would have me killed, the child killed, the doctor killed. I was in a state of absolute panic. I went to see Nestos. I needed a solution, and he provided one.

"You'll have to have an abortion, Toni, what other answer is there?" he asked.

I shook my head. I was crying very softly. I wanted Bill Nestos's child, but I knew there was no way I could have the baby and live.

"We can't get married yet," he went on. "Your father . . . Mooney will have us both dumped in some grave and buried before he'd let something like that become public knowledge. There's no other way, Toni, no other way. I'll arrange it."

I was frightened beyond belief and my voice was quavering as I spoke. "Will you . . . will you handle it yourself, Bill, please?"

He shook his head. "I can't, Toni," he said. "I'm too involved emotionally. I love you . . . if something should happen because I made a mistake . . ."

He put his arm around me and held me close to him. Reassuringly he squeezed me and kissed me lightly on the mouth. "Don't worry, Toni," he said softly. "Everything will be all right. I'll be with you every minute and the day will come when we will have children together."

So I agreed to the abortion. I really had little choice and Bill arranged it. He had the right connections. He had been handling abortions for prostitutes for years.

It was a hot summer day, a Saturday because Nestos thought that would be the safest day in the week. Sam's watchdogs wouldn't be around. They would be too busy watching the nightclub and gambling operations to worry about what I was doing. I remember going to Ogden Avenue to a horrible little office building . . . up a flight of stairs to a small seedy office with an awful little doctor. Here was a man who literally scared the hell out of me just looking at him. He was a licensed physician, but he looked like something out of a horror movie, a character in *Frankenstein*, and that table I was looking at where he normally gave examinations was to be my operating table!

They got everything ready. There was to be no general anaesthesia, just a mild pain-killer.

"Why?" I asked. "I can't stand pain . . . you know that, Bill."

"Toni," Bill answered, "we've all got to walk out of here without showing any signs of what happened. If someone should see and guess . . . and make a call to . . . well, you know what the consequences would be."

I knew, but it didn't help. At the time, I was three-and-a-half months pregnant. Handling an abortion this way was very dangerous. It was almost like getting a D & C (dilatation and curettage) in the hospital, only without all the preparations, without any of the comforts or the pain-killers and sanitary protection. All I had was a saddle block, a local anaesthesia that numbs the area on the outside and just a little bit on the inside of the vaginal tract. Then without warning the doctor drove an instrument inside me to open a path for other instruments that were to follow, and I felt him taking cutting tools of some kind and scraping, cutting away inside of me.

Every turn of the blade, every slice was like a white-hot coal burning away my insides. The pain went from the upper front of my belly to my lower back. I screamed, I yelled, I cried. It was agony—like nothing I had ever encountered before.

My legs were propped up in the air and I could feel another instrument pulling out the fetus and still another being used to scrape the womb to remove the afterbirth. Most upsetting of all were those moments after the operation was over and I was taken to the bathroom and there were the fetus and the afterbirth lying in a bloody, chipped white porcelain pan, waiting to be flushed down the toilet.

There are still nights when I wake up screaming, remembering the agony, reliving that terrible afternoon. Throughout I was begging Nestos not to let me go through this, and he just stood there all during my agony, watching, telling me to be calm, that what was happening was for the best.

He told me he loved me, that I was doing the right thing, and that there was no other way for us. He wasn't married. He didn't want to get married, although at the time I didn't understand that.

Nestos told the doctor who performed the operation that I was a cousin of his, that my name was Nestos, and that there would be no problems for him. Had that doctor known who I was he would never have agreed to do it for the same reason Nestos didn't want to.

Bill knew that if something went wrong and he had handled the operation, Sam would hunt him down and he would probably die the most horrible death imaginable. If something happened to me with the doctor he had hired, Bill could simply have walked out and washed his hands of the responsibility. Whether my father would have accepted that kind of reasoning is questionable, but that was what Nestos thought.

Bill Nestos's fear of a slow and painful death at the hands of Sam and his goons was not unreasonable. I remember a number of years later an article in *Life* magazine written by Sandy Smith that recounted the agonizing death of a three-hundred-pound loan shark, William (Action) Jackson.

Some of Sam's friends, most of whom I knew, recounted with delight the death of Jackson, who they had suspected of being a federal informer. To force him to admit to what he had done, they took him to a Chicago meat-rendering plant where they tied him up, shot him, hung him on a meat hook, and after stripping him, stabbed him with ice picks, beat him with baseball bats, and used an electric cattle prod on his rectum. It took him two days to die.

I guess Bill had heard stories about the way Sam and his enforcers handled people who angered them. Certainly they were common enough after the Kefauver hearings, and some had come out during the McClellan committee labor-racketeering hearings then making headlines across the country. So he was being extra careful.

After the abortion somehow I managed to walk down the stairs to the car, and we returned to Nestos's office, where he gave me some antibiotics, some vitamin K, and a pain-killer. Then we went to a restaurant for coffee and a drink, and as I sat there, I began hemorrhaging. I had to be helped to the bathroom, where I took my dress off, washed the back of it, cleaned myself up, and then eased carefully out of the restaurant with him.

When I returned home, I virtually walked into the house backward, hurried upstairs to my room, closed the door, and changed. Sam was in the house. He noticed something was wrong and followed me up to my room, knocking at the door before he entered.

"Annette . . . you don't look so good," he said.

"I just don't feel good, Dad," I said. "I've got cramps . . . severe cramps, that's all. I'll be all right in the morning . . . really. I just need some rest."

"You sure?" he asked.

"I'm sure," I answered and he left. He never asked any more questions, but I was living on the edge of a sword and I knew it. When I lay in bed that night, I thought of how I could have died on that table and Nestos would have been clean. Sam would have found out nothing about what he had done. The other doctor would have had to take the blame and he probably wouldn't have lived long enough to be questioned by Sam.

It wasn't too long afterward that Sam began to suspect I was having an affair with Nestos. I'm not sure what led him to suspect it. Perhaps it was the late hours I kept, perhaps some of his spies spotted us at motels, or possibly someone had reported to him in more detail on Nestos and his activities.

By that time, however, my relationship with Nestos had begun to cool. I found out that he was running around with an old girl friend, and when I would call to see him, he would give excuses about being tied up. The more I tried to see him, the more he seemed to avoid me. Finally I found out what had happened from an attorney friend of his.

"Look, Toni, Bill's crazy about you but not crazy enough to get himself killed," he said.

"What are you talking about?" I asked.

"You don't know?" he asked.

"Know what?" I answered.

He shook his head and then explained. "Bill didn't want me to say anything, but maybe I'd better. Your father had some of his friends pay Bill a visit. They told him to stay away from you, then they worked him over. Bill spent about a week in the hospital . . . indisposed."

"Oh, God," I said softly.

Nestos and I did get back together for a time, but it wasn't the same. He was a man living in fear and I could sense it. He said nothing about the beating to me and he never formally broke our engagement. It just quietly died.

In December, 1963, William Nestos died, and I found out that

Sam had known all along about his illegal sideline. He had used Nestos to handle at least one abortion. And Gus Alex had filled Sam in on other Nestos activities with prostitutes and hot jewelry and drugs. That's where Sam had gotten some of his information to make the accusations. And it was Alex's friends who taught Nestos a lesson about the dangers of playing around with a Mafia princess.

For a time I hated Bill Nestos for deserting me, just as I hated him for putting me through all the pain of the abortion. But that bitterness softened later, just before my marriage to someone else, when Bill and I met for dinner at an out-of-the-way restaurant. I told him I knew what had happened to him and I was sorry for what my father had done. He understood and wished me happiness in my marriage. If he had said, "Toni, I love you," I would have canceled my wedding on the spot. But he didn't, and it wasn't until years later, after his death, that a relative of his told me that Nestos had loved me till the day he died.

"He was in love with you, Toni," the relative said, "but he was certain your father would kill him and you if he kept seeing you."

I was stunned. I should have known that Bill still loved me, but I was hurt and very immature then, and even if I had known, I'm not certain there was anything we could have done to survive my father's awesome power and terrible anger. Most certainly, Sam would have had one or both of us killed if our affair had continued.

When William Nestos died, part of me died too. In later years I changed my religion to his, Greek Orthodox, and to this day I still place flowers on his grave to commemorate special dates during our turbulent romance.

Angeline Giancana as the young bride of Sam

"Toinette" the model

Marion DeTolve, Sam, Angeline, and Antoinette at a nightclub

Bride Antoinette Giancana

Sam Giancana and Phyllis McGuire in London, England

(Associated Press)

During one of his few courtroom successes, Giancana is seen outside federal court chamber with Anthony Tisci, his son-in-law (husband of Bonnie). Occasion was suit against the FBI for harassment.

Sam Giancana shortly before his murder

Family home in Oak Park, Illinois, where Sam Giancana was slain

Antoinette Giancana in 1978

13

The Slippery Fox

Sam snickered a little, then scowled as he heard Robert F. Kennedy, then chief counsel to the U.S. Senate Select Committee on Improper Activities in the Labor or Management Field, call out the name of Anthony Accardo in that nasal Boston-accented voice of us.

"He's the big boy," Kennedy's nasal voice rasped out over the microphone as he addressed the committee chairman, the Democratic senator from Arkansas, John L. McClellan.

"That little ———," Sam mumbled as he listened to Kennedy, not noticing that I was standing right behind him.

As he watched the TV screen intensely, I could see just the tiniest trace of a smile across Sam's lips when Tony Accardo walked slowly to the witness table with his Washington attorney, H. Clifford Allder. Accardo was wearing dark glasses and searching out any familiar faces in the audience of the Senate hearing room.

KENNEDY: State your name, address, and occupation.
ACCARDO: My name is Anthony J. Accardo. I live at 915 Franklin, River Forest. On my business and occupation I decline to answer on grounds that it might tend to incriminate me.

MCCLELLAN: Do you honestly believe that if you told us your business and occupation it would tend to incriminate you?

ACCARDO: It may incriminate me or lead me into something.

Sam's smile broadened and he began to chuckle as Accardo's attorney asked that the television cameras be turned off only to have McClellan turn down the request. Earlier, Allder and Accardo had tried and lost in U.S. District Court in Chicago to get an injunction to bar Field Enterprises, Inc., publisher of the *Chicago Sun-Times,* and the American Broadcasting Company from telecasting Accardo's appearance.

The questions droned on, 172 of them, and each time Accardo declined to answer. At times Sam seemed bored, at others intensely interested in what was being said and how Accardo was handling himself. Sam had spent three months ducking deputy U.S. marshals, FBI agents, and Senate investigators, who camped outside our home trying to serve a subpoena on Sam to force him to appear before the committee.

Sam's interest picked up when they handed Accardo some photographs and asked him if he could identify the men in the pictures with him. There were Meyer Lansky, the man who Sam once conceded to me was most responsible for his successful investments in Cuba before Fidel Castro appeared on the scene; Charles (Lucky) Luciano, whom he knew very well before and after he was deported from the United States; Paul Ricca, who the committee described as being one of the three most important crime figures in Chicago. Then Kennedy pointed to a figure in a photograph and said:

. . . And the individual to the right is Mooney Giancana, is that correct?

ACCARDO: I decline to answer.

KENNEDY: Now, Mr. Giancana is one of the most important and perhaps one of the two or three most important underworld figures in the Chicago area, and we have been looking for him for quite a while, and I was wondering if you could give us any information as to his whereabouts at the present time?

ACCARDO:	I decline to answer.
KENNEDY:	We understand he is a close associate of yours, and I thought maybe you would help us with that, even if you won't give us some of your own background.
ACCARDO:	I decline to answer.
MCCLELLAN:	Well, you decline to answer as to the whereabouts, whether you know the whereabouts of the other man in this picture; is that correct?
ACCARDO:	Yes, sir.
MCCLELLAN:	On what ground?
ACCARDO:	It may tend to incriminate me or lead me into something that may incriminate me.

Sam chuckled. He had been playing hide-and-seek with federal law-enforcement agents for three months and they still didn't realize that except for some quick trips to Florida, Cuba, and Nevada, he had been home all the time.

"What jerks," he said to himself out loud, still not noticing I was in the room with him.

They asked Accardo about his twenty-two-room mansion with its two bowling alleys, its indoor pool, the pipe organ, and the gold-plated bathroom fixtures they said were worth $500,000. Sam laughed at that. He had always said that Accardo was too flashy, drew too much attention to his style of living because of his big Fourth of July parties for the mob and its families, and because of that mansion which everyone talked about. "It's gonna cause him problems one day," he would say. Now they were talking on national television about the luxury Accardo lived in, and Sam was chuckling over his obvious embarrassment.

The hearings had been going on for months, primarily centering on the Chicago mob's control of the unions and the muscle it applied in taking control of the Chicago Restaurant Association. One of the men who had been used by Sam and Accardo in handling the association and its operation was Sam's attorney, Anthony V. Champagne, who had served as president of the Italian Welfare Council and who had been instrumental in getting my mother to work for the council.

Now Kennedy was questioning one of his own investigators, a

man named LaVern J. Duffy, about a problem Accardo had with Champagne in the association. Duffy was telling the committee of a quarrel between Accardo and Champagne. Sam's eyes were fixed on the screen and I could see him clenching his fists on the arms of his chair as he watched and listened.

"Duffy: There was an argument between Accardo and Champagne. Accardo became disturbed and ordered Champagne murdered forthwith. Through the intervention of friends, Champagne's life was saved and he immediately resigned from the Chicago Restaurant Association. Mr. Champagne formerly was a lawyer with a practice earning him $9,000-a-year. When he went with the Chicago Restaurant Association he was paid $125,000 a year, which is more pay a month than he was making in a year. Then he suddenly resigned."

I didn't know it then—in fact, I didn't find out until years later from Tony Champagne himself before he died—that the person who saved Champagne from Accardo's order to eliminate him was Sam.

After the testimony ended, I looked outside. The cars of the federal agents were still camped near the house, waiting. That night, Sam put on a dark suit, as he had done for months, slipped out a back door and into a two-door Chevrolet sedan he had parked in the garage. Suddenly, howling with laughter, he turned on the ignition of his souped-up car and roared out of the driveway and down the street before any of the startled agents could figure out what had happened.

The frustration in failing to catch Sam and serve him with a subpoena reached a pitch, and perhaps a new low, when Kennedy and some of his investigators decided that they could get at my father through me. They put their strategy into action on July 14, three days after Sam and I had watched Accardo on television.

I was in the kitchen when the doorbell rang and Sam was downstairs in his basement apartment. He, of course, wasn't about to answer the door and the Pernos weren't around, so I, like a dummy, answered it.

As I opened the door, two men, flashing badges, identified themselves as deputy U.S. marshals.

"Is Mr. Giancana home?" they asked.

"No," I answered.

"Do you know when he'll be home?" one of them asked.

"I have no idea, really," I said rather shortly.

"Are you Annette Giancana?" they asked.

"Yes, I am," I answered. "Why do you ask?"

"We have a subpoena for you," the taller of the two men said, handing me a document that ordered me to appear in Washington, D.C., on July 18, 1958, and testify as a witness before the U.S. Senate.

I stood there dumbfounded as the two deputies smiled politely, turned on their heels, and walked away. Slowly I closed the door and after I had locked it, I ran down to the basement shouting, "Dad . . . Dad . . . they've subpoenaed me . . . they've subpoenaed me to that damn committee."

For a moment Sam sat there, stunned, looking at me as if I were crazy. Then he grabbed the subpoena from my hand and looked at it.

"Those lousy bastards . . ." he snapped, "those rotten, lousy . . ."

Sam could see panic written all over my face. At that time I was still being treated by Dr. Parrilli, although I had long since left the hospital. Of course, I was still deeply attached to Dr. Nestos and although Sam didn't know it, I had been with Bebe Rebozo at the Chicago convention only a few weeks earlier. My God, suppose they asked me about that? My mind was conjuring up all kinds of things that they could ask that would embarrass me or embarrass Sam. How would I handle myself? Why even call me? I couldn't tell them anything about Sam's criminal activities, his investments. What does a twenty-three-year-old kid know anyhow?

"Sit down, Annette," Sam said. "Stop worrying. You're not going before any goddam committee, so don't worry about it." Then, as he turned to go to the phone, he muttered, "That little ——— Kennedy . . . he's behind this."

The strategy behind the subpoena was pretty much spelled out in an FBI report dated August 7, 1958, sent from the Chicago office to the FBI headquarters in Washington.

This document was entitled "Anti-Racketeering" and it identified my father, Samuel M. Giancana, as being known also as Russell Paige and Anthony DeBendo (the latter name appearing on the registration belonging to a car my father used when he was at a party at Accardo's home. This car with the same registration was kept parked in our driveway and in our garage too and on occasion it was used by Sam to elude surveillance, that is, when he wasn't using my car.

The report, which was partially blanked out in the version I received under the Freedom of Information Act, began with an attempt to explain why agents were having so little success in identifying Sam, his holdings, and his activities:

"Subject [Giancana] reportedly seen in company of FRANK SINATRA in Las Vegas. Examination of legal records gives no indication subject has financial interest in Villa Venice, large restaurant and lounge northwest of Chicago.

"Subject, using name 'RUSSELL PAIGE,' operated on in May, 1958, for rectal disorder and in April, 1956, for colon disorder, but no indication of malignancy. [Blanked-out sentence] Efforts by Deputy United States Marshals during May–July, 1958, to locate subject to serve subpoena for subject's appearance before McClellan Committee unsuccessful to date. Car driven by subject registered to ANTHONY DE BENDO, Berwyn, Illinois, but efforts to establish existence of this person unsuccessful.

"DETAILS: The title of this report is marked changed to add the aliases RUSSELL PAIGE, used by the subject in connection with his medical and surgical treatment in April, 1956, and in May, 1958, and 'ANTHONY DE BENDO,' shown as the registered owner of the car used by the subject: efforts to establish that such a person exists have not been successful."

Page nine of the report then added that:

"[Identity censored] advised in the latter part of June, 1958, that several months ago, when FRANK SINATRA was appearing at the Sands Hotel show, SAM MOONEY was seen in the company of SINATRA at the El Rancho Veras Hotel in Las Vegas, Nevada. [Blank] MOONEY is a Chicago racketeer whose true name is something other than MOONEY but who is commonly known as 'MOONEY.'"

The report went on to suggest that an undisclosed person was representing the interests of the Chicago mob, especially those of my father, Sam Mooney, "at the Stardust Hotel." The report also quoted a source (blanked-out), as stating that Sam had been in Cuba during part of the time the committee had been conducting hearings.

Then on page fourteen of the report, the FBI described what they said were:

"Current Efforts to Locate the Subject.

"Deputy United States Marshals [identities censored], Chicago, Illinois, advised on various dates during the period May–July 31, 1958, that efforts by them to locate the subject for the purpose of serving him with a subpoena to appear before the Senate Select Committee on Improper Activities in the Labor or Management Field had been unsuccessful to date. Both [blank] and [blank] expressed the view that the publicity given the matter of serving subpoenas on witnesses to appear before the aforementioned committee caused the subject to go into hiding and that numerous inquiries made by them at places the subject is known to have frequented in the past were unsuccessful in developing any information as to the subject's whereabouts."

Then they unveiled their stratagem to flush out Sam by using me.

"On July 14, 1958 [identity censored] advised that he had, on that day, served the subject's daughter, 'TONI,' with a subpoena directing her to appear before the aforementioned Senate committee. He pointed out that this step was taken in the belief that it would encourage the subject to accept serve of the subpoena and appear before the committee rather than subject his daughter to it. [Blank] advised on July 21, 1958, that this plan did not achieve its expected results, as 'TONI' GIANCANA was excused from testifying before the committee after a letter was produced from her doctor, to the effect that it would be injurious to her mental health to testify."

In fact, what had happened was the night I was served with a subpoena, Sam left the house in a cloud of dust to meet with an attorney and with Dr. Parrilli. The next morning he told me I wouldn't be going to Washington and neither would he. He was right. An attorney named Benedict F. Fitzgerald, Jr., whom I never talked to, appeared before the committee. The testimony given before Chief Counsel Kennedy on July 18, 1958, recorded Fitzgerald's appearance and the failed stratagem.

"Mr. Kennedy: Mr. Chairman, we also had expected, or wanted to have, Mr. Mooney Giancana, from Chicago, who is among the first three in the Chicago area in the underworld, and he has important information he can give to the committee. We have been looking for him for a period of some three months. We have been unable to find him. He has left his usual places of operation in Chicago. We have tried to subpoena him at home and have been unable to do so. But we did subpoena his daughter, however, to see whether she could give us any information about the activities of the restaurants in Chicago and the labor unions. His daughter's attorney is here now with a statement to make.

"Mr. Fitzgerald: Mr. Chairman and Mr. Counsel—

"The Chairman: Will you identify yourself?

"Mr. Fitzgerald: My name is Benedict F. Fitzgerald, Jr., attorney-at-law.

"The Chairman: May I inquire if a copy of his statement has been submitted?

"Mr. Kennedy: I believe it is a letter; is it?

"Mr. Fitzgerald: That is right. I have submitted a motion to quash the subpoena, Your Honor, together with a copy of the statement furnished by Dr. William F. Parrilli, M.D. I represent this little lady. I don't represent her father. I have never had the privilege of meeting her father. But she seems pretty ill.

"I have a statement here which indicates that fact.

"The nature of her illness is such that if Your Honor reads this and refuses this, you will be probably wanting to return this to me and not insert it in the record. That was requested by the doctor. He told me not to let this out of my hands. But I thought I would show it to you anyway. If you want any further interrogation on it . . .

"The Chairman: I think, if you have a document there that involves possibly confidential or privileged information as between doctor and patient, that it may be submitted to the members of the committee for their inspection, and, if satisfied that it is a document of that nature, or proper propriety dictates it should not be placed in the record, the committee will not place it in the record. But I cannot pass judgment on it until, at least, the committee has seen it."

As a result of the letter, which wasn't entered in the record of the hearings, my appearance before the committee was killed, but that wasn't the end of it.

Another FBI report on Sam dated March 16, 1959, quoted another, blanked-out source as describing my mental condition quite inaccurately.

". . . that SAMUEL GIANCANA's oldest daughter, ANNETTE, is 'wacky' and has suffered a nervous breakdown on three occasions in recent years. . . . The last time this occurred she was checked at Columbus Memorial Hospital, Chicago, Illinois."

It was the beginning of a number of reports based on surveillances designed to locate Sam that invaded my private life. Agents of the FBI followed me wherever I went and recorded not only the locations but even what buildings I went into and with whom. One of those identified by the FBI was Carmen Manno.

I met Carmen Manno after I had one of my bitter battles with Dr. Nestos at Wesley Memorial Hospital. By then I had had the abortion and I felt Bill was shunting me aside. So we fought constantly. I wanted to be with him. He didn't want me around. It was on one such night that I stormed out of the hospital and drove to André's 213 Club, where I signed the doctor's name to a huge check I ran up for dinner and drinks. Then I headed for the Armory Lounge in Forest Park, a favorite hangout of my father's and of many of the mobsters who worked for him.

I often went to the Armory Lounge either to have a few drinks, to see my father, or just to watch the passing parade of hoods walk in and out to pay him homage. I would always kibitz with the nice old lady who ran the Lounge and who knew Dad quite well. When my father was tightening the purse strings, I would eat there, have a few drinks, and, of course, I would never get a tab. I also knew that was where Sam always held court with his mob friends. All these crazy guys would walk in, all the ones I knew who had been to the house for one reason or another. Most were mobsters, but some were entertainers passing through, who stopped to pay their respects to Sam and sometimes posed for pictures with him and his friends. Others were politicians who came to see Sam to receive their marching orders. And of course there were his various girl friends whom he brought there at one time or another—from the rather plain-looking brunette Bergit Clark, who worked in my uncle Michael DeTolve's envelope company, to Judith Campbell Exner, who admitted in her book, *My Story,* that she had had affairs not only with Sam, but with President Kennedy, whom she had met through Frank Sinatra.

On the night after my fight with Bill Nestos, when I got to the Armory Lounge I started drinking some more. Sam walked in, took one look, and shouted, "Cut her off."

So they cut me off. My nose a little out of joint, I walked out in a huff and headed for a Forest Park bar called the Pink Clock Tavern, where I knew my father used to meet at times with a really beautiful model named Roma. In the building where the tavern was located, Sam maintained an apartment for Roma, whose full name I never learned and who apparently was never identified in the FBI reports.

While I was at the Pink Clock, I noticed this poor guy tending bar. His name was Carmen, Carmen Manno. I was feeling low, and I wanted more than just a drink, I wanted a little conversation, so Carmen and I began to talk.

I'm not sure how, but the conversation got around to the Maywood Sportsmen's Club, a favorite hangout of one of my father's hoodlum enforcers, Joseph (Joey Doves) Aiuppa, and of my cousin James Perno, who lived at my house. Manno told me he was a member of the club.

"Really?" I remarked. "So's my cousin Jimmy Perno."

I had forgotten about that chance meeting with the bartender until about two weeks later when I went to the Maywood Sportsmen's Club for a Sunday outing with my cousin. There, sitting at a table eating alone, was Manno. I don't know why but I felt sorry for him, so I walked over to his table and reintroduced myself.

"So you really are interested in shooting," he said.

I smiled, nodded, and said, "Well, sort of. I'd like to how to handle a pistol first before I get into hunting and using a shotgun."

"Okay, so why don't I teach you?" he suggested.

And that's how our so-called romance began, with an invitation to teach me how to use a pistol, something Sam would never have done because he hated having guns around.

"They're more trouble than they're worth," he said once when I asked if I could have my own gun. "You'll wind up killin' yourself with one of them damn things."

He was probably right. I would have wound up killing myself, but when I began reading FBI reports on his activities after he was murdered by someone using a gun, I felt there was a touch of irony in what he had said. Every FBI report I have ever read on Sam closes with the admonition "Subject should be considered armed and dangerous as he reportedly carries a gun, has been involved in crimes of violence, and has a vicious temperament." Sam undoubtedly was involved in crimes of violence, and he did have a vicious temper, but I never knew him to carry a gun from the time I was old enough to know what a gun was until the day he died. He had a couple of guns hidden in the house, but he never carried them. He was too smart for that. He thought they invited trouble, especially with law-enforcement agents.

After Carmen's invitation to teach me to use a pistol, I began meeting him at the Pink Clock Tavern, where I would pick him up in my car and drive to the Maywood Club. These trips were duly noted time and again by the FBI, who were supposed to be watching for my father, not for me.

There was really nothing sinister about my going to the converted barn at the Sportsmen's Club with Carmen. Quite simply, he had taken me there to give me lessons in handling firearms.

My relationship with Carmen was relatively short. We met in August, became engaged in October, and were married in April, 1959. It wasn't a romance made in heaven, and it wasn't one that Sam was exactly proud of.

To Sam, Carmen was first and foremost a divorced man. He had been married to a nice blond girl, it just hadn't worked out, and they had gotten divorced. But that meant only one thing to Sam, embarrassment. Not only was I unable, in spite of my so-called religious background, to get married in the Catholic Church, but I would be the first daughter of a don in the Chicago crime family not to do so.

That was very upsetting to Sam. It really bothered him, but by this time he had given up on me. He wanted me to settle down and if it was to be with Carmen, who he didn't consider to be terribly bright, so be it. The FBI's informant, who had been quoted as calling me "wacky," and whose identity had been blanked out in the record, also had a low opinion of Carmen. In the FBI report the informant stated: "ANNETTE is scheduled to be married soon to a boy described [identity censored] as 'quiet and stupid.' This individual, described [identity censored], has been previously identified as CARMEN MANNO, who is a bartender at the Pink Clock Lounge."

In the meantime, surveillance by the FBI and other agencies continued unabated.

The FBI records I have reviewed showed that agents watched the Villa Venice, the Cafe Continental, Salerno's Funeral Parlor (where Sam sometimes played cards), the River Road Motel, Mike Fish's Restaurant, the Armory Lounge, our home, and dozens of other locations where they thought Sam might be. Most of the time Sam was home, and when he wanted to meet with someone, he slipped out the way he always did.

An FBI report dated March 16, 1959, spells out dozens of these surveillances and notes that:

"[Identity censored] advised on February 9, 1959, that GIANCANA is at home on most occasions and conducts his business in the usual manner. He can be seen during the dinner hours at the Armory Lounge at 7400 West Roosevelt Road, and takes nightly walks around the block at his home.

"Physical surveillances at the residence of GIANCANA as described above have revealed that GIANCANA maintains at best, very irregular hours and has not been observed on any occasion."

The report went on to note that Sam maintained, according to the FBI's informant, "a lavish apartment on the second floor of the building where the Pink Clock Lounge is located.

"Physical observation of the building [Pink Clock Tavern] . . . revealed that there is one and possibly two apartments located in this building and that the only name on the mailbox is that of G. S. MILLER. Contacts at the Pink Clock Lounge are not considered at this time as being feasible in that the Pink Clock Lounge is owned by one CARMEN TUMINELLO, known associate of GIANCANA, and the bartender is GIANCANA's future son-in-law, CARMEN MANNO."

Still, with all its informants and surveillances, for months the FBI was unable to isolate Sam in any one place long enough so that he could be served with the McClellan committee subpoena. Finally on March 25, 1959, after a year of trying, the FBI finally caught up with Sam at the Desert Inn in Las Vegas, where he had registered under the name of "S. Flood," a name he often borrowed from a relative of ours. In a teletype marked "Urgent" to J. Edgar Hoover at 4:43 P.M., the FBI reported:

SAMUEL M. GIANCANA, AKA. MISSING WITNESS SENATE INVESTIGATING COMMITTEE. [Sentence is blanked out.] SUBJECT AS S. FLOOD REGISTERED WILBER CLARKS DESERT INN HOTEL, LAS VEGAS, NEVADA, NIGHT OF MARCH TWENTYFOURTH INSTANT, GIVING ADDRESS AS ONE EIGHT ZERO ZERO WEST MADISON, CHICAGO, ILLINOIS. [Blank] OBSERVED SUBJECT DESERT INN HOTEL LOBBY COFFEE SHOP NINE A.M. TODAY. INFO FURNISHED DEPUTY US MARSHAL [identity censored], LAS VEGAS, WHO SERVED SUBJECT WITH SUBPOENA ELEVEN THIRTY A.M. TODAY TO APPEAR BEFORE SENATE INVESTIGATING COMMITTEE, WASHINGTON, D.C. FORTHWITH. RUC.

SUBJECT ARMED AND DANGEROUS.

My decision to marry Carmen Manno was what eventually led Sam to make the mistake that resulted in his being trapped and subpoenaed at the Desert Inn. The reason I say that is that I'm certain Sam left Chicago for Nevada because of all the preparations that were under way for the wedding and he just didn't want to be a part of them. He believed if he did, it would lead the federal agents right to him, so he thought that by leaving town for a while, he could still keep them at bay. It's one thing to keep agents at bay in a town that you virtually own, quite another to do it in a casino where you have some interests, in a town where you have limited control—and Sam's control in Las Vegas was limited. There was also the fact that he had gone to Miami Beach with Tony Accardo for a high-level mob meeting. Somehow the FBI had been tipped off that the meeting had taken place and apparently backtracked Sam's movements, finally tracing him to Las Vegas the night he arrived.

Sam really didn't want to be bothered with any of the details of the wedding. He left that up to me and money was no object. The agency I worked with, the agency he approved of, was Weddings, Incorporated, a firm that a friend had recommended, was discreet and efficient.

They coordinated everything, while I did most of the planning from the designing of the cake to ensuring that they sent out invitations in ivory and 14-karat-gold script.

Sam did insist on one thing. He wanted to know exactly who was going to be sent one of the gold engraved invitations to attend the wedding reception, and before each invitation went out he had to approve it personally. Both the wedding, handled by a justice of the peace, and the reception were held at the LaSalle Hotel on April 4, 1959. It was the most lavish reception of its kind held in Chicago in more than a quarter century, I was told.

My wedding dress and my entire trousseau were designed by Momma's designer and my escort to Hollywood, Georgianna Jordan. The gown, white satin with pearllike beads embroidered in soft, flowered patterns, was long and flowing, and I carried an orchid bouquet.

For several days I had been running a high fever, and at one point our physician said that if my temperature didn't go down, the wedding would have to be called off. On the final day I should have been in seclusion to relax. Instead, I had to shop, prepare, and direct the photographer, making sure that last-minute preparations were perfect. Instead of an affair in which everything is taken care of for the bride, my wedding became a nightmare of details that I had to attend to personally to ensure its success.

The wedding itself was a beautiful candlelight ceremony attended by about thirty members of the immediate family. My only attendants were my sisters Bonnie and Francine and a close friend, June Bravos. Sam, dressed in a tailored tuxedo with tails, led me down an improvised aisle. The ceremony was performed by Justice of the Peace David B. Trott of Maywood, Illinois, a man Sam trusted to keep his mouth shut. Then we went from the immediate wedding to the Chicago Room in the hotel for a champagne toast, and then to the Illinois Room for one of the most lavish pre-reception cocktail parties Chicago had seen in years.

Sam may not have wanted Carmen as a son-in-law, but he was

bound and determined to turn my wedding into an affair the
Mafia would long remember. The trouble was it was an affair that
not only the Mafia but all of Chicago became aware of because of
leaks to the press by the police and the FBI. Before the day
ended they turned the event into a circus.

More than seven hundred people crowded into the reception
that day. There were thirty-five cases of French champagne. Hot
and cold hors d'oeuvres of every variety, enormous shrimp, fresh
lobster, and salmon were flown in from the East and West coasts.

After standing in line while hundreds of people walked up to
me to hand me envelopes, we finally went to the grand ballroom
for dinner and dancing where a fifteen-piece orchestra as well as
strolling violinists were on hand to keep everyone amused.

Along with the Mafia's high and mighty were politicians from
New York, Massachusetts, Las Vegas, Milwaukee, Los Angeles,
New Orleans, Florida, people I'd never heard of, much less
knew. Sam dutifully introduced them to me and each, just as dutifully, at some time during the evening handed me an envelope
stuffed with money, which was handed over to an aunt, who in
turn gave it to Sam. More than $130,000 was collected that night
to go with another $40,000 plus that I had received at a shower at
the Ambassador East Hotel.

Altogether more than $200,000 was collected for us by Sam
from his friends. I saw very little of that money in the years that
were to follow.

Problems soon arose in the grand ballroom, where guest tables
were set up with beautiful centerpieces of tea roses and with
gold-engraved invitations identifying each guest. Again, Sandy
Smith of the *Chicago Tribune* had found that place cards of many
of the most important dinner guests had been laid out on a sec-
ond-floor table before the reception dinner began. Smith was
writing down some of the names when Sam discovered him. He
very nearly lost his temper but didn't. Sam was mellower that day
than at any time since before Mother died. Later he broke down
and had an off-the-cuff conversation with Sandy Smith that caused
him a lot of problems later before the McClellan committee.

Sam was absolutely glowing when he watched me in my gown
and with my platinum-blond hair rise to toast him and thank him
for making all this possible. I toasted him, our relatives, and all

his friends, adding, "It's just too bad the lady who should have been here is not . . . so let's all toast my mother as we toast my father."

It was impromptu, but it came from the heart, and I noticed that Sam's eyes grew misty and he blew his nose as we all sipped the champagne. Later when we danced, he whispered to me, "Your mother would have liked that, Annette, and she would have been proud."

The dinner was out of the ordinary, not the typical Italian fare that most expected: cream of fresh pea soup, spring chicken with fresh mushrooms in wine sauce, wild rice croquettes, fresh asparagus tips in drawn butter, and limestone lettuce with sliced avocados. For dessert we had ice cream molded in the shape of wedding bells, slippers, and cupids, and French pastries. The seven-tiered wedding cake was so tall it couldn't be brought into the main ballroom and had to be cut outside the room.

Altogether, Sam's little bash for his eldest daughter cost more than $25,000. In those days that was a lot of money, and he got most of the liquor and the champagne free!

Carmen and I left the party sometime just after midnight for the Ambassador East, where the Frank Sinatra Suite had been reserved for us for the night. The next day we left for San Francisco.

The party never really ended for Sam. Already facing a subpoena to appear before the McClellan committee in Washington, he was slapped with another to appear before a special federal grand jury investigating organized crime. But it was his off-the-cuff discussions with Sandy Smith that would cause him the most problems.

I believe that Sandy Smith was the world's best conman at the time, or that he caught my father when he was feeling mellow and a little sentimental over my marriage and over my toast to Mother.

Sandy had two immediate articles in the *Chicago Tribune* as a result of the wedding. The first was published on April 5, 1959, and detailed the wedding bash and disclosed that place cards he had read showed that some of the underworld's biggest names had attended.

Wrote Smith: "The card of the big boss, Anthony Accardo, was at the head of the table . . . naturally. Other cards bore the names of Philip Alderiso, Gus Alex, Joseph Aiuppa, Joseph Amato, Samuel Battaglia, Louis Briatta, Marshall Caifano, William Daddano, Joseph DiVarco, Frank Ferrara, Albert Frabotta, John Lardino, Charles Nicoletti, and Anthony Perotti, to name a few."

Then he noted that Joey Glimco, a labor-racketeer associate of Sam's, had attended even though he had to leave the wedding reception for his own son at the Edgewater Beach Hotel to be there.

The clincher came in a *Chicago Tribune* article dated April 6, 1959. The FBI chose to send a copy of it to J. Edgar Hoover as part of a report on my father dated May 14, 1959. In that article, Smith wrote:

> Giancana, the number 2 man of the crime syndicate, was forthright.
>
> He gave his views on the organization of syndicates, the place of ex-convicts in society, the Selective Service System, the Senate rackets committee, and crime—a field in which he is an acknowledged expert.
>
> The gambling chief broke his silence when he found observers at the wedding inspecting place cards inscribed with the names of top hoodlums invited to this affair.
>
> Angrily, he scooped up the cards, which were an "honor roll" of the crime syndicate brotherhood, and then said, "Why bother us this way? Sure, some of us are ex-convicts, but are we supposed to suffer forever for a few mistakes we made in our youth?" Giancana went on to say that because of his own experience of being an ex-convict, he knew what he was talking about when he voiced the opinion that the current multiple investigations of organized crime were going to result in "the biggest crime wave ever."
>
> "An ex-convict can't get a job now," he explained. "He has to get a gun and go out and hold up people to get something to eat. There's going to be a lot of crime if this keeps up. It will be worse than Capone. Look at that kid," he added, pointing to his son-in-law, who was helping Antoinette cut a

four foot high wedding cake. "Now everybody is going to hook him up with me. No one will hire him. I'll have to give him a .45 and put him to work for me."

Giancana then switched to another subject, the Senate rackets committee, which finally slapped a subpoena on him in Nevada last week. "They couldn't catch me for a year," he said, "and I was in Chicago all the time. I liked to hide from them. It was fun."

He was asked what he intended to tell the committee and replied, "I'd like to tell them to go to hell, but I guess I'll keep my mouth shut and take the Fifth Amendment."

Giancana then continued by stating: "What's wrong with the syndicate?" he asked. "Two or three of us get together on some deal and everybody says it's a bad thing, but those businessmen do it all the time and nobody squawks."

On June 9, 1959, what Sam had said to Sandy Smith at my reception came back to haunt him. As promised, Sam invoked his Fifth Amendment constitutional rights in refusing to answer questions asked him by Robert Kennedy and the committee. Among those questions were some about his reported income between 1950 and 1957, about the trip to Los Angeles with Accardo and about the name (Mancuso) he had used on that trip and about the interview with Sandy Smith.

He smiled when the committee investigator, Pierre E. G. Salinger, described him as a top figure in Chicago's underworld and as a man who had convictions for burglary and larceny, and for conspiracy in a bootlegging case. He even smiled when Salinger said Sam had been arrested seventeen times. Then Sam got into trouble with Committee Chairman John McClellan. Robert Kennedy was interrogating him.

"Mr. Kennedy: Mr. Giancana, would you give us some information in connection with the meeting you had in Los Angeles with Mr. Tony Pinelli?

"Mr. Giancana: I decline to answer.

"The Chairman: You are ordered to answer. I want to tell you something now. We are not going to put up with this foolishness.

"Mr. Giancana: I decline to answer because I honestly believe my answer might tend to incriminate me.

"The Chairman: You say it that way if you mean it that way. Proceed.

"Mr. Kennedy: Is there something funny about it, Mr. Giancana?

"Mr. Giancana: I decline to answer because I honestly believe . . ."

Sam was still chuckling. Later the questioning centered around the art of murder and my father apparently thought the way Kennedy was asking the question was funny.

"Mr. Kennedy: Would you tell us if you have opposition from anybody, that you dispose of them by having them stuffed in a trunk? Is that what you do, Mr. Giancana?

"Mr. Giancana: I decline to answer because I honestly believe my answer might tend to incriminate me.

"Mr. Kennedy: Would you tell us anything about any of your operations or will you just giggle every time I ask you a question?

"Mr. Giancana: I decline to answer because I honestly believe my answer might tend to incriminate me.

"Mr. Kennedy: "I thought only little girls giggled, Mr. Giancana . . ."

A few questions later my father's testimony ended. He had taken the Fifth Amendment thirty-four times, he had chuckled and giggled, and the government had spent thousands and thousands of dollars for more than a year to get him before the committee to get such responses. It didn't make much sense to me. It seemed like such a waste of money and time.

And Sam? He left for a vacation in Mexico after the hearing ended, but he had learned a valuable lesson. The glare of publicity as a result of my wedding had caused him a lot of unnecessary problems. So on July 4, 1959, when my sister Bonnie and Anthony Tisci, then secretary to Representative Roland Libonati, got married, the wedding was not held in Chicago.

This time Sam got the church ceremony that I couldn't have, and Bonnie and Tony were married in St. Patrick's Church in Miami. The wedding-reception guest list was much smaller and much lower-profile. A total of two-hundred people were invited to the luxurious Fontainebleau Hotel, where they always rolled out the red carpet for Sam.

The Fontainebleau was at its peak as a luxury hotel in those days, and I remember many occasions being there with Sam to watch a show when people would fall over themselves to make sure that he had a ringside table and was ushered back to see the entertainers. In fact, it was at the Fontainebleau where Sam introduced me to Frank Sinatra in his suite quite some time before Sinatra and Dean Martin and Sammy Davis appeared at the Villa Venice.

It's rather amusing to recall an occasion when Dr. Nestos and I were in Florida and I wanted to see the Sinatra show at the Fontainebleau. Bill told me there was no chance of our getting in because the show was sold out.

"Nonsense," I said. "I'll get us in."

He shook his head but he agreed to go along, and when we arrived at show time, I walked up to the maître d' and asked if there was a table for two up front.

The maître d' smirked at me condescendingly as he started to turn away toward another couple.

"I asked you if you had a table for two," I insisted. "The name is Giancana. My father is Sam Giancana."

The maître d' looked at me as if he'd been slapped. His face was as white as a sheet, tan or no tan.

"I'm sorry, madam, I didn't recognize you," he apologized. "Please come this way." And while Nestos looked in wide-eyed amazement, he led us to two front-row tables and sent over a bouquet of roses. To add to that moment of pleasure, we got no check, it was all on the house.

So when Bonnie had her reception at the hotel, it was red carpet all the way. Red-coated waiters with white gloves, a white-tuxedoed strolling string orchestra, tight hotel security to prevent nosy newsmen from getting a list of the guests, all the trappings were there, but the publicity, the extravagance, and the opulence that had attracted so much attention at my wedding were not there in Miami to plague Sam again.

A lot of his friends attended, among them Murray (The Camel) Humphreys, but the police and the FBI didn't know. Sam had planned it carefully so the wedding would coincide not only with Accardo's annual Fourth of July party, which he knew the press and the police would be watching, but also with an expected visit by the Queen of England to Chicago, which would keep the press busy.

Yet there were problems. He had planned to have Frank Sinatra and Dean Martin turn up at the reception, but it couldn't be arranged. I suppose because of all the publicity at the hearings. One minute it was all set; the next they weren't coming. He was mad as hell at both of them for months after that. But while he was angry with them, he was furious with me. I was, of course, expected to show up for the wedding.

"I want you there, Annette," Sam said. "It's not right that you don't come to your own sister's wedding."

"But, Dad, Miami . . . in the summer!" I complained. "Who the hell needs it? Why not here?"

"Didn't I have enough trouble with your wedding?" he shouted. "I don't need no nosy press around."

"Whose fault was that?" I shouted back. "I had a reasonable list, then you started adding all those goddam names . . . all those invitations. What the hell did you expect when you have seven hundred people?"

"Just be there!" he yelled. "You got obligations to Bonnie, to me, to the family. You wanna embarrass me in front of my friends?"

Sam was upset. Two of his daughters married in the same year and because of the McClellan committee and the attendant publicity, he couldn't stage the type of lavish affair that the crime leader he disliked the most had held—Joseph Bonanno.

The Bonanno wedding, at which Salvatore Bonanno married Rosalia Profaci, the daughter of the Brooklyn Mafia leader Joseph (Giuseppe) Profaci, was the most opulent gathering of its kind in Mafia history. It was held at the Hotel Astor in New York City on August 18, 1956, and more than three thousand people, including Sam, our family, Anthony Accardo, and what seemed like the whole world of the Mafia as well as businessmen and politicians, were on hand. Strangely enough, Bonanno encountered none of the problems Sam did when I was married. His timing was better than mine and Sam was infuriated.

Bonnie asked me to come too, no wailing or gnashing of teeth, just a try-to-come-for-my-sake request. I told her I would think about it. I had already made up my mind not to come. For months afterward Sam and my sisters barely talked to me.

So Bonnie and Tony Tisci had their wedding. It wasn't as elaborate as mine, but it was expensive as hell. Sam picked up the tab for most of the guests who flew into Miami for the affair, and the bash at the Fontainebleau cost more than ten thousand dollars. And while Sam didn't have to face another McClellan hearing, the war of wits between him and the nasal-voiced Robert Kennedy was far from over. That would become a long and bitter behind-the-scenes struggle in the years ahead and would lead to my father's downfall and eventual assassination.

14

Travelin' Sam, the Casino Man

From the time I was old enough to vacation in Florida with my parents, I knew that my father was a traveler. What I didn't realize until years later was that Travelin' Sam was an international casino man who spent years and years planting the flags of the Chicago mob all over the world, from Havana to Beirut, from Teheran to the famous "Glitter Gulch" of Las Vegas.

It has taken thousands of pages of government documents, and investigations into my father's criminal activities to help me take bits and pieces of my life with him and fit them into the puzzle of our life together. This, in turn, has provided me with a semblance of understanding of what Sam was doing to increase the power and wealth of Chicago's Mafia. Before I read the documents, I had little idea how widespread his power and that of the Chicago mob had become. All through my life I had only had glimpses of his influence, but without the significance I attach to them now. I used his power, as did my sisters, to achieve minor personal goals. That was the extent of our interest. We were all frozen out of the inside machinations of Mafia politics and plotting.

It has been said at numerous public hearings and by law-enforcement officials that the late Meyer Lansky was the financial genius behind organized crime's infiltration of the casino world, beginning with the early days of the Flamingo Hotel and Benjamin (Buggsy) Siegel in Las Vegas in 1946. More knowledgeable people have identified Lansky also as being behind the corruption of the Battista government in Cuba and the organization and operation of Havana casinos. But it is also quite apparent to me now that while Lansky was undoubtedly behind everything, what made his success possible was the power, the money, and the muscle of members of the Chicago mob—people like Anthony Accardo, Paul Ricca, Charlie and Rocco Fischetti, and my father.

In those early years before my mother died, Sam was constantly hopping a plane from Chicago to Florida, and then he would be off to Havana, Cuba, Bimini, and other Caribbean areas. Sometimes he was with Accardo, or the Fischettis, or Gus Alex, or Johnny Roselli. Roselli managed one of the Cuban hotel casinos, the Sans Souci, with the boss of the Florida crime family, Santos Trafficante.

However, it really wasn't until after Mother died that Sam became a world traveler and Las Vegas his regular haunt. And the place he generally selected to hang his hat when he went to Las Vegas was the Desert Inn, then run by Moe Dalitz.

The Desert Inn was my first introduction to Las Vegas. I'm not sure just how old I was, but it was after Momma died, perhaps a year later, perhaps less. I had been through a difficult time and Sam decided that a little rest and relaxation in Las Vegas was just the right medicine for me. He was right.

I was very impressed with the way Sam was treated in Las Vegas. He was the king of the roost, and the man who practically did cartwheels to keep Sam happy was Moe Dalitz.

From the beginning I liked Dalitz. He was a gentleman and he had class. He was a rather good-looking man, sensuous, well built, with salt-and-pepper hair, and a very engaging smile. He dressed like he was a millionaire—and he probably *was*—but he was polite, well spoken, and always the gentleman when I was around.

I recall quite vividly being brought to Moe's private office where he was sitting at a big horseshoelike desk. Next to him stood a gorgeous woman, his wife, Toni. Both of them were elegantly dressed, but then so were Sam and I.

"Moe, this is my oldest daughter, Toni," my father said.

"Toni?" Moe asked. "Do you spell it T-O-N-I?"

"Yes," I answered. "It's short for Antoinette."

He smiled broadly. "That's very interesting," he answered. "You know my wife here, her first name is Toni too."

Almost immediately I looked at her and my eyes fell on a beautiful diamond pendant she was wearing with her name emblazoned in glittering diamonds.

"Oh, my, those are beautiful," I remarked.

"They are nice," she said. "Moe had them made up *especially* for me."

"You like them?" Moe asked.

"Oh, yes," I answered. "They are very lovely."

Six weeks later I received an identical diamond pendant from him with a gracious note complimenting me on my looks and on being an asset to my father. I still have that piece of jewelry.

While we were there at the Desert Inn, we used the name "Flood." If I wanted to sign for something I bought or for a meal or for some other service, I was under Sam's instructions to sign "Richard G. Flood." That was the full name of an uncle of mine whose last name Sam frequently used.

Normally whenever we went anywhere, Sam paid in cash if there was a bill to be paid, but at the Desert Inn, things were quite different. I had the impression that by signing "Richard Flood" on the chit I was signing something that said in effect, "This is on the house." I don't think I ever saw Sam pay for anything when I was with him at the Desert Inn, whether for the stacks of chips he obtained to gamble with, or for our meals, or for anything that I bought.

For example, Sam liked to gamble. Throwing dice, usually a loser's game, was his favorite, but when he played he was always a winner. I certainly never saw him lose. It was as if he were acting as a shill for the casino. He would walk in, get a stack of chips from the cage—using the name of Richard G. Flood—and walk to the table. Then he would start working the dice, and the chips would begin to pile up in front of him as he won one bet after another. And as he played, a crowd gathered. On one of those occasions he had a huge stack of chips in front of him— thousands and thousands of dollars' worth—and the crowd seemed to be ten-deep around the table.

"He's just shilling for the casino," said one gambler who tried to appear knowledgeable. "When it's over, the casino gets everything back."

I smiled but didn't say a word, certainly nothing about the so-called shill being my father. Finally, when Sam tired of the game, he threw a bunch of chips to the croupier and some to the pit boss, and a casino employee hustled over, gathered up the huge bundle of chips, placed them in a bag, and took them to the cage.

A short time later, the employee came over and handed Sam an enormous wad of bills, and I thought to myself, some shill. I just never consciously registered that maybe Sam was skimming from the casino, that maybe he owned a piece of it. Never, that is, until I read several FBI reports about my father and the Desert Inn. These reports were based on bugged conversations among my father and his associates and on investigations into a Hammond, Indiana, insurance company the FBI believed fronted for Sam and the Chicago mob by investing its money in Las Vegas casinos.

> [Blank] advised in December, 1960, and January, 1961, that SAM GIANCANA, ANTHONY ACCARDO [identity censored], MURRAY HUMPHREYS, and two unidentified individuals from Cleveland, Ohio, one of whom was probably [identity censored] had recently negotiated a "contract" whereby GIANCANA and the Chicago group acquired an undisclosed number of points of shares in a three-way deal, which was not clear to the informant [the bug] but which apparently involved the Riviera, Desert Inn, and Stardust Hotel casinos in Las Vegas, Nevada.
>
> [Blank] that the groundwork for these negotiations was laid a number of years ago by ANTHONY ACCARDO and PAUL DeLUCIA, also known as PAUL "THE WAITER" RICCA. RICCA is currently completing a three-year sentence at the Federal Penitentiary in Terre Haute, Indiana, for income tax evasion.
>
> According to [blank], the kingpin in the negotiations in Las Vegas was GIANCANA, ably assisted by ANTHONY AC-CARDO and MURRAY HUMPHREYS.
>
> —From Chicago FBI report on Samuel Giancana, dated February 15, 1961, for the investigative period November 23, 1960 to January 1, 1961

[Blank] advised in July, 1961, that [blank] was in close contact with SAM GIANCANA during the latter's stay in Las Vegas in July, 1961. The informant [bug] stated that [blank]'s purpose in contacting GIANCANA in Las Vegas was to apprise GIANCANA of the current situation regarding certain operations of gambling casinos in the Las Vegas area. [Blank] has assured GIANCANA that his, GIANCANA's, interests at the Desert Inn and Stardust hotels were being protected.

—From FBI report dated September 18, 1961, for the period July 30 through September 6, 1961

Reference is made to previous information linking GIANCANA with the operation of the Desert Inn Hotel in Las Vegas through manipulation of the so-called "front money" put up by GIANCANA through numerous legitimate channels which eventually reach the establishment in Las Vegas, after which point the benefits from the operation from the gaming casino provides a lucrative source of income for GIANCANA and his associates.

—From FBI report dated January 3, 1962

Of course, I had no way of knowing it, but Sam and Murray Humphreys had negotiated a deal for the Chicago syndicate that gave them interests not just in the Desert Inn but in the Stardust and the Riviera, and this combination resulted in millions of dollars being skimmed from the casino treasuries and delivered to the Chicago underworld, according to articles published later in the Chicago newspapers and in *Life* magazine.

We didn't stay in the best suite in the Desert Inn. That would have been ostentatious and have attracted too much attention. Sam always had a comfortable suite, but nothing elaborate. The only thing elaborate was the service. Employees bowed and scraped and fell all over themselves to please him wherever he went. And so did Moe Dalitz.

The Desert Inn employees and management didn't fall all over themselves to please only Sam, they did it with me or with anyone else he brought there. I know that while he was off meeting someone, I would go to the roulette table and play with some chips that he would leave for me, or I would sign for them using the Richard G. Flood name. I never won or lost much because

I'm not much of a gambler. And while I played, I always played the role of a lady so as not to embarrass Sam. I dressed in the finest clothes, all original designs that he had bought for me, and I wore expensive jewelry, diamonds, emeralds, rubies on my fingers, my ears, my wrist, or around my neck. I never overdressed with the jewelry, but I wore the right amount for the occasion . . . enough for people to know that I was SOMEBODY. Sam liked that. He liked to have me decked out and well dressed in a place like the Desert Inn, and liked to see people pay attention to me because of it.

I was careful about drinking there, although the waitresses were always refilling my glass. I didn't want to embarrass Sam and I never did. I did later in Chicago, but then he wasn't around when it happened. It seemed that no matter where I went, whether to the casino, or to the pool, or to a restaurant, people swarmed all around me trying to please me, to make certain I had whatever I wanted. Only once did I go too far. This happened when, with Dalitz's approval, I used the name "Toni Flood" in a Desert Inn promo that featured a modeling photograph taken of me by Desert Inn photographers. Sam wasn't very happy about that. The daughters of mafiosi aren't supposed to model at casinos, particularly those owned by the mob.

The initial success of the Villa Venice in Chicago was the beginning of Sam's personal involvement in casinos. This and his interests and those of the Chicago organization in the Desert Inn, the Stardust, and other Las Vegas casinos were but modest beginnings for a grandiose scheme by my father and the Outfit to establish the power of the Chicago Mafia in casinos all over the world.

Once Bonnie and I were married, Sam was off and running like an unbridled stallion. It was wine, women, and song, and enough international travel to qualify him as a jet-set playboy. Frannie was at home most of the time under the care of James and Marie Perno. But there were occasions when she went on trips with Sam. One such trip was to Hawaii, a place where he loved to vacation because of the golf courses. Sam was an avid golfer.

Interestingly enough, the FBI took special note of that trip and at least one previous one he took to Hawaii. The reason, apparently, was Frank Sinatra. The FBI was interested in Sam's meetings with Sinatra and was keeping a tally on them.

In a memo dated April 30, 1963, for example, the FBI observed that on February 10, 1963, Sam was in Jilly's restaurant in New York City with Frank Sinatra, Paul (Skinny) D'Amato, and two other men. I knew Jilly's. It was owned by Frank's sidekick and shadow, Jilly Rizzo, and it was a popular hangout for a lot of people. Sam had brought me there once or twice when we were in New York doing the sights. D'Amato I knew was a friend of Sam's from New Jersey—Atlantic City, as I recall. He was also with Frank Sinatra a lot, particularly when Sinatra was a listed owner of the Cal-Neva Lodge in Lake Tahoe, Nevada.

Then in June, 1963, the FBI exchanged a series of teletypes between its Washington, Chicago, and Honolulu offices concerning two Hawaiian trips made by Sam.

On the first trip to Hawaii in May, Sam used the phony name of "J. J. Brackett," one he had used before, to register at the Sheraton Surfrider Hotel, and spent several days playing golf and partying with Frank Sinatra and some of his friends. Then, in a memo dated June 13, 1963, the FBI observed:

"Subject [Giancana] . . . traveled via airport limousine direct to Sheraton Surfrider Hotel, Waikiki, where reservations previously booked by Frank Sinatra May 14 last during period Sinatra and subject were residing same hotel [the Royal Lahaina Lodge]."

The FBI went on to note that Sam had registered the second time under the name of "F. Carson" and had also registered two of his daughters, "Andrea and Francine," in a suite with James Perno and a middle-aged woman. Andrea, of course, wasn't Sam's daughter, she was James and Marie Perno's daughter. Sam had brought the Pernos along to take care of Francine while he played golf with some of his cronies at the Waialae Golf Course. The FBI said it had eyewitnesses, handwriting comparisons, and photographs that positively identified both Carson and J. J. Brackett, the man observed playing golf and partying with Sinatra.

I was too busy having babies and trying to live on a limited budget to wonder about Sam's travels and escapades after 1959.

His travels to Mexico, Jamaica, Italy, Iran, Lebanon, or the Dominican Republic seemed frivolous but understandable. He was just a middle-aged man feeling his oats, trying to regain his youth, doing things and seeing things he had never had the opportunity to see or do before.

I certainly never thought of these trips in terms of international conspiracies or interference in revolutions until the summer of 1963 when Sandy Smith, then working for the *Chicago Sun-Times*, wrote a so-called exclusive story about attempts by the Chicago mob to take over control of multimillion-dollar casinos in the Dominican Republic.

In the spring of 1963, Sam did take a trip to the Dominican Republic. I attached no significance to it even when I read that the country's newly elected president, Juan Bosch, was overthrown at about the time Sam was there. I thought he was vacationing and taking care of some of his investments like he did with his shrimp boat business in Cuba. Even when Sandy Smith's article appeared, I didn't believe what was in it. I had been taught all my life—by my mother, by Sam, by our relatives, and by our friends—never to believe what appeared in the press, either on radio, television, or in print about my father. So my skepticism was always high and Smith's speculations sounded ridiculous.

It took a series of FBI documents, including letters to the White House, to give me some perspective on the situation and make me realize that Sam was more than just a high-living gambler sowing his wild oats around the world. He was building an empire, and this was drawing the attention of a lot of people in high places in government here and in the Caribbean.

An August 5, 1963, FBI memorandum made special notes: "Information received Giancana considering operating gambling interest in Dominican Republic. During stay in Hawaii in May, 1963, Giancana left with, and in daily company of Frank Sinatra . . ."

Through an illegal eavesdropping device the FBI had had in place in the Armory Lounge since 1959, agents learned Sam had gone in May, 1963, to Santo Domingo, the Dominican Republic, to meet with another Chicago hoodlum.

"During this trip," the FBI said, "[identity censored] was extremely active in attempting to negotiate for a large hotel in which a gambling casino could be operated. It was further learned that [identity censored] made several trips during the next several months for the purpose of continuing these negotiations which events fell through."

Then on April 24, 1965, the followers of Juan Bosch, as well as the Communists, revolted against the government. Four days later, President Lyndon B. Johnson ordered the U.S. Marines to intervene against the pro-Bosch forces. On the day that Johnson gave the order, the FBI overheard a conversation concerning the Dominican Republic that was of such significance that it resulted in a special communication from J. Edgar Hoover, the director of the FBI, to Marvin Watson, special assistant to President Johnson, on May 6, 1965.

"Dear Mr. Watson," the letter from Hoover began. "The attached information concerning the Dominican crisis is of possible interest to the President.

"The information relates to reported efforts of Chicago hoodlum figure Samuel M. Giancana and his associates to take advantage of the revolution in the Dominican Republic by organizing gambling casinos in that country to be under the control of the Chicago underworld. It also indicates that Giancana is negotiating with five or six contending groups in order to assure that he will be able to successfully carry out his plans with the group which will ultimately win control of the Dominican Republic."

Attached to the letter was an FBI daily summary of the conversation that had been overheard between my father and a contact man for the Dominican Republic whom the FBI had not been able to identify.

"Apparently arrangements have been made with government which, it is assumed, will take control of Dominican Republic, for Chicago group to open gambling operations as soon as situation quiets down.

"Giancana somewhat apprehensive over which group is to take control of government, feeling that they may have to do business with five or six groups before one becomes strong enough to control country. Unknown advises this possibility present but confident they have made proper contacts.

"Source advised two individuals have been in Dominican Republic for some time making contacts in behalf Chicago group.

"Source advised one of conditions Giancana extremely interested in is arrangement whereby Chicago organization can 'put machines in the city' [Santo Domingo]. Possible reference to 25,000 slot machines reported to be stored in Florida during 1964 [blank] in anticipation of shipment to Dominican Republic at that time."

A month later, another Bureau memorandum added that:

"[Blank] and Sam Giancana met with an individual in Chicago who furnished Giancana with details concerning another attempt by Chicago hoodlum interests to negotiate for gambling interests within the Dominican Republic. At that time it was learned that an individual believed identical to the one [blank] who has a history of association with Chicago hoodlums, was at that time the apparent contact man between the Chicago syndicate and responsible citizens within the Dominican Republic who were involved in the overthrow of the Dominican government in early May 1965. It was learned that the persons fronting for the Chicago hoodlum organizations were apparently dealing with individuals behind the initial revolt which occurred in the Dominican Republic.

"It was further learned that the interference of the Communists in that revolt did not greatly concern the Chicago interests and feelings were that this was actually helping their cause.

"Information has also been received that Giancana has had a representative traveling to Lima, Peru, within the past six months for the purpose of investigating gambling casino sites."

The FBI file on Sam had been marked "classified" until I received it and has never been made public, as far as I know.

I did learn from former FBI Agent William Roemer, who had followed my father for years, that Sam's representatives in the Dominican Republic were the late Les Kruse and Louis Lederer. Both Kruse and Lederer were gamblers and casino experts. In Chicago Lederer had been connected with Rocco Fischetti's "Big Game," a floating dice game for high rollers. Lederer, Roemer said, had opened up the Tropicana Hotel in Las Vegas, and when Frank Costello was shot in a hotel lobby in New York, he was carrying a note in Lederer's handwriting detailing to the penny what the gambling take was from the Tropicana as of April 27, 1957.

I don't believe Lederer was ever convicted of a crime, but his license to operate a Las Vegas casino was revoked by Nevada gaming authorities. He now lives quietly on Lake Shore Drive in Chicago.

I also learned through Roemer that the Dominican Republic official whom Sam and his friends were using to penetrate the island's gambling world was one of its internationally known ambassadors.

Sam's attempts to establish a casino empire that stretched from Las Vegas to Teheran spanned more than seven years of work, most monitored illegally by the FBI. Almost all the plans, so far as I can determine, flopped, probably because the FBI tipped off investigators in other jurisdictions in a way that didn't compromise their listening devices while still providing the necessary evidence to halt Sam's empire-building fantasies.

In January, 1962, the FBI bug recorded a conversation with Sam in which one of his associates told him that he should consider the "possibility of looking into large scale investments in gambling casinos in Puerto Rico which are legitimate and controlled by the Commonwealth Government.

"[Blank] advised informant [the bug] that the possibilities are manifested in Puerto Rico in that there are few large scale operations there at the present time with the largest one being in the Caribe Hilton Hotel in San Juan. [Blank] told the informant that he felt that in view of the fact that gambling has been curiously curtailed in the Chicago area, Puerto Rico would be the logical spot in which to continue to receive profitable returns on their investments.

"[Blank] also indicated to the informant that some time ago he started with the okay of the Commonwealth Government a gambling enterprise in Puerto Rico more or less on the trial basis and at the present time is continuing. [Blank] told the informant that Giancana was only lukewarm to the suggestion of Puerto Rico gambling in that there was tight governmental control and hours are restricted from 8 to 2."

There had also been plots to open a casino in Jamaica if gambling was legalized there. The plan called for using a Milwaukee hotel owner who had Jamaican interests to front for the Chicago group. The hotel owner had agreed until another, unidentified mobster from another area had offered the hotelman one hundred thousand dollar "front money."

The offer angered my father, who instructed one of his enforcers to "get the word back to [blank] that the Milwaukee hotel owner belongs to us; tell him to mind his own business and if he doesn't, that fella is going to get knocked in the head."

The next year found Sam busy scheming the financing and construction of a $9.5 million hotel-casino in Reno, Nevada. The architect for that casino was the same one who Johnny Roselli said had been used for a planned Chicago mob casino in Cuba.

Roselli then came up with a suggestion to use New York Yankee baseball hero Joe (Joltin' Joe) DiMaggio and Leo (The Mouth) Durocher of the Brooklyn Dodgers to front for the mob at the planned casino-hotel.

But as with so many of his and the mob's plans and plots, the Reno plan collapsed. And as persuasive as my father and his organization might be, I don't believe he could have convinced DiMaggio or Durocher to work for him.

Perhaps the most bizarre of the casino flags my father was busy planting was discovered by the FBI in September, 1970, in Teheran. I never even knew that Sam had ever been to Teheran.

The disclosure came first in the form of a partially blanked-out memorandum dated September 17, 1970, which said in part: ". . . Giancana perfected arrangements whereby the Shah of Iran has allowed the construction and operation of a gambling casino to be opened in Teheran, Iran."

That same day J. Edgar Hoover fired off a memo to the director of the Bureau of Intelligence and Research, Department of State. The communication said:

"Enclosed is a memorandum indicating that the captioned individual [Samuel Giancana], a former organized crime figure in Chicago, Illinois, has reportedly made arrangements for the opening of a gambling casino in Teheran, Iran."

The casino opened, but by then Sam was no longer in control.

15

A Filly Named Phyllis—Part I

The first time Sam met Phyllis McGuire was in 1960. She was playing blackjack, a card game sometimes known as twenty-one, between entertainment breaks at the Desert Inn. He had been running around with other women since Momma's death, but none had held a strong attraction for him, at least one that lasted. Phyllis was different. There was a real magnetism that drew Sam to Phyllis as a flower draws a bee. He was like Caesar in Gaul: He had to have her. He had to be able to say, "I came, I saw, I conquered." The trouble was that with Phyllis, Sam couldn't walk away after he conquered, and unwittingly she became a contributing if not a major factor in his downfall.

I first saw Phyllis when she and her sisters, Dorothy and Christine, appeared on Arthur Godfrey's 1952 television hit *Talent Scouts*. They were almost an instant success, and Godfrey, who had practically become a national institution himself, hired them to perform on his weekly variety show.

The three sisters were extremely talented and beautiful, but the most beautiful of all was Phyllis. She had the sort of looks that made other women, older and younger, jealous. And she had personality to go with her beauty. I came to know her, like her, and be jealous of her myself in the years after she met my father.

From the outset the McGuire Sisters' act was a hit. Their first song, "Pretty-Eyed Baby," went right to the top. It was quickly followed by "Picnic," "The Naughty Lady of Shady Lane," and half a dozen other songs that made their records huge successes. So I guess it was natural for them to have gravitated from Godfrey's show to where the big money was—Las Vegas.

The trouble with most entertainers I know who play Las Vegas is that sooner or later they become victims of the casinos they entertain in. Jimmy Durante was one; so were Tommy Leonetti and Vic Damone. They all gambled large sums of money and lost. Some, like Durante and Sinatra, could afford to lose large sums. Others didn't care; still others couldn't absorb the heavy losses.

Phyllis rarely worried about how much she lost, whether she could afford it or not. By the time she and her sisters hit the Desert Inn in 1960 as professional performers, she had changed from the naïve choir singer who first started harmonizing with her sisters at the First Church of God in Middletown, Ohio, to a sophisticated, gorgeous entertainer who thought nothing of betting healthy portions of her considerable uncollected salary at the casino's gaming tables. There was, after all, always more where that came from.

It was under such conditions that Sam first took notice of her as she gambled. He not only noticed her but filled her dressing room with flowers, and he did arrange to have the debt she had run up that night taken care of. However, contrary to reports cited in the media, it was not one hundred thousand dollars. In fact, the debt was never really written off, and a conversation recorded by the FBI on December 6, 1961, between my father and Johnny Roselli confirmed that.

This conversation was primarily over negotiations between my father's criminal group and the group headed by Moe Dalitz to take over a casino. For purposes of brevity, "R" identifies Roselli and "G," my father. In this excerpt from the conversation, Roselli is describing to my father a conversation he had with Dalitz:

R: . . . Now, also, let me ask you. What did the FBI ask you about the loan, I mean the marker with Wonderful [Phyllis McGuire]? Oh, he says, yeah, I forgot to tell you. The FBI went in to see him, he says, and asked him if there was a marker and a half for Phyllis McGuire. He says, I don't know, let me take a look. He looks and says, yes, there is a marker, and they say, has it been paid, and he told them no. So I told him . . .

G: You mean the G [FBI] asked him?

R: Yeah.

G: How come he never sent word out?

R: I even had to ask him. He still hadn't sent word out, until I asked him yesterday. I found this out. I says, tell me about it.

G: I told him, when it first happened, to take the marker off of there . . .

R: Wait a minute, hold on. The reason, he said, I told them she still has the marker, was so if I told them the marker was paid, she would probably have income tax troubles. This way she still owes the marker. So it don't mean anything, which is all right. I agree with that, too, but the only thing I don't agree with is this . . .

G: How did they know that she had a marker?

R: I don't know. Either through some telephone conversation or someplace where they got a lead . . . I don't know. They do more ———— at that joint. They're always there, nosing around. I know this much. The G has been at his house and his office. TEN DIFFERENT TIMES they talked to him. Now the G don't talk to a man ten different times unless they are getting something out of him. I don't say that he's a ———— stoolpigeon, but . . .

G: But he's cooperating with them . . .

R: Something is happening. Either he's cooperating or he's not cooperating, but each time they get a little different story or a little something. They're either trapping him or they're getting something out of him. No G talks to a man ten times. Every time I see them go back two or three different times, I figure something is wrong someplace. I don't discuss things with them. I shoo them the ———— out . . ."

From the moment they met, Phyllis and my father began living in a goldfish bowl. Privacy was more and more elusive largely because the FBI knew my father's every planned movement through the illegal bugs it had installed at Celano's Tailor Shop and in the Armory Lounge.

These weren't however the only illegal eavesdropping the FBI engaged in to keep tabs on his and Phyllis's movements. I learned later that agents listened in on conversations in their bedrooms in Las Vegas, in a motel in Maryland, in Pittsburgh, Atlantic City, and other areas. I have been denied access to those conversations, not through any legal technicality, but largely because the FBI was careful not to index them in its central files, but instead kept those records in outlying offices, such as Las Vegas and Baltimore. What I have learned is that although I have been denied access to them, apparently FBI agents from one end of the country to the other haven't, and many have amused themselves reading about the escapades of Sam and Phyllis. And I have been told that the one who enjoyed reading about their private lives the most was the late J. Edgar Hoover.

Not only were those recordings illegal, but they were of no investigative value for the agents involved. It was just a flagrant invasion of Sam and Phyllis's privacy and part of a deliberate campaign of harassment. I don't defend what my father did as a criminal, but what anyone does in the privacy of the bedroom is of no consequence or legitimate interest to the FBI. Certainly it doesn't provide evidence for prosecution.

Typical of this type of voyeurism by some elements of the FBI is evidenced by documents that disclose the tight surveillance, both physically and electronically, kept on my father and Phyllis beginning in early May, 1961.

The first indication of this surveillance was in a document dated June 30, 1961, directing the attention of agents and J. Edgar Hoover to a report of a special agent whose identity was deleted. The report, originating in Chicago, suggested that there was a "close relationship between Sam Giancana and the well-known entertainer Phyllis McGuire."

Then the report, which covered a period between June 1 and June 27, 1961, noted that "[identity censored] advised on June 14, 1961, that Phyllis McGuire, who as of that date was residing at the Desert Inn Hotel, Las Vegas, Nevada, had been in contact with 'Mr. Flood' at Chicago telephone number Euclid 6-0381. Mr. Flood was not in and returned the call on June 14, 1961. It is noted that Euclid 6-0381 is the telephone number of Sam Giancana, 1147 South Wenonah, Oak Park, Illinois." The report continued: ". . . Giancana presented Phyllis McGuire with a white 1961 Cadillac convertible. This vehicle bore temporary Illinois license plates and was delivered to her at the Desert Inn Hotel by two men . . . possibly connected with the Stardust Hotel in Las Vegas."

On July 6, another report, sent from Las Vegas to the Newark office, stated that "Phyllis McGuire presently has Green Gables Ranch in Paradise Valley near Las Vegas rented for a month during current engagement at Desert Inn Hotel. She spends most of time at ranch and all investigation by Las Vegas thus far indicates subject [Giancana] staying at ranch with her."

A short time later, the agents filed another report and they followed Sam's movements with Phyllis from Las Vegas to Phoenix, Arizona. The report came in the form of a teletype to the FBI director, J. Edgar Hoover.

SUBJECT [GIANCANA], PHYLLIS MCGUIRE AND JOSEPH PIGNATELLO [MY FATHER'S BODYGUARD AND LAS VEGAS ADVANCE MAN FOR SAM] DEPARTED LAS VEGAS APPROXIMATELY 3:40 A.M. [JULY 11] IN MCGUIRE'S 1961 CADILLAC CONVERTIBLE AFTER NUMEROUS EVASIVE TACTICS TO DETERMINE POSSIBILITY OF PHYSICAL SURVEILLANCE. PHYSICAL SURVEILLANCE BY LAS VEGAS PLAYED VERY LOOSE. OBSERVATION [UNIDENTIFIED SOURCE] REFLECTED CADILLAC DRIVEN FROM [GREEN GABLES] RANCH WITHOUT LIGHTS ON DEPARTURE.

PHYSICAL SURVEILLANCE CONDUCTED BY LAS VEGAS TO PHOENIX WHERE TURNED OVER TO PHOENIX [FBI AGENTS] APPROXIMATELY 8:30 A.M. CADILLAC DRIVEN AT SPEEDS UP TO 105 MPH ON OPEN ROAD, BUT NO INDICATION PHYSICAL SURVEILLANCE DETECTED.

Later, a teletype directed to the Newark FBI office advised agents to be alert for "microphone surveillance" of Phyllis and Sam when they arrived in Atlantic City, where she was to perform.

The next day, however, Sam and Phyllis flew from Phoenix to Chicago en route to New York, and there the FBI was waiting, subpoena in hand, to interview Phyllis. It was the beginning of an incident that would have repercussions from O'Hare International Airport to the Oval Office of the White House.

Sam was like a wild man over the FBI's public intrusion on his romance with Phyllis. Up to that moment, I had never seen him in such a state of fury over something done by law-enforcement officials.

As far as Sam was concerned, the FBI had violated all the so-called unwritten rules between law-enforcement agents and organized-crime figures—rules in which mobsters acknowledged that federal agents and police had a job to do and submitted to certain indignities without creating any problems. In return, they expected law-enforcement officials would not embarrass them in front of their families or girl friends, and generally they did not. Certainly girl friends were not to be publicly humiliated. According to Sam, the FBI had broken those rules, and thus he no longer felt bound by discretion in how he dealt with it.

I think that in the forty-eight hours after the airport incident, Sam was in such a mental state that he was capable of ordering the execution of the FBI agents involved. Cooler heads prevailed, however, and the coolest of all was Phyllis. She turned down his temperature so expertly that I'm certain he didn't even realize what she was doing.

The famous airport incident began innocently enough when Sam and Phyllis debarked from their flight from Phoenix on July 12, 1961. On hand to greet them were five agents of the FBI whose identities were deleted from documents they filed as reports. Years later I was made aware of their identities through published reports of the incident and through court records.

The following paragraphs are taken from reports dated July 13 and July 14, 1961:

"Samuel M. Giancana, Chicago racketeer, and his current romantic interest, Phyllis McGuire of the well-known McGuire singing trio, were interviewed separately at O'Hare International Airport by agents of our Chicago office on July 12, 1961. Our agents had been forearmed with a grand jury subpoena for Miss McGuire. The subpoena was not served.

"[Paragraph blanked out] Giancana was exceptionally belligerent and abusive during the interview by our agents and frequently used obscene words in describing authorities who he believed were responsible for the investigation of him. He was extremely bitter regarding what he terms 'persecution of the Italians' and said he 'wasn't going to take this laying down' and 'I am going to light a fire under you guys.'

"He advised he was married to McGuire, however, was flippant in this remark and [it's] noted that McGuire denied being married or contemplating marriage to subject.

"Asked if he had any interests in the Las Vegas, Nevada, area, he flippantly replied: 'I own ninety-nine percent of Las Vegas . . . I also own twenty-five percent of Marshall Field's, Carson's, Goldblatt's [all prominent Chicago department stores].'

"Giancana directed abusive language to the interviewing agents and to any and all passersby who happened to glance in his direction, all of whom he suspected were agents. Agents continuously advised Giancana he was free to go anytime he wished. However, he remained with the agents until the reappearance of McGuire, stating, 'I told them to go to hell, why didn't you, so we could get out of here?' Consensus of Giancana as observed by interviewing agents and observing agents is that he [Giancana] exhibited definite psychotic tendencies, was extremely shaken, and with little provocation would explode."

The agents further observed that they had not found it necessary to serve the subpoena on Phyllis McGuire because they "interviewed her on the spot," and the subpoena was "the door opener to a successful interview."

That wasn't the whole truth, according to what one of the agents admitted later when he was interviewed. The truth is that Phyllis McGuire outsmarted the FBI.

The agents had been authorized to serve a subpoena on her if she didn't cooperate and submit to an interview. What Phyllis did was sweet-talk an FBI agent, who withdrew the subpoena when it seemed she was cooperating. They talked to her about her marker (debt) at the Desert Inn; about whether Sam had told Moe Dalitz to "eat" the marker and the thousands of dollars it covered; about the gifts he had given her, including the car; about a whole range of things. She played the "I'm really not well, but I'll come back to answer all your questions later" routine, and the agent bought it—much to his later chagrin. She never did return voluntarily to talk to them as promised.

One of the agents Sam had argued with and who later tried to interview me was William Roemer, a very persistent man who knew how to needle Sam and seemed to spend his every waking hour keeping tabs on my father and on our entire family.

Sam admitted later that he lost his patience with Roemer at the airport while other agents were questioning Phyllis. To avoid making a mistake such as hitting Roemer and being charged with assaulting a federal officer, Sam reboarded the plane. He said he finally realized that the flight time to New York was approaching and that unless he speeded things up and got Phyllis out of the FBI's clutches, the plane would leave without her.

Sam told me he knew that no matter how angry he was at Phyllis he couldn't leave without her, so he debarked from the plane carrying her purse and some of her garments. That was when the agents began whistling at him and suggesting he was a homosexual because he was carrying women's clothes.

According to some published reports, Sam finally lost his temper and began verbally abusing the agents and threatening them. To me, Sam denied he ever did that, and I had no way knowing whether he was telling me the truth or not until I read an FBI report dated May 11, 1965. This report concerned a conversation recorded at the Armory Lounge between Sam and a person not identified by the FBI.

> Discussion relates to subpoena Giancana has gotten to grand jury which he blames on Paul DeLucia [Ricca] deportation hearings at which DeLucia named too many names as old associates.

GIANCANA: You know this was one time I kept my mouth shut. He [the agent] handed it to me. I got in my car, thank you, and zoom.

UNKNOWN: That's wonderful.

GIANCANA: Maybe I shoulda called them some names again.

UNKNOWN: No. They don't care.

GIANCANA: They don't care? Are you kidding? If they had any backbone about them, if a man would call me what I called them fellows, I'd shoot them right there! I'd shoot them right on the dime and say, well, he pulled a gun. If you can call a MAN the names I called him, why for God's sake, they're not MEN!

UNKNOWN: No, they couldn't be if they take that.

GIANCANA: What I didn't call them. . . . and everything. Holy
———! It is just like a fellow would catch his wife in
bed with another man and not say anything about it.
The same thing. Like he would take it with a grain
of salt and that's it. And these fellows would do the
same. But I shoulda done that again this time. So
they could put it into their report and let them send
it in. Like I'm talking about that time at the airport.
I said, well, ah, tell ROBERT KENNEDY what I
said and you can tell him to. Oh ———! That's
when they put five cars on me. But you see, out
there his boss was with him and he was holding him
back. Ha, ha, ha! You know when you have nothing
to worry about and you're clean, you can call them
all the names under the sun. You can say anything.
When you're clean, you can say to hell with them.
You got money in the bank there, money in the
bank here, go ahead and check.

Sam was furious that the agents had made a fool of him in the
terminal in front of Phyllis and other people, and he said that he
would never forget it, someday he would make the agents pay. It
was just talk. But for a long time, his anger was at such a pitch
that he very nearly made a fatal mistake.

What some of the documents relating to the airport incident
hinted at but didn't explain was that Sam was extremely jealous of
Phyllis and didn't trust her associations with other entertainers, in
particular comedian Dan Rowan.

"Giancana was asked [about] his involvement, if any, in the
wiretapping matter of Dan Rowan's hotel room in Las Vegas and
had no comment. He denied knowing Robert Maheu. Giancana
accused agents of attempting to 'frame' him into the penitentiary."

At the time that Sam's suspicions about Rowan were raised, he
was meeting with Robert Maheu, who has since been identified
in congressional hearings as the Central Intelligence Agency's go-
between, the one who stood between the Agency and the Mafia
in various plots to assassinate Fidel Castro. Maheu had been introduced to Sam by Johnny Roselli, but in October, 1960, Sam

decided to test Maheu and the CIA on what they could do for him while he was helping them in their plotting.

The object of Sam's attention, of course, was Rowan. I suppose Sam could simply have had someone pay a visit to Rowan and beat the hell out of him, or worse, make certain he had a fatal accident. Instead he decided he wanted to know all the intimate details of what Rowan was doing, if anything, with Phyllis, so he told Maheu that he wanted him to use some of the CIA's spying equipment to tap in on what Rowan was doing.

Maheu, who owned a private detective agency in Miami, decided to hire another private detective to electronically monitor Rowan's apartment in Las Vegas. There was only one problem. Maheu's man got caught, and Roselli had to bail him out before Sam was able to find out anything about Rowan. It was embarrassing for Maheu, for the CIA, which had approved of his actions to keep Sam appeased, and for Roselli.

The CIA, of course, wasn't telling the FBI what it was doing, so the Bureau found out with its own illegal listening device. A FBI report dated March 8, 1961, says it believes Sam was behind the illegal bugging.

"Attention is drawn to Las Vegas origin investigation captioned [blanked-out] incident at Las Vegas, Oct. 31, last when [identity censored] was arrested by Clark County Sheriff's office at Las Vegas following the discovery of wire tapping devices in Dan Rowan's room. [The bugging] was at the time that subject Giancana was romantically interested in Phyllis McGuire. This situation is being explored in view of the fact Giancana possibly the prime moving force in having the installations made against Rowan."

Sam never did discuss the Rowan incident with me or with anyone else, as far as I know. What I learned, I learned through the FBI documents I obtained, but Sam suspected everyone by this time of all kinds of things. He trusted no one, not Phyllis, not his daughters, not those he worked with. He was paranoid about being watched, about there being a government agent behind every door, and with some justification. An incident that took place in Maryland, just two months after Sam's airport problems, justifies somewhat the way he thought and acted.

The incident was dutifully related in FBI reports to and from

Director J. Edgar Hoover, revealing that Sam and Phyllis were the targets of not only physical but electronic surveillance.

The first report, dated September 14, 1961, noted that Sam and Phyllis were staying in rooms at the Boxwood Motel on September 13 until they went out to eat at a nearby restaurant. Then they went to the Painters Mill Playhouse "in time for McGuire's evening engagement." The report stated that Sam didn't stay for the performance but remained in the vicinity of the motel until her engagement was over and then picked her up in her new Cadillac convertible.

"They stopped for refreshments at nearby restaurant and then returned to their own rooms at motel where McGuire left instructions not to be disturbed until four P.M. today. Photographs and moving pictures of subject and McGuire obtained during time they were out of motel. Microphone surveillance activated about ten-thirty P.M. on September 13 last. Nothing significant obtained to date. Surveillance continuing."

A second report, dated September 15, noted Sam's justified suspicions that he was being watched. He was in fact so careful that agents called off their watch. The problem was he didn't know how intimate that government surveillance had become.

"Subject and Phyllis McGuire since their arrival in Baltimore have been extremely surveillance conscious and have gone to exaggerated extent to determine if surveillance is being conducted.

"During periods McGuire has been at Painters Mill Playhouse, subject has walked area of motel [Boxwood] and playhouse parking lot to observe cars and persons in the area. Also, he has made no significant contacts and, in view of their remaining in a relatively isolated area northwest of Baltimore, it does not appear that further MISUR [microphone surveillance] or FISUR [physical surveillance] would be productive or advisable. In accordance with instructions, surveillance has been discontinued."

With microphones hidden in their bedrooms and in their telephones, and outside their windows, wherever Sam and Phyllis went, from the summer theaters Phyllis played in, like Painters Mill in Maryland, or playhouses in Delaware, to singing engagements at Atlantic City, to the expensive ranch Sam used at Paradise Valley outside Las Vegas, the FBI was there . . . listening to their every word and, I suspect, to every moment of passion. Even when Phyllis went to Europe on tour and Sam joined her in a carefully planned vacation to Rome, Madrid, and London, the FBI's agencies from London to Madrid kept tabs on their every move. To what end?

If the documents are any indication, there were no great secrets to be learned from Sam in his lady friends' bedrooms. The FBI might learn where Sam and Phyllis were heading the next day, or who they were going out with, but invading their privacy in that manner for that kind of material was hardly justified. It did succeed in one area, however. It made Sam more and more paranoid about his being watched, and that led to his making more and more mistakes, sometimes foolish ones.

In October, 1962, the FBI found out that Sam was trying to get a movie role for Phyllis through Frank Sinatra. That discovery came after two things happened. First, on September 26, 1962, the FBI in Palm Springs, California, watched as Phyllis flew into the Palm Springs airport in the wee hours of the morning to meet with my father. A report dated September 27, 1962, observed: ". . . Phyllis McGuire departed from this plane and was met by three unknown men in a station wagon later determined to be a 1962 Buick station wagon with California license XDP 318. This station wagon is registered to Essex Productions, 9229 Sunset Blvd., Los Angeles, one of Frank Sinatra's enterprises.

"After Phyllis McGuire entered this station wagon it proceeded to the vicinity of the Tamarisk Country Club, Cathedral City, California. This same station wagon was very shortly thereafter observed parked in the carport of the residence of Frank Sinatra." Then the report stated that at 4:55 A.M., an hour and forty minutes after she had arrived, Phyllis was seen returning in the same Buick to the airport with three men, one of them identified as my father. She boarded the plane she had arrived on and left. And Sinatra's car with my father, a black driver, and another unidentified Italian man in a "porkpie" hat were observed returning "to the Frank Sinatra residence in Cathedral City." For some strange reason, however, the FBI was ordered not to continue the usual tight surveillance of my father while he was in Palm Springs. I suppose the Bureau didn't want to embarrass Sinatra who it knew had close contacts with members of the Kennedy family, including President John F. Kennedy. The FBI noted: "Pursuant to instructions of Las Vegas, limited coverage will be afforded Giancana's activities during his stay in Palm Springs."

A few days later FBI agents again noted Phyllis's appearance in Palm Springs. "The Los Angeles Division advised on October 2, 1962, that . . . a white Ford Falcon belonging to Frank Sinatra Enterprises arrived at the Palm Springs airport at 3:40 A.M. . . . and contained one female and two males. Frank Sinatra's airplane bearing number N71DE arrived at the Palm Springs airport at 4:50 A.M. Phyllis McGuire at that time joined the individuals in the Ford Falcon described above. One of the individuals in the Falcon appeared to be Sam Giancana." So much for limited surveillance!

Just two days later, one of the ever-present electronic FBI bugs recorded a conversation between my father and three other persons identified only as an unknown male and two unknown females. The subject of the discussion, according to the FBI report, was a Sinatra movie and a part in that movie that Phyllis was getting.

GIANCANA: . . . guy comes over and we start back and forth . . . happened to be standing there by the elevator, and gives Frank a crack and hits him and bang, right down into the elevator shaft. Right in the script. Looks like a regular hook, and when the guy hits him, the hook goes right in and out.

I didn't see it, but the guy was telling me about it. Then there's another part, where the guy is in the apartment, and who walks in? Her. Looking like a million. [Talk is about a movie apparently in the making with Frank Sinatra (music interrupts conversations).] . . . takes place in the early twenties, something like the Robin Hood thing.

UNKNOWN: Robin Hood? Isn't that the English fairy tale? [FBI observes sarcastically, "Intelligentsia."]

UNKNOWN: . . . Well, couldn't it be the other way, like maybe she don't feel for him like he does for her?

GIANCANA: No, no . . . she still wants to keep her career. She told me she wants to marry me, but under one condition. I want to sing, she says. . . . [Talk is about Frank Sinatra] . . . he has a fabulous place on that lake [an apparent reference to the Cal-Neva Lodge casino at Lake Tahoe, Nevada].

UNKNOWN: You mean Phyllis?

GIANCANA: Yeah.

A month later the FBI was keeping close tabs on both Sam and Frank Sinatra, but this time at the Villa Venice. A surveillance that began on November 27, 1962, and continued into the following morning at the Villa Venice noted that "Frank Sinatra and Dean Martin were observed entering the Villa Venice for the second show at approximately 12:30 A.M. on November 28 accompanied by Joseph Fischetti. Joseph Fischetti is a former Chicago member of the Chicago criminal organization now residing in Miami, Florida, where he is part owner of Puccini's Restaurant in Miami."

The same report made a point of stating that " . . . Frank Sinatra and Eddie Fisher accompanied by Sam Giancana recently flew from Los Angeles, California, to Reno, Nevada, en route to Lake Tahoe, Nevada, in Frank Sinatra's private plane."

Lake Tahoe was the site of a magnificently situated casino, the Cal-Neva Lodge. The lodge was located on the California-Nevada border at the northern end of the lake, and was publicly owned by Sinatra and four other men. According to the FBI, Sinatra held the largest interest in the casino with 36.6 percent.

The Cal-Neva consisted of a beautiful, luxuriously appointed building where the games were played and where entertainers brought in the crowds, plus more than twenty lavishly furnished cottages that cost fifty dollars a day and up. In those days, that was a lot of money, but it was not exorbitant.

The lodge had a huge dining room and a coffee shop on the California side of the building. On the Nevada side were all the gambling paraphernalia—the tables, the slot machines, the credit cage. The Cal-Neva was unique because of its border location, and the beauty of the lake and the surrounding ski resorts and mountains made it a potential goldmine for its owners. The same popular entertainers who appeared in Las Vegas's gambling palaces performed at the Cal-Neva to draw in the crowds. The lodge never really reached its potential in the early 1960s, and I'm not sure if it ever will because of what happened there later.

Typical of the microphone disclosures over the Cal-Neva was a conversation between John Roselli, the Nevada representative of my father and the Chicago Mafia, and Sam.

This conversation was recorded at the Armory Lounge in December, 1961, shortly after Sam had returned from his trip to Europe with Phyllis. It not only identified Sam's interests in the Cal-Neva, but it also described efforts Sinatra made on behalf of my father to have the family of President John F. Kennedy ease the FBI's harassment of Sam. It also suggests that President-Kennedy's father wasn't very successful in living up to a promise to help my father after Sam had donated money to the political campaign of President Kennedy during the Democratic primaries.

ROSELLI: Did you go to Luciano's home [Charles (Lucky) Luciano, the former leader of national syndicate, who was deported to Italy and lived in Rome]?
GIANCANA: No.
ROSELLI: Oh, that's a hell of a place . . . a real nice home. He's a real nice guy.
GIANCANA: I couldn't get out of that country fast enough.
ROSELLI: How do you feel, buddy? Did you have a nice time? Did you get a lot of heat over there?
GIANCANA: What kind of heat?
ROSELLI: Over there.
GIANCANA: Naw.
ROSELLI: Nobody tailed you? Well, Skinny called me, and said get ahold of the guy, he wants to see you. I says, right away, so I calls him back. I went to Vegas after I come back from . . . [The reference to Skinny is to Paul D'Amato, a New Jersey nightclub operator and a close friend of Sinatra's and Giancana's who worked at the Cal-Neva.]

GIANCANA: Who was [it]?

ROSELLI: Frank. You know. So the first week, I didn't see
him. [Then] I saw him, hello, how are you, and
that's all. After his wife left, he sent for me. . . .
Now, I said, Frank, I don't want to be in your
way. I don't want to bother you. He said, I want
you to bunk with me . . . will you do that, he
says, bunk with me? I says, all right. So he says,
when are you going home? I says, today. So
he says, cancel out, I want you to come to my
home.

I says, that'll be fine with me. So he was real nice
to me and offered me some money. I threw it back
at him. I had a chance to quiz him. Towards the end
I took three . . . three thousand I was able to
pay. I said, Frankie, can I ask you one question?
He says [answer blanked out]. I took Sam's name
and wrote it down and told Bobby Kennedy, this is
my buddy. This is my buddy, this is what I want
you to know, Bob.

. . . And he says to me, he says [blank] is he
still with Phyllis? I says, I think he sees her, and
he says, that don't help anything, either. I said, in
what respect? He figures they can always find you
through her.

GIANCANA: What am I supposed to do? If I didn't have her . . .

ROSELLI: They'd [the FBI] follow the next girl.

GIANCANA: In other words, I should stick my head in the sand
with my ——— in the air. Is that it? Or I shouldn't
go no place.

ROSELLI: Between you and I, Frank saw Joe Kennedy three
different times. He called him three times . . . Joe
Kennedy, the father.

GIANCANA: Called who?

ROSELLI: Called Frank [blanked out, but known to be Sin-
atra]. So maybe he's starting to see the light . . .
you're friends. He's got it in his head that they're
not faithful to him. That's what I'm trying to get in
his head.

GIANCANA: In other words, then, the donation that was made [campaign contribution to Kennedy primary fight] . . .

ROSELLI: That's what I was talking about.

GIANCANA: Had to pay for it, regardless.

ROSELLI: That's what made the issue with him. Nothing deliberate, take it back.

GIANCANA: In other words, if I even get a speeding ticket, none of these ——— would know me?

ROSELLI: You told that right, buddy. And I'm for you a hundred percent for that . . .

GIANCANA: . . . they just worry about themselves and keep themselves clean, take the heat off of them.

ROSELLI: Sam, I think you gotta start, you gotta start giving them orders. This is it, Frank, and that's how you got to start.

GIANCANA: No, let him get his own.

ROSELLI: He says, I'll put you on the payroll . . . He says, I'll put you in the Cal-Neva and I'll open up a swinging bar. The boys will bankroll it and, if you can't, come to me. I told him, I'm gonna tell Sam everything . . .

GIANCANA: I sent for [identity censored] and was gonna say, listen, I'm getting sick and tired of this.

ROSELLI: He's not in town, you know.

GIANCANA: I know.

ROSELLI: Aren't you gonna be tied up with Cal-Neva?

GIANCANA: Who gives a ——— about Cal-Neva? ——— him. Don't worry about it. I'm gonna get my money out of there . . . and I'm gonna wind up with half of the joint with no money. Not gonna make any difference.

ROSELLI: If you do that, please send me there, will you . . . to look out for you?

Then on September 19, 1963, the FBI reported that Sam met with two unnamed individuals who held a discussion concerning James Hoffa and the Central States Teamsters pension fund and a three-million-dollar loan that Sam had tried unsuccessfully to obtain from Hoffa and his Teamsters.

Said the FBI: "Giancana was extremely bitter [about not receiving the three-million-dollar loan] and in his comments concerning this, advised the others present that there were times recently when Giancana could obtain any sum of money he desired from the fund, but now with all the heat on he cannot obtain any money or favors.

"'Now all this heat comes on and I can't even get a favor out of him now. I can't do nothing for myself. Ten years ago I can get all the ———— money I want from the guy.'

"In regard to this conversation, it is believed that the request for the three-million-dollar loan was in connection with a request by Frank Sinatra for a similar amount for the purpose of renovating the Cal-Neva Lodge, supposedly owned by Sinatra but believed in actuality to be owned by Giancana."

The "heat" that my father was talking about was largely of his own doing, his and Phyllis's. It all started when Sam flew to Lake Tahoe in mid-July, 1963, to be with Phyllis when she and her sisters opened a ten-day engagement at the Celebrity Room of the Cal-Neva.

Sam tried to keep a low profile by staying in one of the cottages, Chalet 50, overlooking the lake. The cottage had been assigned to Phyllis officially. Apparently, according to published reports, the Nevada State Gaming Control Board was tipped off that he was there, and Sam's presence was a no-no. In fact, Sam was one of eleven crime figures who were blacklisted in Nevada.

Casinos, supplied with the list of names, were supposed to oust him and the other crime figures should they show up. The Cal-Neva and Sinatra didn't live up to that requirement according to a Control Board document filed in 1963 charging that Sinatra tried to intimidate board officials.

The document charged that: ". . . Giancana sojourned in Chalet 50 at the Cal-Neva Lodge at various times between July 17 and July 28, 1963, with the knowledge and consent of the licensee [Sinatra]. Although Chalet 50 was registered to a female performer [Phyllis McGuire] then appearing as part of the entertainment in the Celebrity Room of the license, Giancana is known to have been entertained, harbored, and permitted to remain there and to receive services and courtesies from the licensee, its employees, representatives, agents, and directors."

Things got complicated when Sam threw a punch at one of Phyllis's staff members in the Cal-Neva bar, causing more problems. The incident was witnessed by an employee, who was ordered to testify about the fight but failed to show up at a hearing of the Control Board. At that point the board charged that Sinatra had something to do with the employee's reluctance to appear.

Things got even hotter when the press reported that Sinatra had called Control Board Chairman Edward A. Olsen and used what Olsen described in an eight-page complaint against Sinatra as "vile, intemperate, base, and indecent" language in an attempt to intimidate him. Olsen also reported an attempt by Paul D'Amato to bribe board agents into calling off their investigation. The result was that Sinatra had to sell off his interests in not only the Cal-Neva but also in the Sands Hotel in Las Vegas. Now all is forgiven. Sam is dead and no longer an albatross for Sinatra, and Sinatra is regaled by presidents and attorneys general, and as a result, once again he is allowed to invest in and represent a casino . . . Caesar's Palace.

But that July in 1963 very likely represented the catalyst that not only eroded my father's power as a crime boss, but eventually brought it to an end. For the time being, however, it did little to cool his ardor for Phyllis McGuire.

16

A Filly Named Phyllis—Part II

Paul Ricca loved Sam, but he didn't like Sam's international exploits with Phyllis McGuire. The notoriety, the constant harassment of Mafia hangouts, the loose talk among disgruntled crime-family members, and the never-ending drumbeat of news stories and column items about my father and Phyllis were irritants to a man who believed in the low profile, at home and in the family. At least that was the image Ricca promoted to the day he died, when he received the last rites of the Catholic Church and a priest proclaimed that his family should be consoled by the fact that he "died in the grace of God."

In all the years that I knew Paul Ricca, I never heard about his running around with girl friends. His image was that of a family man, and it was an image he furthered whenever I was in his presence. If he had any women—as I'm sure he must have had since all the Italian stallions of the Chicago mob did—he probably hid them in a closet and had his fun there.

Paul Ricca would never say directly to me that my father was acting like a fool. That would be beneath his dignity and violate the tenets of the respect in which he held Sam, and he did respect, even love Sam in his own way. Instead he would always speak to me in parables. He would explain that men in positions of authority had an obligation to maintain their positions of leadership and esteem with those beneath them and to do that, they must set an example. Then he would look off, as if into space, and remark, "Your father is well, I trust?"

I would give a kind of nod and answer, "I guess so . . . I haven't seen him lately . . . he's been traveling . . ."

Paul would nod knowingly and add, "Ah, yes . . . and I am saddened by what I see and hear these days. So many things are written and talked about that affect others . . ."

An FBI report dated August 8, 1963, reflected the effect that some of the publicity was having on people like Paul Ricca and other members of the mob.

"Current publicity in Chicago papers concerning La Cosa Nostra presently receiving comment from underworld figures. . . . Advise that Giancana in extremely tenuous situation because of publicity and consideration seems to be that Giancana may be replaced as head of Chicago organization.

"As has been pointed out in the past, several names have been set forward as logical successors, however, at this time no singular effort is under way to the knowledge of the Chicago division [of the FBI] to remove Giancana.

"Chicago feels Giancana in Palm Springs [at that time] for two-fold purpose . . . one, to escape possible further surveillance by the FBI and two, to remain away from leading members of Chicago organization who may desire to berate him for his recent activities."

In the beginning, I didn't like Phyllis McGuire. Perhaps it was the circumstances we met under, perhaps it was just jealousy, but from the first moment we met I resented her.

Our meeting took place on a Christmas Eve at my childhood home in Oak Park, three years after I was married. She was using a bedroom on the same floor where mine was, where my mother and father's bedroom had been. I resented her staying there, sharing a room with Sam. At least he had the good taste not to have her stay in the room he had once shared with my mother.

However, I was angry at Sam for having her there, for living with her while my sister Francine was still living at home, and not even the beautiful Somali leopard coat he had bought me as a Christmas present could soothe me. I just didn't think it was right, particularly at Christmas.

Phyllis was a very pretty girl . . . blond, curvaceous, and even without much makeup on, she looked attractive. After I had entered the house, she excused herself, went upstairs, changed her clothes, and put on makeup. When she reappeared she was elegant, absolutely sensational, and I resented her even more.

She too was rather cool and aloof, but that changed as time passed, and we eventually became close enough so that I confided in her very often, and she supported me in arguments that I had with Sam on many occasions.

I suppose Sam treated Phyllis well enough, but there were quite a few occasions when he tried to put her down. Many times I heard him call her stupid in a kidding sort of way when she would express an opinion on something worldly. So often he was demeaning in the way he treated her, as if she was an inferior. But she had a talent for rising above it. Phyllis was really strong, and she knew how to handle him. She talked back to him in a way no other woman had ever talked back to him, not even my mother. When he called her stupid, she would snap back without hesitation, "Well, Sam, I've done pretty well in life without you." Or, "I didn't need you to get where I am, and don't forget it."

Sometimes she used the strange hold she had on my father to make him dance through hoops. At least one conversation recorded by the FBI indicated my father was worried about how Phyllis might react to other women and situations. The conversation was recorded at the Armory Lounge on October 4, 1962, between Sam and an unknown woman.

GIANCANA: . . . What do you think happened? We went to this restaurant, and whose picture do you think is sitting right above us?

UNKNOWN: Keeley Smith?

GIANCANA: No. Wilma's.

UNKNOWN: Does she know her?

GIANCANA: Yeah. I told them to take that picture down . . . please. I says, give me one more chance [to Phyllis McGuire] . . . that's up to you.

UNKNOWN: Who's Wilma? Is she in show business?

GIANCANA: No. She was a girl I knew. Someone told her when she was in Vegas. Someone pointed her out. Then she sat down and talked to the girl. Somebody sent her [McGuire] one of Winchell's columns, about a month ago. The article said, Love is fading away . . . Keeley [Smith] was in Atlantic City with Frank Sinatra, and I was there and was all over her. He's given up McGuire and is going back to Keeley. So someone from New York sent her the clipping.

For a time Sam wore a toupee because it made him look younger and because Phyllis liked it. Sam wouldn't have done it for any other woman except perhaps my mother, and normally he would have been very self-conscious about using such a thing. But Phyllis made Sam feel good about wearing it, and surprisingly enough he mentioned it in a conversation at the Armory Lounge on April 28, 1965.

At the time Sam was planning to see an old and close friend of his, comedian Joe E. Lewis, perform at the Camellia House. Of course, the FBI turned up and noticed that Sam was with another girl friend, a secretary to my uncle Michael DeTolve at the envelope company that carried Sam on its payroll as an employee.

The Joe E. Lewis meeting is worth mentioning at this point because it illustrates just how open Sam had become in going out with various women, not just Phyllis, and how those activities drew FBI agents like flies.

Sam had been dating the secretary who worked for my uncle, but I never understood why he was so stuck on her. Certainly she wasn't as beautiful as Phyllis McGuire or many of the other professional entertainers and models he went out with, but there was an attraction that had lasted over the years, and he would go out with her on different occasions. On April 25, 1964, the FBI, with the advance knowledge of where Sam was going that its electronic bugs provided, was at the Camellia House, watching . . . and listening.

The FBI reported that its surveillance found "Sam Giancana to be present in the company of three other persons, one of whom was identified as being Bergit Clark, a female with whom Giancana has maintained an acquaintance for several years."

The surveillance agents observed that Sam and Joe E. Lewis spent about twenty minutes talking together at a small bar, and that after Lewis performed at the Camellia House, he changed clothing and returned to Sam's ringside table to join him and his group.

Then the agents noted that Sam spotted them and "smiled in acknowledgment" when he saw them. Sam pointed out their presence to Lewis and was overheard telling Lewis, "Those are G guys."

With a smile on his face, Sam introduced Lewis to the agents. While the report doesn't say so, it was Sam's way of showcasing the agents to everyone in the vicinity who might not know who or what they were. It was also his way of letting the agents know that he had lots of friends in high places, from politics to the entertainment world, who weren't ashamed to be seen with him. The April 27, 1964, report said:

"Following the introductions, Giancana made a statement to Lewis, which was apparently being made for the second time and which Lewis had not answered previously, to the effect that Lewis should consider retiring from show business and go on a trip to Johannesburg, South Africa, with Giancana. When Giancana was queried as to the seriousness of his intentions [concerning such a] trip, he answered that he plans to take such a trip and continued that he is now going to start enjoying life.

"Giancana made it a point to stress the fact on several occasions that the FBI was aware of all his movements and he felt it useless to try and keep them secret any longer. In this regard, Giancana admitted, without prompting, his presence at the Camellia House the previous evening in the company of [blank] and Ross Prio [a high-ranking Chicago mobster].

"The conversation was terminated when Lewis was advised that it was time to commence his first performance of the evening. Giancana remained in the company of the agents for approximately two to three minutes following Lewis's departure and then proceeded to return to his table. As he was departing, Giancana said to the agents, 'Well, you guys keep on working for a living, and I'll steal for mine.'"

The report then pointed out that as my father left the club, he showed his first "signs of irritation" when he saw an agent leaving a telephone booth he was about to use. The report stated that Sam "specifically stated to SA [Special Agent] . . . that the agents should be sure to put in their report that they observed Sam Giancana at the Camellia House and they should tell their boss that he could then perform an obscene act with this report. Giancana continued to be extremely loud and vulgar while departing the hotel with Clark. No rejoinder was made to Giancana at this point."

It was incidents of that type which irritated Paul Ricca and other important members of the Outfit. The FBI was everywhere . . . watching . . . recording . . . identifying people, all because Sam was flaunting his associations with various women. It wasn't good for business.

While my father partied with a variety of women, Phyllis McGuire was the one woman he stayed with over a long period of time, and although she frequently told him that she had gotten to where she was in life without him or his influence, he still tried to do things for her, including getting her movie roles.

Sam loved Phyllis in his own way. He wanted to marry her at one point, but as close as they were, and they were almost inseparable for years, there was something missing, something Sam looked for but couldn't find.

This was made clear by a somewhat circumspect conversation my father had with a close friend on December 13, 1963, at the Armory Lounge. Although the FBI does not identify who the person was, I know it was someone close to my father because Sam was freely discussing not only his romances with various women but what he was searching for in a woman.

"[Identity censored] and Moe [Sam Giancana] discuss his love life. They discuss Keeley [Smith], Judy [Campbell], Roman [not further identified but apparently a former entertainment personality], Phyllis [McGuire]. The conversation centered around how [blank] felt about each one of these women.

"[Blank] thinks Keeley never wanted marriage and that she is Moe's type . . . lots of fun, etc. [Blank] thinks Phyllis is the pretty one of the more recent girls. With this statement, Moe says: 'Oh, you haven't seen the hidden ones.' [Blank] was surprised at 'Roman's looks that last time she was in [blank] she used to be so attractive, now she is nothing.'

"[Blank] thinks Moe should think more about marriage. [Blank] thinks Moe is a 'lost cause' because he doesn't know what he wants.

"Moe goes into a long dissertation about what he likes in a woman. He thinks she should be very handy around the house (in case people come in for a visit during the early hours of the morning) and she should have the ability to make a man feel at ease. He doesn't think he will find the woman to fit the bill."

The FBI agents' observation didn't surprise me, but it may surprise *them* to learn that the woman he was describing who was handy around the house, who could entertain his friends in the wee hours of the morning, and could make him feel at ease was my mother. She was the only woman who ever filled that bill for him. The others were all interludes, women who fulfilled his sexual fantasies and needs or made him feel younger than he really was. None of them, regardless of how pleasant, beautiful, or sensual, had the qualities that Mother had and that Sam had come to expect in their life together. That small comment in the FBI report unknowingly bared Sam's soul . . . and his loneliness. He was searching for someone he would never find and in a moment of candor, he admitted it.

While Phyllis and Sam were playing international hopscotch and Sam's mob was stirring uncomfortably over the pressure the couple's cavorting was causing Chicago's underworld as a result of increased FBI surveillances, I was busy having babies, one after another.

My first was Samuel Paul Manno, born February 6, 1960. After that, it was one a year for the next four years: Carmen Zachary, March 11, 1961; Scott John, February 19, 1962; Carl Antony, March 15, 1963; and Philip Morris, September 4, 1964. The quick succession of children, Sam's apparent lack of interest in me and the kids, a marriage that was never really happy . . . all those things and the feeling that I was in a prison from which there was no escape led to a severe case of postnatal depression in January, 1965, and another trip to a psychiatric ward, this time at an out-of-town hospital where the press would not know about me or that Sam had a daughter with mental problems. Sam was so paranoid he thought every newspaper in the Chicago area would pick it up if I checked into a local hospital. So I went to St. Mary's of the Hill in Milwaukee, Wisconsin.

I had become an alcoholic. I would walk to the local liquor store with just a little Mickey Mouse dress on, the type old ladies wear, and my appearance was terribly disheveled. With no makeup on, my hair virtually uncombed, I would pick up my bottle of booze, go home, and drink it down. Carmen would find the liquor and throw it out, but instead of trying to help me or understand what I was going through, he would give me a belt, and call me a drunk and a whore and anything else he could think of. In fact, I *was* pretty disgusting, although I wasn't whoring around, I wasn't even fooling around or flirting then. Things got to the point where I would keep two bottles, one diluted with water, the other filled with the real booze, and make sure he would find the diluted bottle. Then when he left the house, I would drink it down. My children were being neglected, and I know I put them through hell letting them see me in that state.

St. Mary's of the Hill was a god-awful place. Big iron doors banging behind me . . . being locked in a cage like an animal . . . nothing in my room at all except soft items. There were no mirrors, no utensils, no brushes to brush my hair, nothing. If I wanted to smoke, I had to ask the matron for a light. I felt like I was in jail. There were nights when I screamed for help, for death . . . for anything, and no one listened. I had an overwhelming desire to take my life, to end it all. Knowing that I couldn't made it all the worse. It took me nearly nine months to come out of St. Mary's and get my life straightened out, and if it hadn't been for the help and love of a sweet little nun, Sister Michele, and the letters I received from Phyllis McGuire, I'm not sure I would have made it.

I had seen Phyllis at least once a year, sometimes more after that first meeting until Sam died. We corresponded often, particularly when I became ill and once again had to receive electric shock treatments.

Sam had been a sometimes father-grandfather, not very happy over either role, and more often than not impatient when the boys were a little noisy as small boys are. I always believed he felt that being a grandfather cramped his style as a man-about-town, a jet-setter. But he was generous to a fault in other ways with the boys, with me, and with Carmen. When we bought a new home in St. Charles, a rather quiet upper-middle-class suburban community outside of Chicago, Sam gave us more than twenty thousand dollars for the down payment. The one-hundred-thousand-dollar home, a large, almost plantation-style five-bedroom house with a huge circular driveway, stood on a corner plot of more than two acres surrounded by houses of similar or even higher cost. And there were bonds for the boys' futures, expensive new furniture, cash when we needed it, all courtesy of Sam Giancana. It was the only way Sam knew how to show love—pay for it, shower us all with gifts.

I recall one Christmas when Sam sent Phyllis, my sister Bonnie, and me to New York on a shopping spree. We were there for three days. He gave Bonnie the money to hold, about ten thousand dollars in cash, and I bought three gorgeous suits, one with chinchilla trim and another with mink trim at an exclusive Park Avenue shop called Martha's. They cost over three thousand dollars. Bonnie got a designer dress for about the same amount. That was typical of Sam's generosity with us.

Phyllis showed her affection in a different way, though she was also generous with gifts. She tried to mend the breach growing between Sam and me. She also tried to express his feeling for me where he had failed to. A letter, written January 17, 1965, from New York where she was taping a television show, *On Broadway Tonight,* reached me at the hospital and momentarily helped lift my spirits.

It said in part:

> Your father is truly concerned and loves you VERY, VERY MUCH. It would make him and all of us so happy to see you come through with flying colors and able to face anything that life has to dish out. Honey, we all have our problems, believe me, so keep your chin up and I know everything will work out for you. Remember, your doctor knows best at this time. Listen to him and trust him. He wants to help you. Please write soon again—
>
> Love,
> Phyllis

Phyllis came to Chicago for Christmas almost every year except perhaps the year Sam went to jail for refusing to talk to a federal grand jury, and later when Sam had moved from Chicago to

Cuernavaca to avoid federal agents and the possibility of more grand jury appearances.

She came because Sam spent his Christmases traditionally, with the family around him at home in Oak Park. For a while, Christmas without Phyllis there was like no Christmas at all. I looked forward to seeing her, talking with her about a lot of things, not the least of which were my growing marital problems.

When I came out of St. Mary's after nine months, I started to straighten myself out at home. Living the life I had led with Carmen and the kids wasn't that unusual. A lot of other people have had to live through worse. But what was different in my case was my special status as a Mafia princess. Whenever anything went wrong and I was hospitalized, it was under an assumed name. When I wanted to pursue a career in modeling or acting, it was under an assumed name. When I went out with men, again an assumed name. I couldn't live with the name of Giancana. I was worse off than the fairy tale princess locked in her castle. I was a princess without a castle whose father, the king, wanted her locked away. Sam was always afraid of disgrace: Sam Giancana, the crime boss, has an alcoholic, a case for the nuthouse as a daughter. If I had been a Kennedy and had had a nervous breakdown or been an alcoholic, it would have been in the paper, and that would be the end of it, no big deal. With me, nobody could know, it might cast doubt on my father's mental capabilities or on his decisions.

I had riches, luxuries, a nice house, fur coats, cars, private schools—but I paid for it all in one way or another. I am still paying for it.

It was 1971 when Phyllis and I became very close, and shared a secret that could very well have cost us both our lives had Sam learned about it.

Carmen and I had been battling as usual, and I was seriously considering a divorce. The mere mention of the word sent Sam into a rage, so I couldn't talk to him about it. And Carmen couldn't be reasoned with. When he didn't like what I had to say, or thought I was getting too familiar with someone at a party, there was no discussion, just a belt in the mouth or a punch in the stomach. On one occasion a dentist whom I had known for years made the mistake of keeping his arm around my waist for too long at a party at the Villa Venice. Carmen said nothing to the dentist but later, after we had left the party, he knocked me around until I was black-and-blue. When I made the mistake of complaining to Sam about the treatment I was getting from Carmen, he just snickered and cracked: "You probably deserved it."

Sam always sided with Carmen. It was a man's world. He told me more than once that I had made my own bed by marrying a divorced man like Carmen, now I had to lie in it.

Carmen had been a wife-beater almost from the beginning of our marriage. He would beat me when he thought I was flirting with another man, or when I sassed him back, or when he found out I had gone over his head to Sam, or if I made a fool of him at some affair in front of his friends. The verbal battle would start there, continue into the car, and then the blows would come when we reached home, or sometimes even before then. I am the first to admit that I had been spoiled. I wanted what I wanted when I wanted it, and I wouldn't take no for an answer. But in the final analysis, the primary reason for his beating me was jealousy, a motivation that was without any real provocation during the years he was keeping me barefoot and pregnant. We would go to weddings, family get-togethers, mob parties, and he would watch me like a hawk. If a man became friendly with me, Carmen would accuse me of having a wild affair with him, and I really wasn't . . . not then.

It was during this period of marital unrest that I met again and fell in love with the young midshipman I had first encountered on my train trip to California to study acting. Only Bob was no longer a midshipman, he was an Annapolis graduate, a submarine captain, and very much married.

Our meeting came about by chance in Milwaukee when I was in the hospital, and later we had additional meetings and a liaison. We began our affair in the St. Charles area where Bob came to see me while he was on assignment at a nearby naval-ordnance depot. This was no passing fancy, no one-night stand for the thrill of the moment. Bob and I have kept our relationship close, intimate, and loving in all the years since, but we have been unable to break the bonds that keep us separated—his marriage. I have had to content myself with weekends, sometimes a little longer, in hotels and motels in cities throughout the Midwest, knowing full well that Bob will never leave his wife, yet also knowing that in his way he does love me and has ever since that first affair in St. Charles.

Eventually, Carmen did discover what had been taking place. He secretly taped telephone conversations I had with Bob and found and seized the letters and photographs I had from and with Bob as a result of our many meetings. Those discoveries eventually led to a divorce to which I consented under terms dictated to me by my husband. It was either that or have the whole affair tried in court with the letters and recorded conversations and photographs made public, which would not only embarrass Sam but would destroy my children and the love we shared, as well as Bob and his marriage. I couldn't have that happen, and it didn't.

But before we reached that point, I became pregnant again and I wasn't certain whether the father was Carmen or Bob, or anyone else. I had suddenly gone crazy over the constant beatings and fights and sought solace and sex with anybody who was interested, even with the husbands of women who had befriended me. I'm ashamed of that now, but it happened and I can't take it back. The net result, however, was that I became pregnant and I didn't want another child . . . I couldn't have handled another child, so I sought help from the only person I felt I could trust and who I believed understood what I was going through, Phyllis McGuire.

Phyllis had told me on many occasions that if things got too difficult at home to come to Las Vegas and stay with her. I knew my marriage was crumbling at the time, and things were very bad, so I turned to her for company and advice.

My husband suspected nothing when I said I wanted to go to Las Vegas to be with Phyllis. He really loved Phyllis and enjoyed her company, so he readily agreed, as long as I had the money to make the trip. He wasn't about to provide the money. I told him I had it. In a way that was true. I had, without his knowledge, sold one of my children's one-thousand-dollar bonds. These bonds had been put away for my kids when they were born—they were gifts from family friends, friends of their father's, friends of Sam's—for their education. It was a terrible thing to do, but I had to get away from Carmen, the kids, everyone.

At the time I did not know I was pregnant. I felt rather strange, but I didn't question it. Sometimes you play dumb, I guess, you don't want to admit things to yourself. It wasn't until I got to Las

Vegas and stayed at Phyllis's estate that I knew definitely. Phyllis called her doctor who gave me a pregnancy test and confirmed it.

Before that occurred, however, I spent a week with Phyllis having the time of my life. There were three houses on the estate: the main house where Phyllis lived, the guesthouse where I stayed, and the maid's house. The guesthouse was big enough to take care of a small-sized family. It had two bedrooms, a huge living room, a large dining room, and a fully stocked kitchen with all the equipment a gourmet cook would need to turn out a dish for the gods. Despite the best of intentions, I didn't do any cooking. I ate at the main house with her and her guests. There was also a small swimming pool at the guesthouse, but Phyllis wouldn't hear of my using it. She usually reserved that pool for Johnny Carson's musicians or other guests who she thought wanted to be isolated from the main house. She wanted me to use the giant main-house pool, which could be reached from the guesthouse via a walkway and a bridge.

When I wasn't in the pool, I was playing tennis with Phyllis, an avid tennis player, Pancho Gonzales, whom she invited over for dinner with his son, and oil millionaire Mike Davis, a man Phyllis often saw when she wasn't going out with Sam.

I wasn't a very good tennis player, and I suppose I looked a little foolish trying to compete with experienced players, but Phyllis commented later on the manner in which I had related to Pancho Gonzales.

"You were really quite marvelous today," she said.

"Why?" I asked. "What did I do right? It couldn't have been tennis . . . I was simply awful."

She smiled. "Oh . . . I'm not talking about that," she answered. "It's the first time I've ever seen Pancho talk that much to anybody. You really got him out of his shell."

It was a nice compliment and I appreciated it, just as I appreciated the shows, the restaurants, the clubs, and even the hairdresser Phyllis treated me to. Without her, I would have been miserable and broke and unable to deal with what was ahead.

A week after I arrived and her doctor confirmed that I was pregnant, I knew I had to do something. I told Phyllis I just couldn't bear to have another child, not now. She understood and made a call to another doctor she knew, who made arrangements for me to see some California physicians operating a clinic near Los Angeles.

With Phyllis's help and about seven hundred dollars I had left, I flew to Los Angeles to have my second abortion. It was not a memory I cherish. It was cold and lonely, but at least it wasn't the agonizing experience I had gone through the first time.

I didn't know what to expect when I arrived at the clinic, which was located in a suburb outside of Los Angeles. I was examined, told to fill out some forms, given some prescriptions, and then required to sit and wait in a room with some other girls all of whom had terrible stories about how they had been left in the lurch by boyfriends, or were going out with men who didn't want children, or were afraid, as I was, to tell their husbands they were pregnant again. Abortion mills are terribly depressing places, and I found myself crying for some of the girls who had to lose children they wanted and crying also for myself because I hated what I was doing.

The next day I returned to Las Vegas and was picked up at the airport by Phyllis's chauffeur in her pink Rolls-Royce. But Phyllis wasn't home. She was in the hospital battling hepatitis. I was unable to see her, and the following day I left for home. A short time later, on August 15, 1971, Phyllis wrote from her sickbed to apologize and remind me to get the necessary shots to protect myself against hepatitis.

She apologized because my visit to her ranch had ended the way it had and promised that "it will never happen again." She asked me to return for another visit, noting that the people I had met at her home had remarked on how alive and fun-loving I was. I had tried desperately not to let anyone other than Phyllis know how really unhappy I was. Apparently I had succeeded.

Phyllis's illness, however, made her concerned about my well-being. She was afraid there was a chance that I might be infected by the hepatitis virus, and closed her letter with an emphatic "GET YOUR SHOT" in capital letters, then signed it, "Love, Phyllis."

Two weeks later, after I wrote her that I felt there was no other answer to my marital problems but divorce, she wrote again from Albuquerque, New Mexico, this time having a friend type the letter because she was too weak to write at length in her own hand.

Phyllis was saddened deeply "to see any family break up," but she said she understood that I believed what I was doing was best for both Carmen and me.

She reminded me that she knew exactly what I was feeling and what I was going through and how difficult it was for me.

Then Phyllis added that Sam "loves you deeply" and was very concerned about what happened to me in every way. I found that difficult to understand even when she reminded me that "some people are only capable of expressing just so much love, but that does not mean that they do not feel deeply." She believed Sam felt deeply about me, and I guess he did, but he was so violently opposed even to the mention of divorce that it was difficult if not impossible for me to believe what she was saying.

Once again she reminded me to get a shot to protect myself against the infectious hepatitis she was recovering from. She added that everyone in Las Vegas missed me, even "Tiger Mike" Davis, her oil-millionaire escort, who had gradually been taking my father's place as Phyllis's beau after the FBI had forced Sam to abandon his leadership of the Chicago Mafia and move to Mexico to avoid federal grand juries and jail.

Phyllis McGuire had turned out to be more than just a headliner girl friend of my father's. She had been a good friend to me. She had counseled me when I needed somebody, she had comforted me in time of stress, and she had literally risked her life to help me obtain a secret abortion.

There are some who might cast stones at her because of her relationship with Sam, but they'll never know what a warm and really decent human being she is.

If Phyllis's romance with my father led to his downfall, he had only himself to blame. Phyllis McGuire had never promised him a rose garden, but she did let him smell the roses. He just didn't learn to do it in private.

17

Sam and His Shadow

The erosion of my father's stature and power as a crime boss may have begun with his relationship with Phyllis McGuire, but it was his continuing public confrontations with the FBI and behind-the-scenes warfare with U.S. Attorney General Robert F. Kennedy that finally led to his demise as a boss.

Phyllis was, as stated, just one of many women whom he chased following my mother's death. Not all of them were entertainers. One was a blond waitress from Florida whose husband, a well-known Chicago burglar, just never came home one night. Though there was no proof, the FBI circulated the story that Sam had had the woman's husband killed so he could continue his affair with her undisturbed.

The story goes that about six weeks after the blonde's husband disappeared, she discovered she was pregnant. So Sam bought a house for her, using a fake name, and she had the child. The baby wasn't Sam's, however, it was her husband's, but the tale circulated that it was my father's, and that he had taken care of her because of what he had done to her husband, whose body was never found.

I'm not sure who circulated the story in 1959, but I know it was repeated by agents as well as by people in the underworld. I don't know if there was any truth to it because Sam never discussed his affairs with me, but like so many tales of his conquests of other women, the story gave rise to more and more rumors and complaints about Sam not paying attention to the affairs of the mob.

He was, suggested one agent, "pussy-whipped," that is, all he thought about was sex, and business suffered because of it. Certainly he made mistakes and the FBI capitalized on them.

One of those mistakes took place when he returned from Mexico in 1959 following Bonnie's wedding. United States Customs was on hand to greet him and search him, and when they did they found a list. According to testimony given by FBI Agent William Roemer, the list contained the names of all the leading Chicago hoodlums in code, and after each of those names was a figure. Roemer testified that the FBI discovered later that the names and figures comprised the points that those identified would have in a racetrack my father had been negotiating to buy in Mexico.

One of the names on the list, according to Roemer, was that of John D'Arco, then a Democratic alderman of the First Ward and still an influential committeeman of that ward.

I think that under normal conditions Sam would have been more careful and would not have had such a list on his person when he knew he might encounter Customs. That mistake led the FBI down avenues of surveillance that helped it unravel the intricate web of intrigue and power between the Chicago mob and the politicians of the Windy City, particularly those in the First Ward. For not only did the FBI plant electronic listening devices in Celano's Tailor Shop and in the Armory Lounge to listen in on my father and his cronies, but Bureau agents planted another one in the headquarters of the Democratic First Ward at 100 North LaSalle across the street from City Hall.

It was there that the FBI learned and documented how much power my father, Murray (The Camel) Humphreys, and Anthony Accardo wielded in the First Ward, and it was also there it learned that not only did John D'Arco answer to them, but so did Pasqualino Marchone, a very personable politician who was better known as Pat Marcy.

I knew Marcy quite well. I knew he and Sam were close, that, like Sam, he had grown up in the Patch, and that they often socialized together. But it took FBI documents and the recent testimony of Agent Roemer before a 1983 U.S. Permanent Senate Subcommittee on Investigations in Chicago for me to learn that Marcy was not only the mob's political arm and conduit to City Hall, but he was actually a member of the crime family. It was through Marcy that many of the city's public officials and judges and police got their orders from the mob, according to Roemer and FBI documents. Marcy is still alive and though not as active politically as he once was, he is still influential in the political arena.

Pat Marcy met frequently with Sam, who took the precaution of sending his bodyguard-social secretary, Dominic (Butch) Blasi, to pick up Marcy and bring him to meeting places which Sam kept secret until the last minute. The problem was that my father's secrets were about as confidential as the evening news television broadcast, what with the FBI listening and watching. The FBI had in effect become Sam's shadow, strolling down every avenue he took.

Sam used Blasi as more than just a bodyguard. He was Sam's driver, his confidant, his appointment secretary, the man that even Ross Prio or Tony Accardo had to contact in order to see my father.

That somewhat feeble security measure didn't present any problems to the FBI. The Bureau was bugging Sam and following him, and it seemed to Sam as if it even knew his thoughts.

Among those so-called thoughts was his professed hatred of the Kennedy family for forgetting what he believed were their obligations to him. Some of those thoughts surfaced during three conversations carefully noted by the FBI in memorandums dated December 9, 11, and 21, 1961.

The first conversation was reported in an FBI teletype on December 9, 1961, in a daily summary from the Chicago office. The memorandum stated:

"[Blank] advised yesterday that [blank] was in conference with Giancana yesterday and related to Giancana the story of a recent visit which [blank] had to the home of [blank] in California. [Blank] states he questioned [blank] as to the progress which [blank] has made if any in an attempt to intercede with the Kennedys on behalf of Giancana. [Blank] has attempted to persuade [blank] could work on the Kennedys through Kennedy, Sr.

"However, [blank] did not feel that the Kennedys were faithful to Kennedy, Sr. In that respect, however, [blank] believed otherwise and was trying to persuade [blank] that he could work on Kennedy, Sr. [Blank] related to Giancana that Kennedy, Sr., called [blank] three times during visit with [blank].

"'I wrote Sam's name down and took it to Bobby, do you understand?'"

"Concerning the next presidential campaign, Giancana indicated that he would not donate one penny toward any such campaign and furthermore stated that that ' ———— better not think of taking this ———— state.' Giancana claimed that he made a donation to the recent presidential campaign of Kennedy and was not getting his money's worth because if he got a speeding ticket 'none of those ———— would know me.' The informant further related that [blank], in an attempt to persuade Giancana that [blank] had attempted to intercede for Giancana, stated [blank] 'says to me . . . he [Giancana] ain't being bothered.'

"Giancana then screamed, 'I got more ———— on my ———— than any other ———— in the country.' He continued raving and stated that everyplace he goes there are 'twenty guys next door, upstairs, downstairs' and he is surrounded.

"[Blank] asked him where this took place and he said, 'Right here in Russia . . . Chicago, New York, and Phoenix.'"

Two days later, FBI Director J. Edgar Hoover wrote to Attorney General Robert Kennedy on the subject "Gambling Activities, Las Vegas, Nevada." The letter read in part:

> Information has been received that persons connected with gambling activities in Las Vegas are becoming increasingly apprehensive concerning the intensity of investigations into gambling.
>
> In this connection, information has been received indicating that Samuel M. Giancana, a hoodlum figure, has sought to enlist [the identity of Sinatra was blanked out here, according to Roemer] to act as an intermediary to intercede on Giancana's behalf with the Attorney General. In this regard, conversation was allegedly given to making such overtures

through the father of the Attorney General. However, [blank] is reported to have rejected this idea.

Information has been received that Giancana complained bitterly concerning the intensity of investigation being conducted of his activities and that he made a donation to the campaign of President Kennedy but was not getting his money's worth.

Giancana allegedly indicated he would not donate one penny toward any future campaign.

This is being furnished for your personal information.

It was a clever move by Hoover. With that memorandum he put Bobby Kennedy and the entire Kennedy family in an untenable position. Thereafter, the Kennedy family severed their formerly close relationship with Sinatra without ever publicly stating why. If there had been any hesitancy in supporting the FBI's attack on my father, it was certainly eliminated with that memorandum. To resist the FBI's assault on Sam and the Chicago mob would be like saying you were against motherhood and owned by the mob.

Sam's bitterness over Kennedy's rejection came in a conversation I mentioned in an earlier chapter. The FBI memo dated December 21, 1961, recorded a conversation between my father and Johnny Roselli. The donation referred to is one Sam reportedly made to the campaign of John F. Kennedy when he was running for the Democratic nomination for President in West Virginia.

While the amount of the donation isn't mentioned, the conversation, reportedly overheard by the FBI on December 21, 1961, related to what Roselli alleged were calls by Joseph Kennedy to Frank Sinatra concerning problems Sam was having and wanted the Kennedys to take care of now that they were in office.

At one point in the conversation, Roselli and Sam discussed problems they were having with Sinatra:

ROSELLI: . . . He's got big ideas, Frank does, about being ambassador or something. You know Pierre Salinger [then John F. Kennedy's press secretary] and them guys . . . they don't want him. They treat [him] like they treat a whore. You ——— them, you pay

them, and then they're through. You got the right
idea [Sam], go the other way. ——— everybody,
every———, we'll use them every . . . way we can.
They only know one way. Now let them see the other
side of you.

At another point in the conversation, Sam expressed his anger
over Robert Kennedy and the incident that took place with FBI
agents at O'Hare International Airport in Chicago.

GIANCANA: . . . Like they called a guy in the other day, for
bookmaking. He says, well, I haven't been bookmaking. The FBI guy says, you know who's the
cause of all this? Here's the guy that's the cause of
all this, and came up with my picture, and said,
Robert Kennedy has the ——— for him. You know
why, don't you? When they met me at the airplane, I said, why don't you get the ——— out
of here? And I said, ——— you and your boss
and your superboss, you bunch of ———, you.
He said, Who's my superboss? And I said, Robert
Kennedy, you ———, get out of here. I said, go
straight back to him, you ———. Trying to put
me in the penitentiary anyway. That'll give them
reason.

ROSELLI: Oh, they gotta have more than that.

GIANCANA: Oh, I'm just saying that.

There was more and it reflected his influence in Chicago's political arena. An FBI memorandum dated January 13, 1962, detailed a conversation between Sam and an unknown person
concerning Frank Annunzio, a ward committeeman, and Robert
Kennedy. Because Annunzio had allowed Kennedy a spot in a
Columbus Day parade, Sam wrote off Annunzio as a mover in the
political structure.

UNKNOWN: Now if you don't mind, Sam, I don't know whether
he belongs in the organization or not, but as a ward

committeeman, I don't think there is a finer talker
and speaker than Frank Annunzio.

GIANCANA: He's no ———— good.

UNKNOWN: He's dead?

GIANCANA: He's dead. He's a left-handed ————. I tried to let
him see the light two years ago and he just can't
keep his mouth shut. He's too smart for himself.
He'll run right over himself. He had a lot of ————
nerve Columbus Day when he let Robert Kennedy
come in and be his guest in the parade.

UNKNOWN: He told Bob Kennedy?

GIANCANA: Sure, you read it. How do you like a ———— like
that?

UNKNOWN: He'd be a hell of a man.

GIANCANA: Sure, he'd be a hell of a man. He makes a mistake
once, twice, and then you can forget him, but the
third time and you're out . . . and that's off the
record.

UNKNOWN: It is, Moe. Don't worry about it.

Sam's bitterness with the Kennedys and his harassment by the
FBI became further aggravated by 1963 when the Bureau decided, with Kennedy's approval, on a new tactic to harass Sam, a
tactic that became known as the "lockstep surveillance."

Beginning in June, 1963, the FBI's so-called lockstep surveillance was a twenty-four-hour watch of my father's every move
and, for that matter, the moves of everyone in his family: my
sisters, the Perno family who lived at Sam's house, and anyone
who regularly saw or was with Sam. Apparently that did not include me, since FBI records reflected few reports of my activity.
That does not mean that agents didn't try from time to time to
determine who I was seeing or what I was doing. I just wasn't
part of the lockstep-surveillance activity.

Before this the FBI had already installed illegal bugs in motels
and hotels and private homes all over the country to listen in on
Sam's love life in the remote hope of hearing him make some slip
about his criminal life—and those are only the illegal bugs I have
learned about. Lord knows how many other illegal electronic lis-

tening devices were used by the federal government in its almost insatiable quest for evidence against my father.

The lockstep surveillance attracted a lot of public attention because Sam went public with it. His decision wasn't really a rational one. It was based on his anger over the FBI being on his back, at home, in a nightclub, or on the golf course, and on the advice of Tony Tisci to whom he listened now far more than he should have.

Tony convinced him that if he took J. Edgar Hoover and the FBI to court and charged them with violating his civil rights, he could win—or at least force them to reduce their activity. So Sam hired attorney George N. Leighton, while Tisci acted as an assistant counsel and sued the government on June 28, 1963.

It was really a stupid thing to do, particularly for a man who was the boss of a crime family. Not only did it bring the spotlight of publicity on Sam, but also on Tisci, who was criticized in the newspapers for collecting his $985-a-month salary as secretary to Congressman Roland Libonati while appearing in federal court on Sam's behalf.

Chicago-American newspaper reporter Sam Blair wrote a story pointing out Tisci's dual role at taxpayer expense, and quoted Libonati as seeing nothing wrong in having his secretary serve as attorney for a Mafia boss.

"As a matter of fact I ought to compliment him [Tisci] for doing a good job," Libonati was quoted by Blair as saying. And Tony told Blair that he saw no conflict of interest in drawing government pay while representing my father against the Federal Bureau of Investigation. Blair quoted Tony as quipping: "I imagine a lot of other congressional secretaries do the same thing."

The whole event turned into a circus.

Sandy Smith, the same reporter who had had a field day with Sam at my wedding, did a tongue-in-cheek, day-in-the-life-of-Sam that was published in a number of newspapers. And Sandy used the court record to make my father look foolish. For example, the following was printed in the Long Island newspaper *Newsday* under Sandy Smith's byline on July 22, 1963:

"Chicago—In his $50,000 home in a peaceful suburb, Salvatore (Momo) Giancana, 53, the big boss of Chicago crime, rolled out of bed on the wrong side.

"It was Saturday, June 29. The day was balmy and clear. For Momo, however, it was black Saturday—the 19th day of his hot pursuit by agents of the Federal Bureau of Investigation. Since June 10, when he flew home from a Hawaiian vacation, the FBI had been all over Momo. He was under the tightest surveillance ever clamped on a gangster by the United States government. The G-men were everywhere. If he drove, they were behind his car, bumper to bumper. If he set out on foot, they kept pace. They trailed him to mob hangouts. When he holed up at home to brood, they waited patiently outside.

"For Giancana, such togetherness with the government was a plague. It made him, in fact, a gangland leper, shunned by his fellow mobsters. The FBI had cut him off from his underworld syndicate that controls vice, gambling and other rackets—you name it, Momo's got it—in the nation's second city. In the Chicago mob, Giancana has a fearsome reputation. He was arrested three times for murder while he was in his teens (the slaying of the state's chief witness collapsed one murder case against him); he went to jail for burglary and to prison for auto theft and moonshining; he was rejected for Army service as a psychopath for telling his draftboard that he stole for a living.

"But now, his inability to shake off the G-men was spoiling his gangland image.

"How does a day go when the FBI is hot on the trail? Well, according to Momo himself, no day was darker than June 29. And here was how that day went:

"10 A.M.—Momo is up and stirring. He lifts a windowblind to see if the FBI is still outside. They are. He shuts the blind.

"12:30 P.M.—He's off, zooming out of his garage in a brown Pontiac Tempest after getting word from his lawyers that the court, at this point, refused to enjoin the FBI from watching Momo. A government agent waves to Giancana. He returns the greeting with an indecent gesture. Two FBI cars pull in behind him.

"12:45 P.M.—On a busy thoroughfare teeming with autos and trucks, Momo slams his car to a stop and throws it into reverse, attempting to ram the FBI tail car. The agents avoid a smashup.

"1 P.M.—In an effort to elude his followers, Momo wheels into a car wash where he is a regular customer. As he guns his auto along the wash rack, the washers shout: 'Go, Mo, go.' He goes out the back entrance—to find the FBI waiting.

"1:30 P.M.—It's a day for golf, the agents discover. Momo pulls into Fresh Meadows Golf Course, 20 miles west of the Loop.

"1:45 P.M.—Is it golf, or a gang conclave? The agents aren't sure. At the first tee are Giancana and a dozen gangsters. Whatever it is, three foursomes or a twelvesome, it's motorized. The hoodlums have four golf carts.

"Four of Giancana's golf partners are Charles (Chuckie) English, a labor racketeer and a partner with Momo in bookie joints, and three lesser hoodlums, Dominic (Butch) Blasi, Tarquin (Queenie) Simonelli and Johnny (Haircuts) Campanale. Haircuts is nicknamed for his duck-tail hairdo. English is easy to spot. He's the one in the red Bermuda shorts.

"2:05 P.M.—More evasive action by Momo. He decides to play the back nine first. English and two other men are in the foursome. Queenie, Haircuts and Butch take off in golf carts to the clubhouse. All three take up positions at a public telephone.

"2:30 P.M.—At the 14th hole—they're playing backwards, remember—it is discovered that Momo has set up a mobile command post for the syndicate. His command car is a golf cart. Out from the clubhouse telephone booth come Haircuts and Butch, with telephone messages. The couriers return to the clubhouse to make still more phone calls, apparently flash the word of the boss to the mob.

"3 P.M.—Lunch time. Queenie shows up in a golf cart stacked with sandwiches and beer. The gangsters picnic in the rough.

"3:45 P.M.—Giancana hooks his drive off the fairway. Finding his ball in the rough, Momo looks back to see if Chuckie is watching. Chuckie isn't because he's deep in a bunker. Momo picks up his ball and casually tosses it 30 yards on the fairway. Then he strokes into cup on the green.

"4:15 P.M.—Momo is nervous. He takes 18 putts on the 6th green. (Later, his lawyer explained in court that harassing by FBI agents had ruined Moe's putting.)

"5:30 P.M.—Momo is home for only 10 minutes before the reason for his haste is disclosed. A taxi pulls up to his door. A girl steps out and goes into the house. Some agents say she resembles his sweetheart, singer Phyllis McGuire. Others aren't sure. Whoever she is, she stays for dinner.

"10:30 P.M.—Just when the agents thought he might have bedded down for the night, Giancana comes out the back door on the run. He throws up the garage door, jumps in his car and zips away. The agents follow.

"10:32 P.M.—The eccentric gang chief is back. He took a spin around the block. He attempts to back his auto into the garage at high speed. Bam! He rams the side of the entrance, crumpling a fender. He gets out to survey the damage but forgets to set the brake. The car rolls down into the street.

"Giancana, cursing, retrieves it. He makes another pass at the garage, driving slowly. He makes it this time. He retires to his home.

"It definitely wasn't one of Momo's good days. Later, Momo was able to get the court to limit FBI surveillance. But it didn't do any good. The sheriff started watching him."

The press was having a field day at my father's expense and I didn't like it, but Sam told me to stay away from the courthouse and I did. Meanwhile, there were disclosures that Sam had had movies taken of the FBI following him at St. Bernardine Catholic Church and at Mt. Carmel Catholic Cemetery, where he said FBI cars blocked off both exits. He also testified in court that he had taken pictures of the FBI, in particular of Roemer, at the Fresh Meadows Golf Course, and the FBI had played in a foursome behind him, driving balls so close to him as to upset his game.

All the courtroom antics led to an unexpected meeting between FBI agents, Chuckie English, and Tony Tisci. There was a message that my father wanted the agents to transmit to Robert Kennedy. That meeting was detailed in an FBI report dated July 1, 1963.

"On 6/29/63, Giancana again played golf at the Fresh Meadows Golf Course in the company of Chuckie English, Anthony Tisci, and Sam Pardel. During the early evening hours, Giancana proceded to the Armory Lounge. Shortly after his arrival at 7 P.M., a car, registered to Jerry Dolezal, the state representative from Cicero, Illinois, arrived at the Armory Lounge with four elderly, well-dressed male occupants. It is noted that Jerry Dolezal is a politically influential politician who is known to give his support to the 'West Side Bloc.'

"Approximately five minutes after this group entered the

lounge, Giancana was observed to depart and travel within a six or seven block area of the Armory and thence returned to the restaurant. The purpose of this maneuver was apparently an attempt by Giancana to lose any possible surveillance. However, there was no attempt of entrapment on the part of Giancana as to further his picture taking.

"At approximately 7:30 P.M., Giancana, in the company of Chuck English, Anthony Tisci and Tisci's wife, departed the Armory Lounge and proceeded to the Czech Lounge where they were observed to dine for the next two and a half hours.

"On the return trip from the Czech Lounge to the Armory Lounge, English, who was driving the group, pulled alongside of a Bureau car which was stopped at a red light and stated that he desired to talk to the agents. SAs [identities censored] were most discreet in their comments to English and advised English that they were willing to listen to any comments that he desired to make. English then proceeded to the parking lot of the Armory Lounge. The rest of the party with English entered the Armory Lounge and English remained in his car in the parking lot. A discussion ensued with English for approximately 30 minutes in the parking lot at which time the discussion centered around various activities of English and of the FBI investigation into the Lormar Distributing Company which is owned by the English brothers. [Three lines are blanked out.]

"After approximately one half hour, English requested the agents accompany him into the Armory Lounge where they could sit and continue their discussion. [Three lines are blanked out.] It is noted that the Armory Lounge is a public eating place which is frequented by legitimate people as well as West Side hoodlums.

"Upon arriving inside the lounge, the agents continued their conversation with English. [Six lines are blanked out.] Following approximately one half hour's conversation, English called to Anthony Tisci who was also present at the Lounge and requested that he join the conversation. Tisci at first was cool toward the agents but after some fifteen minutes' conversation indicated to the agents that the reason for Giancana attempting to obtain an injunction against FBI surveillance was a last resort and according to Tisci they were 'throwing all the eggs into one basket.' Tisci attempted, at one point, to point out to the agents that through the use of binoculars they were spying on females within the Giancana residence, but upon being berated by the agents for taking this point of view, he admitted that this was extremely unlikely.

"One particular point that should be noted was the fact that English had requested to meet with the agent conducting the investigation into the Lormar Distributing Company and will discuss with him any questions that this agent had.

"English further contended that he is a legitimate businessman, but did not attempt to deny that during his past years he had made his money through gambling ventures. English further contended that he has grown up with Giancana and Giancana has always been one of his closest friends and for that reason he would never leave Giancana or close out Giancana's friendship. [Five lines are deleted.]

"English suggested that he intercede with Giancana and set up an interview between Giancana, English and agents [identities censored]. English was observed to proceed to the table at which Giancana was seated with two unknown males and talk with Giancana for two or three minutes. Following this period, English returned to the agents and advised them that Giancana was not interested in talking with the agents at this time.

"A second item of extreme value obtained by the agents during their entry into the Armory was the information obtained to the effect that Giancana now 'holds court' at a table located just to the inside of the entrance, which location is removed from the location of [the bug]. It was further learned from the discussion with English that Giancana can always be found at this table just inside the door.

"Based on the foregoing, the Chicago Division is considering requesting Bureau authority concerning relocation of this source.

"Following the departure of the two agents from the Armory Lounge, English ran from the Lounge and hailed them as they were beginning to drive away from the area and told them that Giancana had wished a message be related to them that 'IF BOBBY KENNEDY WANTS TO TALK TO ME I'LL BE GLAD TO TALK TO HIM AND HE KNOWS WHO TO GO THROUGH.'

"'You must be talking about Sinatra,' Agent William Roemer said to English.

"'You said that, not me,' answered English."

Sam managed to get a temporary restraining order requiring the FBI to stay at least two foursomes back of him at the golf course. And Federal Judge Richard B. Austin also ruled that the FBI could use only one car to shadow Sam. He even cited one FBI agent, Marlin Johnson, for contempt of court for refusing to answer questions under a claim of executive privilege. Johnson was fined five hundred dollars, but at best Sam had won what was really a Pyrrhic victory.

The FBI agents who had been watching and eavesdropping on Sam for all those months were furious, largely I suppose because the government attorneys had failed to question him when he was on the witness stand. They had their orders from Kennedy. The Department of Justice position, according to its own documents, was that Judge Austin should not have even heard the case, that the U.S. District Court lacked the jurisdiction to do so, and that my father in effect had no civil rights that were being violated.

While the Bureau's agents were temporarily limited in their surveillances—the fact that they had illegal electronic bugs never came out in the court case—this didn't prevent Sheriff Richard Ogilvie from turning his deputies loose on Sam and our family. And hundreds of curious tourists flocked to the area after hearing and reading the publicity about the gangster who was suing the government for watching him. It was horrible, and Sam, for the first time I can recall, began losing his composure. There were more and more confrontations with law-enforcement officers, some federal, some local.

He drove like a madman more often than not. I can recall many times his getting into the car simply to drive to a telephone booth to make a call. He would never make any calls from the house. He was very paranoid that way, even when he was in Mexico. Nobody could say anything over the phone. If I ever mentioned anything over the phone, he would be down my throat for being so stupid. He believed our phone at home was tapped. He never realized that all along, the FBI was bugging his office at the Armory Lounge.

Sometimes Sam would kibitz with some of the men who followed him. He would go up to their cars and talk to them quietly. He would ask them how they were doing, how they felt, how their families were, what they were reading. When I asked him why he did that with men who followed him, he shrugged and said, "Aw . . . they're just doin' a job." Then he said that he was at a point in his life when he was sick of having people follow him, so sometimes he would give them an itinerary of his plans for the day. They would follow, anyway, but the idea was to be one step ahead of them. If he gave them the information first, they didn't have to find it out from his going somewhere, or by questioning some of his friends. The incidents at the golf course were different. The Bureau agents were interfering with his relaxation and his golf games, which he loved, and they were costing him money because Sam's golf games were more than fun, they were big money events. Sam played golf with big money bets as an expression of his high status.

The publicity generated by Sam's suing the government exacted a bigger cost in terms of the respect and power he held in the crime family. I didn't know it then, but he was on shaky footing with the mob. There were many rumblings, and one came from a man my father trusted more than anyone else, Dominic Blasi.

Blasi, FBI records disclosed, went to Frank (Strongy) Ferraro and told him about my father's message to FBI Agent Roemer. The conversation was duly recorded by the FBI, according to Roemer.

"Wait till you hear this," Blasi said. "I'm so sick I could jump out your window [which was on the fifty-first floor]. Would you believe [Sam] sent a message to Roemer through Charlie McCarthy [Charles English] that if Kennedy wants to talk to [Sam] he's got to go through Sinatra."

Roemer said that that meeting and others which followed suggested that Sam had become "goofy" and was no longer capable of making rational decisions for Chicago's underworld. They urged Paul Ricca and Anthony Accardo, who were the powers behind my father's throne, to step in and take control of the family away from Sam. For the time being, nothing was done, but the erosion of Sam's power as a boss had begun.

In the end, a higher federal court reversed Judge Austin's ruling, and Sam's victory, one he had relished and basked in, was short-lived. However, he had released a genie from a bottle that he could not recork, and the genie was not one that would grant him three wishes. It would instead lead to the fall of the house of Giancana.

18

The Fall of the House of Giancana

It came without warning for me . . . and it was unexpected.

"Crime boss jailed for clamming up," a radio announcer said, breaking into a musical program I was listening to at home.

"Salvatore (Momo) Giancana, reputed boss of the Chicago crime syndicate, was ordered jailed indefinitely today after he refused to answer questions before a grand jury."

I listened in stunned silence as the announcer read from what was a United Press International wire story. There it was on the radio, no one had called me. Sam was in jail.

"The mob chief made the refusal even though he had been promised immunity from prosecution arising from any of his testimony," the announcer continued. "Giancana had promised Chief U.S. District Judge William J. Campbell that he would answer the grand jury's questions. But U.S. Attorney Edward Hanrahan said Giancana wouldn't even give the grand jury his telephone number."

The announcer droned on, and I remember going to the telephone and calling someone. I'm not sure whether it was my husband, Carmen, or one of my sisters.

"Is it true?" I asked. "Is he really in jail?"

The voice at the other end answered that it was, and that's all I remember.

The date was June 1, 1965, and it marked the beginning of the end of my father, of his rule as Chicago's crime leader, and in the years ahead, of his life.

When Sam took the government to court he had set in motion an irreversible vendetta between himself and the U.S. Department of Justice. Robert Kennedy had turned loose his warriors with orders to get Sam, and though Kennedy was not there at the finish, he accomplished his purpose. He destroyed Sam just as he destroyed Sam's former friend, James Hoffa of the International Brotherhood of Teamsters union. Kennedy was not a man to trifle with or challenge publicly.

In October, 1963, federal informer Joseph Valachi began testifying before the U.S. Senate's Permanent Subcommittee on Investigations. He identified on television the existence of what he called "Our Thing," and what the FBI forever after referred to as "La Cosa Nostra." Orchestrating that media spectacle was Robert Kennedy, who moved witnesses from the federal establishment and from local law enforcement in and out of the hearings like chessmen.

Although Valachi wouldn't have known Sam if he had fallen over him, my father was angered by his appearance and the stupidity of his counterparts in New York for letting this informer live long enough to testify. When I asked him who Valachi was to have all this knowledge, Sam just shook his head.

"It's all a lotta crap," he said testily. "You shouldn't be watchin' that kinda stuff. Valachi's a nobody. He's part of the fiction that lousy little bastard . . . that Kennedy . . . is pumping out. Now, mind your business and take care of your husband and kids."

I asked no more questions, but I kept watching in the confines of my own home, not Sam's. As far as I know, Sam didn't spend any time glued to his television set watching the hearings. He was too busy playing golf to be bothered.

Joseph Valachi really had very little to say about the Chicago mob or about Sam. He said something about the mob having strong political and police connections, but that was all. It was Chicago Police Superintendent O. W. Wilson and William J. Duffy, then police director of intelligence, who detailed the whole sordid history of the Chicago crime syndicate, including its then record 976 gangland slayings. Duffy called Sam's "family" "The Chicago Italian Organization" and also referred to a non-Mafia-associated group which belonged to the Chicago syndicate but were not members of the organization headed by Sam. The powers behind Sam were identified as Paul Ricca and Anthony Accardo, both of whom, like Sam and others, had appeared before previous congressional committees investigating organized crime in Chicago.

The hearing was far less damaging, I think, to Chicago than to other areas of the country, such as New York, but nevertheless it was a cause of concern, as evidenced by an FBI electronic intercept of a conversation my father had with an unidentified person at the Armory Lounge. The intercept was recorded in memorandum form on October 11, 1963.

"[Blank] advised that Giancana held conversation with [blank] concerning Valachi testimony before Senate committee. Both agreed that Valachi unable to hurt any of Chicago organization, but felt that he was doing a great deal of harm to New York mobsters. Biggest fear held by [blank] was that government would be able to capitalize on this type of situation in the future in obtaining of other informants, being able to show that they went along with Valachi and did not hold him accountable for his crimes.

"In explaining significance of this type of hearing to [blank] it was explained that even though this information did not put anyone in jail it caused irreparable harm to their reputations in their respective communities. Source advised Giancana again playing golf on a daily basis with Chuckie English as one of his playing partners."

Though Valachi hadn't provided any inside information to the committee about Sam, Duffy had testified about my father, and on a chart made for the committee, he had placed him in the position of authority as boss.

Testified Duffy: "Salvatore Giancana, currently resides at 1147 South Wenonah Avenue, in Oak Park, Illinois. He has aliases of 'Sam Gincani,' 'Albert Mancuso,' 'Sam Mooney,' 'Sam Flood,' 'Salvatore Giancona.' He is an ex-convict. He was arrested and rearrested on three murder investigations before he was 20 years old. He has served time for larceny of auto, burglary, and illegal moonshining. Subject has been arrested over 60 times for various charges."

Then on October 14, 1963, Sam was with another group of men in the Armory Lounge. The FBI noted that the television was turned on at 8:26 P.M., "very close to [the] source [electronic bug]." Part of the conversation related to Valachi and Kennedy.

"9:46 P.M. Group continued talking of Knights of Columbus, saying there are a couple of Italian councils, St. Francis Xavier, which is 100 percent Italian, and one in Roseland. They talk of Bobby Kennedy coming here [to Chicago] for the B'nai B'rith affair yesterday [October 13], but he wouldn't come for Columbus Day. They said ——— Jews downtown were beaming like a ———. They then speak of Baker [Bobby G. Baker, Democratic secretary of the U.S. Senate], Lyndon Johnson's protégé, got [blank] up. Didn't do anything to him . . . just resigned his job. He must have come out with a ton of money. He was too smart for them.

"Asked if they saw the chart that [O. W.] Wilson brought to Washington. On the top he had an Italian organization. Didn't see the American [newspaper] [identity censored]. Moretti was named on the Valachi shit. They speak of [blank] and how if he said if they checked Mr. Wilson as thoroughly as Mr. [Joey] Glimco, Wilson would be in jail and so would Bob Kennedy. [All laugh.] Chuck [English] speaks of the Teamsters probably going back into the CIO, saying they are gonna shove that down [labor leader Walter] Reuther's throat. They said it will hurt Kennedy if they take Hoffa back."

The hearings just meant more headlines, more tourists gawking at our Oak Park home—and more surveillances, although the FBI, under restraint by the court, was more discreet.

Sam, having had previous experience with congressional committees and no desire to return to the limelight on national television, spent a lot of time at the home of the family of Mary Colucci in River Forest, Illinois. Mary had taken care of family members at various times during Momma's frequent illnesses, and our families were very close. The Colucci home wasn't far from Paul Ricca's or from mine, but Sam was seeking obscurity, at least temporarily. Another FBI memorandum dated October 16, 1963, noted that:

". . . Giancana spends a great deal of time at the residence of the Coluccis. . . . In this regard it is pointed out that Giancana was observed in the evening of October 9, 1963, to be transported to this residence during the late evening hours."

Then the FBI observed: "It was learned at this time that Giancana did not desire to have his return known and limited this information to a few close friends. Based on the observation of Giancana's visit to the Colucci residence on October 9, 1963, at a time when it was known that Giancana desired to have his whereabouts kept secret for fear of being served with a subpoena to appear before the McClellan [Valachi] hearings, it is assumed that Giancana is utilizing the Colucci residence as an alternate residence while in the Chicago area."

And so it went. Sam had been warned a year earlier, according to FBI bugged conversations, by Paul Ricca and Accardo about his confrontations with the FBI. That discussion, which occurred on November 30, 1962, at 3:30 P.M., was over Sam's confrontation with Bureau agents at the Czech Lounge while he was with John D'Arco, and centered principally on whether they were going to let D'Arco run for higher public office or a relative of my father's. Sam favored the relative.

DELUCIA (RICCA):   Don't let nobody tell you what to do.
GIANCANA: I'm not.
ACCARDO: And you can't go giving these guys [FBI] abuse. You got to talk to them.

Sam's choice of candidate, supported reluctantly by Accardo and Ricca, proved to be a bad selection. The newspapers cut his candidate to ribbons after he made himself difficult to interview, and they hung a nickname on him, "Busy, Busy," because he told reporters he was so busy he didn't have time to meet with them regularly.

The die had been cast. If the government couldn't get Sam one way, they would get him another. The publicity buildup was part of the campaign, but in May, 1965, the key element of their objective surfaced in the form of a federal grand jury that began calling in everyone in the mob who had anything to do with Sam.

It was a *Who's Who* of organized crime, politics, the judiciary, and the entertainment world, and the newspapers had a field day while U.S. Attorney Edward Hanrahan and prosecutor David Schippers pulled the strings to haul in Sam's friends.

Robert Kennedy was no longer around as U.S. Attorney General, having been replaced by Nicholas Katzenbach, but I'm convinced that what was done was planned by Kennedy, and it was illegal. There is no doubt in my mind that the information used to get to Sam and to question those around him was information gleaned from those illegal listening devices that had been planted all over the country years before, devices that the prosecution did not admit existed when they presented evidence to the grand jury and to the judge who eventually sent Sam to jail.

For weeks a parade of witnesses, including my brother-in-law, Tisci, his congressional mentor, Roland Libonati, and a host of other Chicago political bigwigs were called in before the jury as were some of Sam's Mafia confidants, like Blasi, Richard Cain, Frank and Fifi Buccieri, and the man who eventually succeeded Sam as Chicago's mob boss, Jackie (The Lackey) Cerone. And of course they called in Phyllis McGuire, who after she appeared held a streetside press conference announcing to the world that she had cooperated with the federal grand jury. It was a three-ring circus, and Sam was smarting from what was taking place, although he admitted it to no one.

From the beginning the real target throughout had been Sam. The government's plan, as the media later detailed, was a new strategy. They were going to subpoena Sam before the grand jury, grant him immunity from prosecution, and then try to force him to answer hundreds of questions based on information Bureau agents and others had obtained on surveillances, from informants, and through their illegal microphones.

When finally Sam was ordered to appear before the federal grand jury to answer questions about the Chicago syndicate, it was "catch-22." If he answered the questions, he would violate the very Mafia rule of silence he had enforced for others and he would be killed. If he answered the questions and lied in the answers, he would be charged and convicted of perjury, and sent to jail. And if he refused to answer the questions, he would be cited for contempt—and go to jail anyway. Sam chose the only course he could choose. He followed the Mafia rule of silence, refused to talk, and was cited for contempt.

When I recovered from the shock of hearing that Sam had been jailed, I suddenly felt very proud of him, something that I hadn't felt for years. I said to friends who offered their sympathy, "Hey . . . my father is a very honorable man. He's in jail because he won't talk about his friends. What's wrong about that?"

When I went to the Cook County jail to see him I was literally bursting with pride that he had had the courage to take jail rather than be another Valachi. I was proud I was his daughter, and I told everyone exactly how I felt, including people at the county jail.

In spite of these feelings, I never said a word to him about how I felt when I saw him in prison just as he had never told me he loved me when I had been in the hospital for electric shock treatments. I just went to see him, to cheer him up, and say, "Hi, how are you," and tell him that I missed him and that I loved him.

But I botched that. I started to shed some tears.

At first, he smiled a little, then he got upset. "There's nothing to cry about," he said. "What are you doing . . . crying crocodile tears for me?"

Anything to humor me and stop me. He was so sensitive when I cried. He hated tears.

Christmas, 1965, was the worst Yuletide I can remember. Sam's home, my home, was dark. There were no colored lights or sparkling trees or gaily festooned Christmas decorations lighting up the house at 1147 South Wenonah. And there was no gathering of the family or handing out of gifts to and from Sam. In fact, at many of the homes of his friends, people like Chuckie English and Sam (Teets) Battaglia, who was ordered to run things for Sam while he was in prison, or at Paul Ricca's home, there were few, if any, bright lights.

I didn't know it then, I learned about it later, but it was around this time that Paul Ricca started to get senile. He would go to O'Hare International Airport and just sit at the terminal watching people come in and go out for hours for no apparent reason. He wasn't even conscious of being watched by FBI agents, who thought at first he might be arranging for meetings with smugglers of contraband or drugs. If the agents had had any knowledge of Paul, they would have known that the last thing in the world he would get involved with was drugs. Paul Ricca had been Sam's staunchest supporter, his strongest ally. He also, I am told, had agreed that Sam had to be replaced as the boss of the Chicago family both while he was in jail and after he came out, and to that end, he sided with Anthony Accardo in the choice of Jackie Cerone.

Even Accardo toned down his usually flamboyant Christmas celebrating. Once, he had installed a carillon that sent Christmas carols echoing through his rather sedate River Forest neighborhood, much to the chagrin of his neighbors who dared not complain. But Christmas, 1965, was quiet, even for him.

Sam's Christmas joy consisted of stringing popcorn on a tree and opening a few small gifts he received from the family. There was no big family gathering or endless trays of Italian delicacies, just jail fare.

But if Sam couldn't enjoy the comforts of home, he did find a way of bringing some of those comforts to his prison cell, and with them a scandal of sorts. Cook County Sheriff Richard B. Ogilvie went public with charges that my father was running the Chicago rackets from jail.

That was plainly ridiculous, since the Chicago mob had designated Battaglia to run things for Sam while he was in prison, and Accardo was calling the tune. There was truth to Ogilvie's charge that Sam was paying off guards to bring him dollar Havana cigars, provide him with food from the outside, handle his laundry, and let him out of his cell at night to watch television in another room. There were also charges that Sam used the prison shower room to hold conferences with couriers who carried messages outside.

The net result was that the newspapers gave a public spanking to Ogilvie's 250-pound warden, Jack Johnson, and there was an investigation of the jail's two hundred guards and workers—all political appointees. In the end a prison guard captain and two other guards were fired, but life went on for Sam—perhaps with fewer perks.

While Sam was in jail, Murray Humphreys, his number one man to take care of politicians, collapsed from a heart attack, and my brother-in-law, Anthony Tisci, who also had heart trouble, quit his job as congressional aide to Frank Annunzio, the man who had replaced Libonati. Tony was only a little more than thirty-six at the time, but he had heart problems that forced him to cut down his activity.

Sam never cracked during his year-long stay in jail, but there were suggestions in the press and charges and countercharges between Washington and U.S. Attorney Hanrahan about whether my father was to be released from jail in June legitimately or whether he would be indicted or charged with contempt again. In the end Sam was freed and the newspapers were filled with stories that a fix had been put in, but in truth nothing happened, to my knowledge. Time had simply run out, and Hanrahan or Washington had no real evidence to press more charges against Sam.

When he was released, he decided to go to Mexico for an extended vacation. He was no longer the boss of Chicago. He had been told to leave the country by our friend Ricca and by Accardo, and to keep a low profile.

The man Sam chose to bring with him as his personal aide was Richard Cain. Cain was a brilliant man, a discredited policeman who had been with the Chicago police, had later trained with Cuban nationals for the planned Bay of Pigs invasion. He was also the chief investigator for Sheriff Ogilvie—all while secretly being a member of Chicago's mob. It all caught up with him when he was indicted in Chicago after a phony drug raid his friends in organized crime had arranged. Sam chose him to go to Mexico because he considered him to be trustworthy and because he was fluent in a number of languages, including Spanish. Sam needed Cain's language expertise to help him negotiate his investments and more gambling ventures, one of which I learned later was in offshore gambling ships, floating casinos.

I met Cain when I went to Cuernavaca where Sam was staying at his beautiful estate called San Cristóbal. Although under Mexican law, Americans can't own property in Mexico, Sam's ownership was arranged through the Mexican attorney Cain and Sam used to arrange all their investments.

Cain was there with his wife, a singer. He was assigned to chauffeur me around wherever I wanted to go while Sam and Carmen and whoever else was there played golf.

Cain was Sam's driver, his negotiator, his interpreter, his companion, even his protector. He was likable and he was very shrewd. Nothing escaped him. But I liked him all the same and Sam had a strange trust in him.

The house itself had cost my father a small fortune by 1969 standards. I think he paid nearly $170,000 for the place, maybe more. I was never able to find out exactly how much, or what happened to the money that he had invested in it. It certainly never showed up in his estate after he was murdered.

On one level the house had a kitchen and a laundry, and at pool level there was another kitchen and a bar. The first floor also had a kitchen, a breakfast room, a dining room, a living room, and three bedrooms with baths attached. And then there was the upper level where you could look out over the breathtaking countryside and the lights of the town at night.

At the top level, Sam had his bedroom and a telescope. He was an amateur astronomer and loved to spend hours watching the sky, stargazing, and of course watching the approaches to the house for any strangers who might be coming. Below the house were native Mexican Indians in the hills, moving along what looked like cave sites, and they intrigued him. He really got a big bang out of watching them through the telescope. He loved to talk about them.

The house was meticulously and expensively furnished. It was filled with silver—gorgeous silver plates, flatware, a coffee service, and serving pieces. His china was of the finest, and his pottery was made for him at a local pottery shop in a special design and color. And everywhere there were magnificent oil paintings by some of Mexico's finest artists as well as by American artists.

For several years Sam lived in Mexico without Richard Cain. Cain had returned to Chicago to defend himself in a federal court trial in which he was charged with hiding information about a felony. This case also involved one of Sam's oldest friends, Willie Potatoes Daddano. Both men were found guilty, but Willie got the longest sentence, fifteen years. I imagine it was because he was thought to have been behind the murder of a suspected informant who had implicated Willie in an earlier bank robbery. Cain received four years, and when he was freed in 1971 from a Texas prison, he returned to Sam in Mexico.

My father traveled a lot in those years, and in the early 1970s he went to such exotic places as Beirut, Teheran, Jamaica, and

Central and South America. From FBI records it appears the quest was always to establish gambling ventures, either on land or at sea.

For Cain the adventure ended very violently in Chicago, where he was shotgunned to death in December, 1973. No explanation was ever given, but there were reports by FBI agents that Cain and my father had spent large sums of money setting up cruise-ship casino gambling and had refused to share the profits with the Chicago mob, now headed by Joseph (Joey Doves) Aiuppa.

All this happened at a time when my father and I had virtually stopped talking. I had told Sam that I was going to divorce Carmen, that I couldn't live with the beatings, with the constant fights, with the terrible unhappiness I had to endure.

"You made your bed, goddammit," he shouted, "now you lie in it! No goddam daughter of mine is gonna get a divorce . . . you're not going to make a fool of me that way too."

He just wouldn't listen to reason. I was bringing shame on the House of Giancana.

It had never happened in the Chicago mob before. Divorce among the children of Mafia members was unheard of, and among bosses—it was sacrilege.

When I filed for divorce, I had become a heavy drinker, and I had been carrying on a number of affairs with men in St. Charles where we lived. I spent eighteen months undergoing treatment by a clinical psychologist named James M. Lytton. On September 18, 1973, Lytton wrote a report that was submitted to the court when I filed for divorce. It said in part:

"I have been seeing Mrs. Manno for approximately 18 months. During that time, I have observed her problems regarding her husband and children.

"In my opinion, Mrs. Manno's home situation is most unfortunate. On several occasions, she arrived at my office showing unmistakable signs of having been physically abused. Her explanation was that her husband had become angry and beat her. I urged her to press charges, which she did do. The result was that Mr. Manno was found guilty of assault and was fined. To understand Mrs. Manno, her home situation must be considered. Their marriage was apparently very stormy from the start. Pressure from Antoinette's family was effective in restraining her desires to end the marriage. The advent of children had the effect of keeping the marriage together 'for the children's sake.' The marriage is and apparently always was a bad match.

"These two people are completely different with little if anything in common. This obvious mismatch and resulting marital turmoil has had serious effects on the children.

"I gave Antoinette a standardized personality test to get an objective measure of her present personality variables. She scored within the normal range on all aspects of the test. Of special significance was her high energy level and high sociability. Thus Antoinette likes people and has the drive and energy to enable her to achieve things and to enjoy her friends. She showed no signs of neurosis or psychosis. However, Antoinette does have her own problems as do most people."

Lytton found that I was capable of handling my children and that there was no reason I should not be awarded their custody.

I had to settle on Carmen's terms because he threatened to make the divorce a front-page scandal. He knew about my affairs with the naval captain and with some other men and he was going to use that information unless I came to terms, his terms. Rather than have the whole sordid affair aired in the newspapers and made even worse for the family, I agreed, and we settled the divorce without a trial, quietly.

For a time I retained custody of the children and I kept the house, but I couldn't keep it forever. I had only some small savings, family heirlooms, jewelry, and the kids' inheritance to sustain me and pay the bills, and I did my damndest not to touch the kids' money. I didn't always succeed, but I didn't spend all that had been put away for them by Sam, by uncles and aunts, and by Carmen and me. But we had to eat, and there were times when I couldn't live without a drink. Those were horrible days. Finally, I lost the house, and I had to give up custody of the kids to Carmen for their own well-being. I've never really recovered from that and I never will.

And Sam . . . he never forgave me. From the day I decided on divorce to the day he was murdered, I never saw him again . . . alive.

June 23, 1975, should have been the happiest day of my life, but it wasn't. It was a nightmare.

I was forty years old and this was to have been a moment of celebration, a day on which my father and I were to be reunited on a picture-postcard, Mississippi-style riverboat ride along the Fox River in Illinois. But there was no paddle steamer where I was now. It was tied up at a pier in St. Charles. And I wasn't clapping my hands or dancing to the familiar beat of an Italian tarantella with my father while the family watched. Instead I was standing silently in the depressing, somber surroundings of a funeral parlor.

I held back the tears and tried to overcome the nausea I felt from the sickeningly sweet smell of the funeral flower sprays, and every fiber of my body ached with regret. As I watched relatives and a few close friends pass silently by my father's casket, I was almost overwhelmed by heartbreak and the deep sense of guilt I felt.

Had I failed him once again? Should I have called him the night of my vision in Wisconsin Dells? Would that call have prevented the brutal assassination of the father I both loved and hated? Would he have listened to me or refused to talk to me as he had for more than a year?

At that moment I felt helplessly empty as I stood close to the open bronze casket and looked down at his face. His hands were folded carefully in prayerlike repose across his blue business suit, and a black-beaded rosary was draped over his lifeless fingers. I couldn't help thinking that it was probably the first time he had held a rosary since he was a child.

My eyes were brimming with tears, and with my guilt I felt a deep sorrow that he had died the way he had, that a friend, someone he had trusted enough to invite into his home, to bring to his very private cellar retreat, had, like a coward, shot Sam in the back of the head. And not content with that, he had rolled my father over and fired bullets from under his chin into his jaw and brain.

The police said there had been seven shots in all from a .22-caliber automatic with a silencer, a weapon that had become a favorite in the assassination of informers, drug dealers, and gangland members across the country. Looking at Sam's carefully made-up face, I still found it difficult to believe that he was dead. It was all a terrible nightmare from which I would soon wake to find that he was alive and that my planned reunion with him would take place as planned.

I wanted to cut out my tongue, take back the bitter words I had spoken to Chicago television newscaster Bill Kurtis of CBS when he called my sister Francine DePalma's home the day Sam's body had been found. I recall being surprised that Bill had found me at Francine's, particularly since her telephone was unlisted.

Bill Curtis had been a close friend for years. He was one of the few newsmen I had found to be honest in what he reported and who was genuinely concerned about my feelings and welfare. He wasn't calling just for a story, but simply to extend his sympathies. I was touched.

"I'm sorry, Toni, really sorry that it had to happen this way," he said. "It's a terrible way to have to die."

"It's horrible, Bill, just horrible," I said. I was numbed by the pain of what had taken place and I suppose I wasn't thinking very clearly about the effect they would have on others when I added some words I deeply regret having said, words that turned my children and relatives against me and made me seem to the public like an ungrateful witch.

"You know, Bill, the way you live is the way you die," I added rather coolly as Francine's eyes widened in disbelief behind her thick glasses. "Sam lived by the gun, so he died by the gun."

It was a terrible thing to say, no matter that it was true, that Sam had once been the most feared criminal in Chicago, and that he had ordered or been responsible for the deaths of others, according to the FBI and other law-enforcement agencies.

As I spoke to Bill, my mind was wandering, trying to piece together answers on who might have been behind the murder of Sam.

Was it Accardo, who had once been boss, had retired in favor of Sam, and then forced Sam to step down before he left for Mexico? Was it Sam's successor, Joey Aiuppa, the sportsman who loved hunting ducks or rabbits with a shotgun but was more circumspect in his dealings with fellow mob members? What about Jackie Cerone or . . . ?

No, none of them would have had the guts, at least not face-to-face. They might have sent a messenger, someone Sam trusted, but who? Dominic Blasi, Sam's chauffeur and former social secretary? I couldn't believe Dominic was the man. He was loyal to the organization, and he had been with Sam the night of the slaying, but he wouldn't have killed him, nor would Chuckie English who also saw Sam that night, as did my sister Francine, her husband, Jerry DePalma, and their daughter. They had all had dinner together and left, hours before the killer had gained entrance.

Why would the mob Sam had led want him dead? Were they afraid he would talk, as was suggested by the newspapers, if he faced another jail sentence for failing to answer the questions of another federal grand jury investigating him? Were they angry enough, as the FBI's experts suggested, to have ordered Sam's death because he had refused to share the proceeds from his investments in luxurious floating casinos that held the promise of enormous profits?

Was it the Central Intelligence Agency? Had they sent an assassin, someone close to Johnny Roselli, whom Dad did like and trusted enough to work with him in the plots to eliminate Fidel Castro? Were they afraid that Sam might say too much? He knew too much about their plots to kill Castro, Castro's brother, and revolutionary Che Guevara. He was scheduled to appear before a U.S. Senate committee headed by Senator Frank Church, an Idaho Democrat who was busy investigating CIA plots to assassinate world leaders.

I said nothing of these thoughts to Bill Kurtis, but my brain was spinning, desperately trying by process of elimination and analysis to determine who had killed my father and why. I came to no firm conclusion—I still haven't—but suddenly I was sick to my stomach. I barely heard Bill ask did I mind if he quoted what I said.

"No," I mumbled. "Say whatever you think appropriate."

Now at the funeral I saw friends and relatives alike look at me with contempt. I was a pariah, alone among dozens of people I had known all my life. I could see the unspoken accusations in their eyes. I could almost hear them say, "Why are you here? You don't deserve to be here after what you said."

I said nothing. I had said too much that night on the phone with Kurtis. I should have kept my mouth shut, but I never could keep silent. That had been part of the trouble between Sam and me, not keeping my mouth shut, and he had hated that. It tarnished the image of secrecy that was his world, the code of silence that he lived by and went to jail for.

Tears rolled down singer Keeley Smith's face as she whispered gently to me, "I'm sorry, Toni . . . God, I'm really so sorry."

Keeley was a sweet person. Many times I had watched her and her husband, Louis Prima, perform for affairs my father had sponsored. She had been a good friend, a dear friend of Sam's, and I found it difficult to say more than thanks as she embraced me and then walked toward the door.

Nearby was Phyllis McGuire. She was still very beautiful, almost spectacularly so. If she was hurt by his death, it wasn't apparent then.

Phyllis had arrived in Chicago from Paris, complete with her fawning entourage, to pay her last respects. She and Sam hadn't been close for a long, long while. He had been seeing another woman, a California millionairess, at the time of his death.

Phyllis and I didn't speak, but I thought to myself that at least she had the courage to face all those cameras and newsmen who were swarming like locusts outside the funeral home. And she had come with millionaire Mike Davis, the owner of the Tiger Oil Company, whom I had met at her Las Vegas estate.

As often as Phyllis and I didn't see eye to eye, I had always had a grudging respect for her. She had loved Sam openly, in the glare of publicity, with few reservations despite warnings that her affair with him could ruin her career, despite my early antagonism and that of other members of my family. Worse, their private moments of love had not been very private.

Now, as she and Davis stepped out the door and ran toward their waiting limousine while newsmen pushed, screaming their lurid questions, snapping at her heels like wild dogs, I found myself honestly feeling sorry for her and the terrible publicity that would follow her for appearing at Sam's funeral. She drove off in the waiting limousine, her eyes masked by dark glasses while flashguns popped and cameras whirred.

It was my turn now and that of Bonnie and Francine. I could hear the frantic shouts of television announcers and photographers, and, occasionally, I could hear a sickening thud as one of them was hit by one of the angry young sons or nephews of Willie Potatoes Daddano.

One of those boys, Louis Daddano, my godchild's brother, bitterly resented the press for what it had done to his father, for hounding him with their public tales of his violence, even after he was behind bars. Now Louis and the others were venting their fury, getting a small measure of revenge while showing their respect for Sam as they beat down cameras and slugged newsmen who got in their way.

The air was filled with screams and shouts and vile language as Louis and the boys blocked all attempts to photograph Sam's casket while it was being carried toward the waiting hearse.

"You ———— scum . . . get outta here, you lousy bastards!" one shouted. "One more picture and I'll smash your ———— face," said another. "Ain't you got no ———— decency?" still another asked.

It was almost ludicrous. A solemn, sad moment, a funeral was fast becoming an exercise in foul language and near violence. I just wanted it all to end.

On July 21, 1974, Mexican immigration agents had literally kidnapped Sam from his San Cristóbal home as he was ministering to his plants, clad only in pajamas and a robe. They had dragged him to a waiting car, driven him 150 miles to Juarez, and pushed him across the border at El Paso, Texas, into the waiting arms of U.S. Customs and FBI agents. He was then brought to Chicago for grand jury investigations and for questioning in the murder of Richard Cain (Scalzetti), who had been killed on December 20, 1973, by two shotgun-armed killers.

After his return I told him that I had filed for divorce, and Sam was true to his word that he would disown me, that my name would never be spoken again in the family.

Sam had been in the country only briefly before that to visit his California friend, Carolyn Morris, a former roommate of Broadway star Lauren Bacall and the ex-wife of music publisher Edwyn Morris. I never met Mrs. Morris, of whom Sam was apparently very fond, and she didn't appear at his funeral. I didn't even know when he was taken to Methodist Hospital in Houston, Texas, in 1975 for a gall-bladder operation performed by Dr. Michael E. DeBakey. My sisters and Mrs. Morris were with him, but he didn't want to see me.

"Get out!" he yelled. "Get out of this house and don't ever

come back. You are not my daughter. Do not ever talk to me again."

His rejection of me was complete. He not only turned his back on me, but he ordered his attorney to draw up a new will, disinheriting me. Although his initial intention was to cut me off without a cent, he had a change of heart when he saw the document. I learned before he died that he couldn't bring himself to sign it.

His decision not to disinherit me signaled a glimmer of distant hope that we might be able to reconcile our differences and maybe talk to each other again. Oh, how much I wanted that. After all, he was my father and whatever his or my faults, we were family and I loved him.

I knew that I would have to be the one to make the first move, that Sam could make no direct approach. It would have to be done obliquely so that he could preserve his sense of honor.

If there was one thing Sam might attend, it would be a gathering of the immediate family, a celebration of a significant event within the clan. The only such event, which was about to take place in June, 1975, was my birthday.

There was almost desperation on my part in planning an event that would provide me with a means to patch up our differences. It is hard, even now, to explain the love I had for Sam, because there were hate and violence all mixed up with that love. But the fact was that I did love him despite all the misery I had lived with from the moment I clung to his knee as a distraught five-year-old begging not to be sent away from home to a Catholic boarding school to the moment that he shouted he was disowning me for obtaining a divorce. All I had ever really wanted from Sam Giancana was his love. That would have been his most precious gift to me, but it was a gift he could never really give.

With the help of several close friends, I began planning a very private, very festive birthday celebration. Those festivities would take place on a cruise along the Fox River on the *Belle of St. Charles,* a vintage paddle steamer and the area's biggest tourist attraction.

My plan was to cruise slowly up the river just as if we were aboard a Mississippi River boat, spend a few hours eating and drinking and dancing to the music of an accordionist before returning to St. Charles late that evening. I had invited forty people, mostly family and a few of my closest friends from St. Charles who had really been nice to me when I needed support the most. The accordion player would play in Dick Cantino's style because Cantino was one of Sam's favorite entertainers.

I had high hopes that Sam would attend the party largely because of the efforts of a dear girl friend, Barbara, who lived in St. Charles. Barbara had helped me shop for special over-sized invitation cards on which she wrote in script.

It was Barbara who not only was composing the invitations but handling their distribution, and on the card she sent my father she had written a special message suggesting that he let bygones be bygones, that after all I was his firstborn daughter and that I would be heartbroken if he didn't attend. The invitation was composed in such a way as to make Sam believe that Barbara was throwing the family party for me, and it was mailed out.

During the week to ten days preceding the party, I had busied myself preparing for it. I had carefully planned the menu with Barbara, including chicken, fried the way Sam loved it, Jell-O molds that were made the way Momma had made them for him; homemade lasagna, meatballs, sausage, sauces, and specially prepared roast beef. And of course the special decorations and the accordionist were all designed to give the Italian family flavor to the whole event.

As the time neared, I was close to exhaustion, my nerves were on edge, and I imagined I looked like warmed-over death to some of my friends. One of those friends was Howard Ryerson, a wonderful man who was distantly related to my mother by marriage.

"Toni, why don't you take a break, relax a little before you collapse?" Howard said. "Get away from everything for a while and take the kids to Wisconsin Dells with our family."

I knew he was right, that it would help me be better prepared for what was to come. I also knew the kids would love the trip. So I agreed and I drove to Wisconsin with Howard and his family.

For several days all I did was relax at the motel where we stayed several miles from the village. I was beginning to feel physically and mentally relaxed for the first time in months. On June 17, the night before I planned to return to St. Charles, the kids and I went to the village.

The first place the children headed for was the outdoor arcade

where they could play with the pinball machines. I tried joining
them for a while, but I felt restless, driven by a strange sense of
urgency that I couldn't explain.

I told the kids I was going to sit on a bench across the street
from the arcade, and I gave them enough money to keep them
entertained for a time. As I left, I picked up a pamphlet on a wax
museum.

While the children played with the pinball machines, I sat
quietly on the lovely streetside bench and began thumbing
through the pamphlet. All the while, I felt a strange, unexplainable urgency that nagged and nagged at me.

Suddenly I reached a page in the pamphlet that pictured a
woman placing hairs in the wax head of Richard Nixon, and the
feeling that had been nagging at me heightened in intensity, and
cold chills ran up my spine. All at once, the head was no longer
Nixon's head. Instead I saw the woman putting hairs in my father's head. I rubbed my eyes, but it was still Sam's face staring
at me, not Nixon's.

I flipped to another page . . . and another . . . and another.
They were all the same. The face on every wax figure was my
father's face. I heard myself saying, "Good God, Sam's going to
die!," and looked around to see if anyone had heard me. But no
one was paying any attention. No one had heard anything.

I tried to shrug off the dark feeling and said nothing to the
children or my friends when we returned to the motel. After I
put the kids to bed and saw that they were sleeping, I tried to go
to sleep myself, but I was unable to shake off what I had experienced. I tried to reassure myself that what I had seen in the pamphlet was caused by being overtired. After all, Nixon wasn't dead,
it was just a picture of a wax figure.

The next day we drove back to St. Charles. I tried not to think
of the vision, but Sam's face kept haunting me. It was late when
we arrived home and after sending the children to bed, I sat
down in the living room, reached into my purse, and pulled out
the pamphlet once again.

Again all the figures were topped by Sam's face . . . and I
knew.

"I've got to call Sam!" I cried out. "I've got to warn him. He's
in grave danger."

As I reached for the telephone, I looked down again at one of the wax figures and the face was covered with blood. Then I saw nothing. All I felt was a sharp yet distinct chill course through my entire body.

At that moment I knew, but wouldn't admit to myself that Sam was dead. I looked at my watch. It was 2:00 A.M., perhaps just a little later, on the morning of June 19.

At 4:30 A.M., the telephone next to my bed shattered the silence of my room, rousing me from a deep, drugged sleep—I had taken a pill to get the sleep I was too unnerved to get naturally.

I picked up the receiver and mumbled a groggy hello to the caller. It was Carmen. We had rarely talked since we had split up, and he had never called me that late at night. Panic set in immediately. I sat bolt upright in my bed, and before he uttered a word I knew what he was going to say.

"He's dead, isn't he?" I cried. "Sam's dead!"

"Yeah, Toni, he's dead," Carmen said softly. "I'm sorry, really sorry."

I was sobbing softly now and I was making up excuses I knew weren't true to explain away his death.

"It was cancer, wasn't it?" I asked, knowing full well Sam didn't have cancer. He had recovered nicely from the operation in Houston. He was down to 150 pounds and didn't look so great, but the doctors had found no sign of cancer and I knew that.

"You'll read it in the paper anyhow," Carmen said brushing aside my question. "He was killed in the basement. They don't know who did it. He was killed about two hours ago."

As I put down the receiver, I screamed into the night: "Your fault, Toni, your fault!"

I was crying almost hysterically now. I shouted it over and over again: "Why didn't you call him . . . why?"

No one answered, but I knew that for all the days of my life I would carry a terrible guilt about Sam's assassination. I had failed him one time too often.

Epilogue

Sam's body was hardly cold before my family descended on the house and began stripping portions of his office and the rooms upstairs of their valuables and records they wanted no one to see. Exactly what was taken, what the value was, and what secret records disappeared, I'll never really know. It happened before I arrived at the house—before, during, and while the police were checking the crime scene.

The first person to find Sam was Joseph DiPersio, my father's lifelong friend, gardener, housekeeper, and sometime chauffeur. Joe had been with Sam for thirty-one years. A hustler and onetime thief who grew up making a fast buck on the streets of Cicero in the heyday of Al Capone and his mob, Joe had worked as a steerer for a Capone mob gambling house when he first met my father. And for the thirty-one years after Joe went to work for Sam, he was the one man Sam knew he could trust . . . with his family, with his valuables, with his documents, and with many of his secrets. Joe was a man who would never talk and never has.

Joe was the last known person to see Sam alive before the killer arrived, and the first to find my father after the killer left. But he didn't see the killer. If he had, knowing Joe the way I do, I think, as old as he was (eighty-one) when Sam was killed, he would have tried to exact revenge for what was done to Sam. Since he didn't know, he couldn't and didn't.

Years later, Joe recalled the events of that night in an interview with me and my coauthor.

Sam was wearing a blue-and-white checked sports shirt, brown slacks, and black house slippers when Joe last saw him as he worked on a leaky water pipe early in the evening. When Joe had finished, he asked Sam if he had anything more he wanted him to do. Sam told him he didn't, that he would call him if he needed him. They were the last words Joe was to hear from Sam.

Joe said he went upstairs and watched the *Tonight* show. Then, before going to bed, he called downstairs to see if Sam wanted anything. There was no response and Joe decided to investigate.

"I was so shocked when I went down there and saw him," Joe recalled. "I said, 'Mooney, what happened?' I thought he'd passed out at first." He called for assistance from fire rescue workers and police, and he called the family, not believing that Sam was dead at first. He turned off a gas stove on which Sam had apparently been warming up a dish of sausage and spinach when he was killed. The food wasn't burned, so the killer had probably left only a short time before Joe checked on Sam.

"He was like a brother," Joe said. "We'd been together for thirty-one years . . . like a brother . . . I couldn't believe he was dead." It was then he recalled how he and Sam had met.

"I met Sam in a clip joint in Cicero," Joe told us. "It was an old wire room (a bookmaker's) in what later became a post office. They had big sheets on the wall and eight poker tables going twenty-four hours a day. For every guy I brought in and steered to the game, I got five or ten bucks and then when they left, I was out to steal and rob them.

"That whole street was wide open," he recalled. "They paid off right after the race and just one poker game took in so much money in twelve hours that they brought it out in suitcases.

"The cops busted me one night for stealing a load of coats. I sent word out with an outgoing prisoner to tell someone I was in the can. That night Mooney came in with five guys. He looked me over and he said, 'I'm gonna give you a good job.'

"I said, 'How you gonna give me a good job? I'm here . . . in jail.' The next thing I knew he had paid off a precinct captain and he had paid off downtown [police headquarters] because he had to . . . I was in serious trouble. When I got out of jail, I was sent to Mooney's home on Monitor. I said, 'What the hell am I gonna do there?' Then he told me he was gonna have me take care of his places and stay outta trouble. He told me he didn't want me to steal no more, that I'd never have to worry about a thing as long as I stuck with him. We was like brothers after that."

Sam had meant it. He wanted Joe taken care of for the rest of his life. He had trusted Joe with hundreds of thousands of dollars of cash in the house, and Joe knew where all Sam's secret caches were.

Until he died in October 1983, Joe and his wife, Ann, were in a nursing home. They received nothing from Sam's estate, not even the three thousand dollars in cash they said they had left in the house before he died, nor the salary they had coming to them, nor the money they had spent, including their own food stamps, to provide food in the house for Sam and themselves.

Joe had been a thief when Sam knew him, but in his life with Sam and our family, he was one of the most *honest* men I ever had the pleasure of knowing. There wasn't anything my father didn't trust him with.

Sam regularly gave Joe money to deposit in one of his banks, money he would claim he had won at the racetrack and later, investigators at the crime scene said that they found records indicating he won better than 70 percent of the time at the track. The records, the investigators said, were apparently an elaborate ruse to fool the Internal Revenue Service and make them believe that the money Sam had deposited in certain banks had been won at the track instead of having come from illegal syndicate business ventures. One of those bank accounts alone contained $69,000, but when Sam's will was probated all of his three identified savings accounts with the St. Paul Federal Savings Bank combined didn't contain that much. The largest account had only twenty thousand dollars in it.

Joe knew about sacks of gold coins that Sam kept in his desk, coins that had great numismatic value as well as gold content value. There were golden double eagles, in all sorts of denominations both American and Mexican, but they were never found. There were old silver dollars, many of them collectors' items, others from casinos he had played at.

Joe knew of drawers where great wads of hundred-dollar bills were kept, as much as one hundred thousand dollars at a time. He knew of a secret compartment behind a drawer underneath a breadbox behind a cellar kitchen stove where Sam kept large amounts of currency, fifty thousand dollars or more at a time. And he knew about a safe, perhaps ten inches long and weighing more than one hundred pounds, where Sam kept many confidential papers and other valuables. There were other hiding places— upstairs on the main floor, in Sam's bedroom. Sam hid money all over the house . . . all the time. But when police tallied the total amount of cash found at the house that night all they could account for was $1,429 found in a money clip in Sam's pocket and $300 in coins, according to the probated estate filed with the Cook County Circuit Court's probate division by Administrative Attorney Alfred P. Fredo.

By the time I arrived at the house, Joe and his wife were under strict instructions from my sisters not to let me into the cellar where the police were.

"Make sure Annette doesn't get downstairs," they told Joe and Ann. "We don't want her stirring things up."

So I was detained upstairs, on a couch, not allowed to see what was happening downstairs or elsewhere. Later, when I saw the probated will and the room-by-room itemization of the house contents, I saw no record of the 18-karat gold plate set Sam had— twenty to twenty-four pieces—and there was nothing about a magnificent silverware set. Those two sets alone were probably worth over thirty thousand dollars. I have never been able to determine what happened to them, or to priceless items of jade and other jewelry that also never turned up in the itemized household accounting.

I certainly doubt that Sam sold them or gave them away. I'm even more certain that Joe DiPersio got nothing, although he was entitled not only to the money he and his wife had in the house, but to the thousands of dollars in unpaid salary and money that they had taken out of their own pockets for food, repairs, and Sam's needs. My curiosity over the disappearance of these items has never been satisfied by the police, the state's attorney, or my family, and I have never talked to my former husband about it.

When I asked my sisters what happened to Sam's money, I was

told to mind my own business, to keep my mouth shut. They reminded me that he had been about to cut me out of his will and that I should be grateful that I got anything.

What I got was a total of $56,637.64 and of that, $6,124.60 went for inheritance taxes. My sisters received equal amounts, although their inheritance taxes were higher, so their net was only $45,051.44. That was what was left out of the total cash receipts of $390,024. Court documents, property taxes, utility bills, attorney's fees, and other miscellaneous costs took $215,102.72 from the total.

Francine, as estate administrator, received an added $13,500, and the Monclair Funeral Home, which handled Sam's funeral, picked up $8,595. The attorneys also got something: Fredo received $18,200 plus $3,065 for a trip to Mexico to dispose of Sam's $146,000 worth of property in Cuernavaca, and Anthony V. Champagne, who had been Sam's personal attorney for years, got $5,000.

There were also some trusts that my sons had shares in along with other members of my family. These included the Lawrence River Road trusts, set up by Sam to cover property and partnerships valued at some $600,000. One trust included the site of a Burger King fast-food franchise lease. Another trust concerned property, valued in 1975 at well over $150,000 and located in Melrose Park, containing a car dealership and a beef stand formerly owned by Dominic Blasi.

There were other interests: a beef outlet known as Ben's Beef Stand, Ltd., owned by a Ben Tedesco with Blasi and leased from Sam; the proceeds from an insurance claim for a restaurant bar which had burned down and the restaurant property that the White Castle System wanted to purchase; and a partnership agreement between Sam and Charles and Sam English in the Lormar Distributing Company. In this company Sam held, through the trusteeship, 50 percent ownership, and the English brothers each held 25 percent.

All told, the trusts were worth about $600,000. They were originally set up with Bonnie, Francine, and me as equal shareholders, but when I divorced Carmen, Sam cut me out and gave my share to our five sons.

So, Sam's estate totaled nearly $1,000,000, but this in no way represented the millions my father had acquired. An investigation by *Chicago Tribune* reporter Ronald Koziol suggested that Sam's fortune should have totaled more than $25 million.

Mr. Koziol claimed that investigators he had talked to told him that Sam had received a 12 percent cut of all gambling activities in Cook County. And of course there were all those casino proceeds from Las Vegas, from the offshore gambling ships, from investments he was believed to have had in Mexico, Cuba, Lebanon, Central and South America, Europe, and who knows where else.

Wherever these funds were, whatever they were, I was and still have been unable to determine what happened to them. I have been stonewalled by bureaucratic roadblocks thrown up by the Drug Enforcement Administration, the Central Intelligence Agency, the State Department, and the Internal Revenue Service in my efforts to seek, through the Freedom of Information Act, government documents on Sam, his associations, and business activities, although I am entitled to them. Only the FBI, after nearly two years, came up with documents in their possession. They have refused to turn over more than two thousand pages and have not been candid about other documents in their possession they obtained through illegal eavesdropping on Phyllis McGuire and Sam.

In an article Mr. Koziol quoted Fredo as saying that when my sister Francine hired him to probate my father's estate, he "heard all kinds of stories about hidden money." He said that FBI agents visited him several times to inquire about information he might have uncovered regarding Sam's trips to Beirut. "From what I was told," Fredo said, "the FBI apparently followed Giancana to Beirut more than once. They were certainly interested in anything along those lines that I might have found." But Fredo said he didn't have the resources to find out if Sam did have financial interests in Lebanon or in any other country he frequented, including Venezuela, Panama, Guatemala, Puerto Rico, Jamaica, the Dominican Republic, the Bahamas, England, and France. He was also puzzled by a safe deposit box that Sam kept in a suburban bank under the name of "Sam DeTolve" which Fredo said "looked like it had been hosed out . . . that's how clean it was."

Not only have I never been able to determine what happened

to the assets Sam was supposed to have, but I have never been able to get any of the items that were seized in the house by investigators on the day of the murder.

There were, for example, tape recordings Sam had, pictures of our family taken with him and Dean Martin, Frank Sinatra, Jerry Lewis, Jimmy Durante, and dozens of other entertainers. There were papers I never saw, records of expenses, and other documents that might have given me some clue to investments that I and my children might have had a vested interest in. None of those were returned to me. They were all given to Francine and her husband, and they refused to give any of them to me.

It's been nearly nine years since his murder now, and I'm still searching, still looking in the cracks of my father's life to unravel some of the mystery. I'm still looking for that fortune everyone said he had hidden but which has never been found. But most of all, I'm trying to understand my father better through documents, through the conversations he had, through his life with others. Maybe someday it will help me find the peace I could never find while he was alive.

Appendix

CHICAGO CRIME
DIRECTORY
(Major Crime Figures)

ACCARDO, ANTHONY JOSEPH. ALIASES: Joe Batters, Big Tuna. DATE OF BIRTH: April 28, 1906. Former boss and Chicago-mob elder statesman. Still considered the power behind the Chicago Outfit's throne and its chief adviser. Ex-bodyguard and enforcer for Al Capone. Cited by Chicago Crime Commission in 1931 as suspect in the St. Valentine's Day Massacre. More than thirty arrests on charges ranging from gambling and extortion to kidnapping, murder, contempt of Congress, and tax evasion. Identified in U.S. Senate crime committee hearings, including the Kefauver, McClellan, Valachi, and the 1983 Senate Subcommittee on Investigations hearings.

AIUPPA, JOSEPH. ALIASES: Joey Doves, Joey O'Brien. DATE OF BIRTH: December 1, 1907. Number two to Accardo in stature and power. Former boss, now in semi-retirement. Acts as adviser to current leader, John (Jackie the Lackey) Cerone. Former muscle for Capone. Record dates back to 1935. Convictions in gambling case; illegally transporting more than five hundred mourning doves (thus earning his nickname); and contempt of Congress (later reversed). Identified in U.S. Senate crime committee hearings, including those of Kefauver and McClellan, and the 1983 Senate Subcommittee on Investigations.

ALDERISO, FELIX ANTHONY. ALIAS: Milwaukee Phil. Deceased. DATE OF BIRTH: April 26, 1912.   Controlled prostitution in Milwaukee for Chicago mob. Was major figure in narcotics, loan sharking (juice rackets), contract killing, and gambling. Record, beginning in 1929, included more than thirty-six arrests on charges ranging from auto theft and extortion to narcotics, loan sharking, and murder. Suspect in fourteen homicides.

ALEX, GUS. ALIASES: Gussy, Sam Taylor, Slim, The Muscle. DATE OF BIRTH: April 1, 1916.   Record of more than twenty-five arrests for bribery, assault, manslaughter, kidnapping. Identified as suspect in several murders. Identified in U.S. Senate crime committee hearings including those of McClellan, Valachi, and the 1983 Senate Subcommittee on Investigations. Major crime figure in Chicago's Loop with contacts among politicians, public officials, labor leaders, and members of the judiciary.

ANASTASIA, ALBERT. ALIASES: The Executioner, Boom Boom.   Murdered in New York in barber's chair, October 25, 1957. Former boss of Murder Inc., and of what later became the Carlo Gambino crime family.

BARBARA, JOSEPH, SR. Deceased.   Ex-bootlegger, murder suspect, and member of the Stefano Magaddino crime family of Buffalo, New York. Hosted the infamous Apalachin crime enclave in both 1956 and 1957 (when it was raided by police).

BATTAGLIA, SAM. ALIASES: Teets, Joe Rock, Sam Rice. Deceased.   At one time heir to the throne of Sam Giancana. Had record of more than twenty-five arrests for burglary, robbery, larceny, assault, and attempted murder. Was suspect in more than seven murders, and a major figure in narcotics, loan sharking, and gambling.

BLASI, DOMINIC. ALIASES: Butch, Joe Bantone. DATE OF BIRTH: September 9, 1911.   Permanent residence: River Forest, Illinois. Record for larceny. Identified in Valachi hearings. Was trusted aide, bodyguard, and former driver-appointment "secretary" for Sam Giancana. Was with Giancana the night he was murdered, and questioned by police as a suspect in that homicide. Leading FBI experts and Giancana's daughter, Antoinette, do not consider him Giancana's killer, however.

BONANNO, JOSEPH. ALIAS: Joe Bananas. DATE OF BIRTH: January 18, 1905.   Primary residence: Tucson, Arizona. Former boss of the New York-based Joseph Bonanno crime family. Convicted on federal conspiracy to obstruct governmental justice. Acknowledged member of what he terms the Sicilian "tradition." Deposed as crime boss by Cosa Nostra (American Mafia) commission (ruling body of crime leaders). Author of *A Man of Honor: The Autobiography of Joseph Bonanno*.

BONANNO, SALVATORE. ALIAS: Bill. DATE OF BIRTH: November 5, 1932.   Primary residence: San Jose, California. Son of Joseph Bonanno. Former consigliere (adviser) of Bonanno crime family. Convictions for conspiracy, mail fraud, perjury, loan sharking.

BUCCIERI, FIORE. ALIAS: Fifi. Deceased.   Former Chicago mob arsonist and professional assassin. Criminal record included charges of bribery, murder, carrying a concealed weapon, burglary. Was major figure in labor and loan shark rackets.

CAPONE, ALPHONSE. ALIASES: Big Al, Scarface. Deceased.   Former head of Chicago mob during Prohibition. His organization was the base from which the current Chicago Outfit grew, influencing and often controlling the politics not only of Chicago but of Illinois as well. One of crime's most vicious and most publicized criminals. Died of syphilis.

CAIFANO, JOHN MICHAEL. ALIASES: Marshall Caifano, Shoes, Heels. Legally changed name to John M. Marshall in 1955. DATE OF BIRTH: August 19, 1911.   Serving twenty-year federal term for racketeering. Prior convictions for extortion, burglary, bank robbery, and fraud. Suspect in the murder of Richard Cain and in at least nine other slayings. Identified in McClellan and Valachi hearings.

CAIFANO, LEONARD. ALIAS: Fat Lenny. Murdered in 1951.   Former enforcer for Giancana. Brother of Marshall Caifano. Long criminal record.

CAIN, RICHARD (true name RICCARDO SCALZETTI). Murdered December 20, 1973.   Member of Chicago Outfit, main job was to infiltrate law enforcement. Served with Chicago police and as chief investigator of Cook County Sheriff's office. Well educated, a linguist, was confidant of Giancana until his murder in Chicago.

CAMPAGNA, LOUIS. ALIAS: Little New York. Deceased.
Former high-level member of the old Capone mob. Became respected adviser to the Outfit and was a close friend and booster of Giancana's succession to the mob's leadership.

CERONE, JOHN PHILLIP. ALIASES: Jackie the Lackey, John Cironi. DATE OF BIRTH: July 7, 1914.   Identified in 1983 U.S. Senate Subcommittee on Investigations hearings as the Outfit boss. However, seeks advice from both Accardo and Aiuppa. Record of more than twenty arrests on charges ranging from bookmaking to armed robbery. Leading political fixer and former Accardo chauffeur.

COLOMBO, JOSEPH. Deceased.   Former crime boss and successor to Joseph (Giuseppe) Profaci. Victim of assassination attempt that eventually caused his death. Led mob-controlled Italian Civil Rights movement, which picked the pockets of well-meaning Italian Americans of more than two million dollars.

DADDANO, WILLIAM, SR. ALIAS: Willie Potatoes. Deceased.
Close associate of Giancana and major member of the Outfit. Died in prison. Identified as an assassin and torturer. Was major figure in loan shark rackets and distribution of jukeboxes.

DELUCIA, PAUL. ALIAS: Paul (The Waiter) Ricca. Deceased.
Former boss of the Capone mob, successor to Frank Nitti. Became major adviser to Accardo and Giancana, and was chief supporter of Giancana's ascension to the leadership. Known for his manners and attire, DeLucia was a traditional mafioso.

DEMORA, VINCENZO. ALIAS: Machinegun Jack McGurn. Deceased.   Capone mob machine-gun assassin for Al Capone who helped Giancana in his early years of crime. Known as a vicious killer of the Capone organization.

DESTEFANO, SAM. ALIAS: Mike Step. Murdered April 14,

1973.   Was a member of Giancana's old 42s gang and considered one of the most vicious and demented of all Outfit killers. Record of more than forty arrests included robbery, burglary, rape, bank robbery, intimidation of a federal judge. Infamous for torturing his victims, letting them die slow and excruciatingly painful deaths. Probably the most hated of all Chicago's gangsters.

DiVARCO, JOSEPH VINCENT. ALIAS: Little Caesar. DATE OF BIRTH: July 27, 1911.   Boss of Chicago's Rush Street nightclub district, DiVarco is a respected lieutenant in the Outfit and has arrests for bribing a juror, counterfeiting, voter fraud. Identified in the McClellan, Valachi, and 1983 U.S. Senate Subcommittee on Investigations hearings.

ENGLISH, CHARLES CARMEN (changed from Inglese). ALIAS: Chuckie. DATE OF BIRTH: November 7, 1914.   Record includes arrests for extortion, counterfeiting phonograph record trademarks, robbery. Invoked the Fifth repeatedly before McClellan labor rackets committee, identified in Valachi and the 1983 U.S. Senate Subcommittee on Investigations hearings. Once a top lieutenant of Giancana, English has been identified as a soldier who served Joseph (Joey the Clown) Lombardo until his conviction in a labor racketeering case in 1983.

FISCHETTI, CHARLES. One of the most powerful and violent of the three Fischetti brothers, cousin to Capone, and member of the Capone mob before he died. Fischetti was a major mob figure in Las Vegas and Havana casino gambling circles. Brother Rocco and brother Joseph were also major gambling figures with the Chicago mob, and Joseph Fischetti was particularly known for his close relationship to entertainer Frank Sinatra. All were identified in the Kefauver, McClellan, and Valachi hearings. All are now deceased.

GAMBINO, CARLO. Deceased.   Former boss of what has come to be known as the Gambino crime family of New York, the largest single Cosa Nostra family in the United States. Gambino succeeded Albert Anastasia, who was slain in New York in 1957.

GIOE, CHARLES. ALIAS: Cherry Nose.   A powerful Capone

mob member who before his death was responsible, along with Paul DeLucia (Ricca), Rocco Fischetti, Frank Nitti, Louis Campagna, and others, for shaking down the movie industry in a cele- brated extortion case at which Willie Bioff testified, who was later slain for his efforts.

GLIMCO, JOSEPH PAUL (true name Giuseppe Glielmi). ALIASES: Joey Clinco, Giuseppe Primavera. Deceased.   Record of thirty-six arrests. Identified in Kefauver, McClellan, and Valachi hearings as a major labor rackets figure in Chicago, where he bossed more than a dozen Teamster locals and dominated the taxicab industry.

HUMPHREYS, MURRAY. ALIASES: Murray the Camel, Joseph Burns.   One of the most important fixers of the Chicago syndicate. Succeeded Capone mob fixer Jake Guzik in the late 1950s when Guzik died. Humphreys, a Welshman, now deceased, together with Gus Alex, a Greek, provided the Chicago mob with strong ties to labor leaders, public officials, judges, police, and businessmen.

KRUSE, LESTER. ALIASES: Killer Kane, The Kid.   Twice arrested for murder, his arrest record was ordered destroyed by court order before his death. Was a major gambling figure used by Giancana in the Dominican Republic and other areas to establish casinos for the mob. Ex-bodyguard for Jake Guzik and gambling partner of Rocco Fischetti.

LANSKY, MEYER. Deceased.   Known as the mob's financial wizard, it was Lansky who initiated and arranged for the mob's control of casinos in areas from Las Vegas to Havana, from Antigua to Greece. Was considered a genius at laundering mob money and was scrupulously honest in his dealing with Mafia figures with whom he worked. Got his start in the Bugs and Meyer mob in New York with sidekick Benjamin (Buggsy) Siegel, who was eventually ordered slain on the orders of Lansky and the Mafia for cheating the mob in opening the Flamingo Hotel in Las Vegas.

LaROCCA, SEBASTIAN JOHN. DATE OF BIRTH: December 19, 1901.   Attendee at Apalachin. Controls Cosa Nostra rackets in southwestern Pennsylvania. Identified by the Pennsylvania Crime Commission and at the Valachi hearings as the Cosa Nostra boss of the Pittsburgh-southwestern Pennsylvania area.

LUCCHESE, THOMAS. ALIAS: Three-Finger Brown. Deceased. Former boss of what has been identified by law-enforcement officials as the Lucchese crime family, which is primarily based in Long Island, New York, and is now led by Anthony (Tony Ducks) Corallo. Both Brown and Corallo have been identified in McClellan and Valachi crime hearings and have had numerous arrests.

LUCIANO, CHARLES (true name Salvatore Lucana). ALIAS: Charlie Lucky. Deceased. The architect of what is now the current structure of the Cosa Nostra, the Americanized version of the Mafia. Was deeply involved with Lansky in Havana in establishing mob control of casinos in Cuba before the advent of Fidel Castro.

MAGADDINO, STEFANO. ALIASES: The Boss, the Old Man. Deceased. Former boss of the Magaddino crime family of Buffalo. Was responsible for the ill-fated Apalachin meeting and arranged the kidnapping and eventual release of Joseph Bonanno.

NITTI, FRANK. ALIAS: The Enforcer. Committed suicide. Chief enforcer and successor to Chicago boss Al Capone, Nitti killed himself rather than face jail in the movie industry extortion scandal with Paul DeLucia (Ricca), Louis Campagna, Charles Gioe, and John Roselli.

PRIO, ROSS. ALIAS: Rosario Fabricini. Deceased. Capone mob member and major suspect in numerous murders. Was questioned in connection with several bombings and cited for contempt of Congress after he took the Fifth before the McClellan committee. Was a major political fixer, boss of a multi-million-dollar policy racket, and named by informer Joseph Valachi as a major power broker in Chicago mob. Had major interests in the milk, cheese, and canned whipped-topping businesses.

PROFACI, JOSEPH (GIUSEPPE). Deceased. Former boss of what is now known as the Joseph Colombo crime family. Died of natural causes following a violent gang war in Brooklyn resulting from the rebellion of the Joseph Gallo faction of his crime family.

ROSELLI, JOHN. Murdered following his testimony in congressional hearings about his and Sam Giancana's roles in the Central Intelligence Agency plot to murder Cuban dictator Fidel Castro. Was Giancana's representative in Las Vegas and in the entertainment industry and wielded enormous power. Faced deportation prior to his congressional testimony, and was found later in a bullet-riddled barrel in Florida waters.

ZERILLI, JOSEPH. Deceased.   Former boss of the Detroit Mafia and closely allied with the Chicago crime family prior to Giancana's assassination. Zerilli's mob was considered the Chief conduit to former Teamster president James Riddle Hoffa, and members of his family were believed responsible in the conspiracy that resulted in the abduction and murder of Hoffa, whose body was never found.

This Appendix is based upon government and law-enforcement records, including those in the text and those reviewed by Thomas C. Renner during his more than twenty years of investigating organized crime.

Index

Accardo, Anthony Joseph (Joe Batters), 16, 17, 19, 20, 21–22, 29, 30, 32–33, 34, 36, 45, 72–73, 86, 88, 99, 118, 122, 130–131, 138, 142, 148, 149, 157–159, 175–177, 187, 191, 192, 194, 195, 198, 200, 246, 247, 259, 263, 265, 268, 269, 274, 291

Adducci, James J., 74–75, 102, 142

Aiuppa, Joseph (Joey Doves), 184, 191, 271, 274, 291–292

Alderiso, Felix Anthony (Milwaukee Phil), 33, 34, 115, 143, 191, 292

Alex, Gus, 166, 191, 198, 292

Anastasia, Albert (The Executioner), 157, 292

Annunzio, Frank, 104, 250–251, 268

Austin, Richard B., 258, 259

Barbara, Joseph, Sr., 151, 155, 292

Battaglia, Sam (Teets), 33, 45, 72–73, 191, 267, 292

Bioff, Willie, 83, 86–88

Black policy rackets, takeover by Giancana and "42s," 29, 40, 71, 72, 80, 86, 117

Blasi, Dominic (Butch), 72, 247, 254, 259, 266, 274–275, 292–293

Bonanno, Joseph (Joe Bananas), 155, 156–159, 195, 293

Bonanno, Salvatore, 158–159, 195, 293

Bouchay, Alfred (Papa), 109, 112

Brown, Tommy. See Lucchese, Thomas

Burba, Alex, 32–33

Caifano, Leonard (Fat Leonard), 29, 33,

45, 72, 80; death of, 39–40, 71; relationship with Giancana family, 37–39, 293

Caifano, Marshall, 33, 39, 45, 72, 88, 115, 191, 293

Cain, Richard, 79, 266, 269–270, 271, 294

Cal-Neva Lodge, Lake Tahoe, 13, 107, 113, 222–227

Campagna, Charlotte, 72, 102, 141

Campagna, Louis (Little New York), 49, 72, 77, 87–88, 102, 103–104, 121–122, 141, 294

Capone, Alphonse, 16, 17, 20, 21, 33, 36, 45, 77, 86, 87, 99, 100, 103, 121–122, 131, 132, 150, 291, 293

Castro, Fidel, 176, 275, 298; assassination plot against, 9, 13–14, 15, 18–20, 23–25, 217–218

Catholic Church, Mafia and, 59, 67–68, 91, 118–119

Central Intelligence Agency. See CIA

Cerone, John Phillip (Jackie the Lackey), 59, 142, 266, 268, 291, 294

Champagne, Anthony V., 100, 177, 178, 287

Chesrow, Dr. Eugene J., 41, 42, 100, 138–139

Chicago Crime Commission, 78–79, 84–86

Chicago Stadium, Giancana acquires for "Night of Stars," 102, 104

Chicago Tribune, 33, 90, 115, 189, 190–192

Church, Frank, 18, 24, 275

CIA: and plots to assassinate international leaders, 9, 13–14, 15, 18–20, 23–25, 217–218; Giancana and, 218, 275
Clark, Bergit, 184, 232–233
Colombo, Joseph, 106, 294
Colucci, Mary, 264–265
Corngold, Joe, 34, 143
Costello, Frank, 122, 206
Cuernavaca, Mexico, 48, 50, 69
Curtis, Bill, 274, 275

D'Amato, Paul (Skinny), 109, 203, 227
D'Andrea, Phil, 88, 104
D'Arco, John, 102–104, 142, 246, 265
Daddano, Mary, 81–82
Daddano, William (Willie Potatoes), 33, 72, 78–80, 115, 191, 270, 276
Dalitz, Moe, 198–199, 201, 202, 215
Davis, Mike, 241, 276
Davis, Sammy, Jr., 94, 111, 113–114, 115
DeLucia, Paul. See Ricca, Paul
DeMora, Vincenzo. See McGurn, Jack (Machinegun)
DeSimmona, Antonia (grandmother), 30
DeStefano, Sam, 33, 45, 142, 294–295
DeTolve, Andrew, 52
DeTolve, Angeline, 51; wedding of, 55–56. See also Giancana, Angeline
DeTolve, Anna, 52
DeTolve, Anthony J., 52, 104
DeTolve, Francescantonio (maternal grandfather), 36, 52, 54, 55–56
DeTolve, Joseph, 36, 52, 56
DeTolve, Maria, 36
DeTolve, Michael, 36, 52, 63, 70, 184, 232
DeTolve, Rose, 52, 56
DiPersio, Joseph, 127, 155, 283–287
DiVarco, Joseph Vincent, 191, 295
Divis, Edward, 33
Dominican Republic, Giancana's efforts to establish gambling casinos in, 204–207
Duffy, LaVern J., 177–178
Duffy, William J., 262–264
Durante, Jimmy, 8, 94–95, 101, 105, 111, 210

English, Charles Carmen (Chuckie), 41–42, 80, 254, 255–259, 263, 267, 275, 295
Eulo, Frank and Rose, 140, 141
Exner, Judith Campbell, 161, 184

Father Joe (pseudonym), 89–90, 91–92, 134; affair with Antoinette, 124, 126–128; and Antoinette's acceptance at Ladywood, 120; Giancana and, 118–119

FBI; on Adduci, 74–75; and Antoinette's marriage to Manno, 185–186; on Antoinette's mental condition, 183; articles on Giancana by Sandy Smith and, 191–192; on attendance at funeral for Giancana's father, 143; electronic surveillance of First Ward, 246–247; electronic surveillance of Giancana, 210–211, 219–220; on Fischetti, 77; on Francine Giancana, 57; on gambling operations at Villa Venice, 115; and Giancana's activities in Dominican Republic, 204–207; and Giancana's attitude toward Kennedy family, 247–251, 255–259; on Giancana's donations to Church, 67–68; on Giancana's influence on First Ward politics, 102–104; on Giancana's influence in Hollywood, 95, 204–207; and Giancana's interest in Desert Inn, 200–201; and Giancana's meeting with Sinatra, 202–203; on Giancana's rejection for military service, 90; and Giancana's relationships with women, 246; and Guzik kidnapping, 73; and Italian Welfare Council of Chicago, 99; on Jones, 70–72; lockstep surveillance of Giancana, 251–259; on Moretti's death, 75–76; and plot to assassinate Castro, 25; and seizure of Giancana's list by U.S. Customs, 246; on subpoena for Antoinette, 179–183; subpoenas of Phyllis McGuire, 213–217; surveillance of Antoinette, 183, 185; surveillance of Giancana, 15, 16, 17, 84–86, 122, 186–187, 232–234; surveillance of Giancana and Phyllis McGuire, 210–215, 220–221; surveillance of Giancana and Sinatra, 222–225; taped conversations of Giancana, 107–108, 156, 158–159; telegrams on assassination plot against Castro, 13–14, 24–25; on Villa Venice, 109–114; on wiretapping of Rowan, 218
Ferraro, Frank (Strongy), 138, 191, 259
Fischetti, Charles, 77, 198, 295
Fischetti, Joseph, 76, 77, 101, 115, 222
Fischetti, Rocco, 76–78, 86, 101, 118, 198, 206
Fisher, Eddie, 111, 114, 122
Fitzgerald, Benedict F., Jr., 181–183
Formosa, Johnny, 107–108
Fosco, Peter, 103, 104
Frabotta, Albert (Obie), 45, 143, 191
Fredo, Alfred P., 286, 288–289

Gambino, Carlo, 157, 295
Giancana, Angeline (Mrs. Sam Giancana), 15, 18, 19, 21, 27, 81, 177, 190, 235; and Antoinette's career ambitions, 92, 94, 132–134; Antoinette's relationship with Tisci and, 125; attitude toward sex, 126; attitude toward Sulwk, 136–137; and birth of Antoinette, 41, 42–43; Charlotte Campagna and, 72; cooking skills, 73–74; death of, 33, 58, 106, 137–142; and Durante, 94–95, 105; family background, 51–52; Francine and, 118; Georgianna Jordan and, 89; Giancana's donation to Church after death of, 67; during husband's imprisonment, 36–40; illnesses of, 52–53, 57–58, 132; and Italian Welfare Council of Chicago, 99–107, 117; life-style of, 70; and precautions in home, 45–46; relationship with Antoinette, 63–64, 95, 96–97; relationship with husband, 54–56, 57–58; religion and, 60–61
Giancana, Antoinette: abortions, 161–165, 240–241, 242; affair with Bob, 239–240; alcoholism, 235–236; ambition to become actress, 92–93; attitude toward Daddano, 78–80; attitude toward Fischetti, 76–78; attitude toward Moretti, 75–76; behavior at Desert Inn, Las Vegas, 198–202; birth of, 41–43; Bonnie's wedding and, 195–196; in California, 88–89, 92–97; childhood, 8–9, 35–36, 69–70; Dalitz and, 198–199; decides on divorce, 242–243, 271–272; decision to attend Ladywood, 89–90, 91–92, 118, 119–120; desire to become nun, 66; efforts to obtain information on father's funds, 288–289; efforts to reconcile with father, 278–280; estrangement from father, 9; family background, 30–32; family vacation in Rhinelander, Wisconsin, 42–43; father arranges MGM tour for, 83–84, 95–96; and father's "business associates," 73–80; father's reaction to divorce, 277–278; father's reaction to friends of, 46–47; FBI surveillance of, 183; fear of professional killers, 44–46; first holy communion, 66–67; gives custody of children to ex-husband, 272; ignorance of father's criminal activities, 8–9, 30–31, 43–44, 80–81; inheritance of, 287; at Ladywood, 120–126; learns of father's death, 281; life-style of, 10; marriage to Manno, 184–190; meets

Rebozo, 160–161; modeling jobs, 132–134; nervous breakdowns, 145–148, 235–236; and "Night of Stars" events, 105–106; plastic surgery, 129–130; poverty of, 9–10; premonition of father's death, 280–281; punished by father, 49–50; reaction to father's crimes, 8; reaction to father's death, 272–277; reaction to father's imprisonment, 28–29, 36–40; reaction to mother's death, 9, 137–142; relationship with Daddano family, 81–82; relationship with father, 7, 17–20, 22–24, 41; relationship with Father Joe, 91–92, 124, 126–128; relationship with husband, 238–239; relationship with mother, 132; relationship with Nestos, 151–155, 159–160, 161–166; relationship with Phyllis McGuire, 230–231, 236–243; sent to Catholic boarding school, 63–66; sent to Miami, 159–161; Sinatra and, 113–114; subpoenaed by McClellan committee, 178–183; Sulwk and, 135–137; and Tisci, 124–125; volunteers at USO, 135–136
Giancana, Antonio. *See* Giangana, Antonio
Giancana, Bonnie, 18, 22, 27, 34, 43, 44, 53, 56, 118, 125, 129, 142, 188, 237, 246, 276, 287; wedding of, 193, 194–196
Giancana, Charlie, 30, 32
Giancana, Francine, 18, 30, 32, 53, 56–57, 61, 62, 67, 118, 129, 142, 188, 202, 203, 230, 275, 276, 287, 288, 289
Giancana, Lena, 30
Giancana, Mary Leonardi, 30, 32
Giancana, Sam: Accardo and, 20, 21–22, 130–131; affairs of, 57, 58, 139–140, 183–184; Alex and, 150–153; aliases used by, 32, 53–54, 180, 203; allows Antoinette to volunteer at USO, 135; ambitions for Antoinette, 92; anonymous contributions of, 68; antique and art collection of, 47–48, 49; Antoinette's premonition of death of, 280–281; Antoinette's relationship with Nestos and, 153–155; Antoinette's relationship with Tisci and, 125; Antoinette's suicide attempt and, 146–147, 148; and Antoinette's trip to California, 88–89; Antoinette's wedding and, 188–190; Apalachin meeting, 155–159; appearance before grand jury, 266–267; appearance before McClellan committee, 192–193;

Giancana, Sam *(cont.)*
  arrest record, 32–33, 53–54, 263–264;
  articles by Sandy Smith on, 190–192;
  assassination of, 16; and attempted
  takeover of black policy rackets,
  39–40, 71–72; attitude toward Antoinette's divorce, 243; attitude toward
  Antoinette's male friends, 22–23; attitude toward Antoinette's marriage to
  Manno, 185–186; attitude toward Antoinette's mental problems, 239;
  attitude toward family, 8; attitude
  toward government agents, 216–217;
  attitude toward guns, 184–185; attitude toward priests, 89–90, 91;
  attitude toward psychiatrists, 90–91;
  attitude toward Sulwk, 136–137; attitude toward surveillance, 84–86;
  attitude toward women, 19, 135,
  234–235; audience with Pope Pius
  XII, 68; automobile of, 85; on avoiding
  draft, 90; avoids McClellan subpoena,
  264–265; Bonnie's wedding and, 193,
  194–196; burial place of, 68; "business
  associates," 73–75; Catholic Church
  and, 59–63; Champagne and, 178;
  character of, 15–16, 34; charity and,
  100–101; Clark and, 232–233; conference room of, 15; conflicting
  birthdates for, 30; control of children's
  friendships, 46–47; court case against
  government for surveillance, 252–259;
  Daddano and, 79–80, 81; death of
  Caifano and, 40; and death of wife,
  106, 141–143; decline as Chicago
  Mafia leader, 229–230; Desert Inn,
  Las Vegas, and, 198–202; and Desmond, 105; DiPersio and, 283–287;
  disappearance of money after death,
  285–288; donation to Kennedy campaign, 248–249; driving skills, 16–17;
  efforts to control casinos in Dominican
  Republic, 204–207; efforts to establish
  gambling ventures, 270–271; efforts to
  obtain loan from Hoffa and Teamsters,
  225–226; electronic surveillance of
  Rowan, 217–218; English and, 41–42;
  erosion of power of, 245–259; estate
  of, 285–289; evasion of subpoenas,
  148, 149, 176–177, 178–179, 180–182,
  186–187; family background, 29–32;
  and Father Joe, 118–119, 126, 128;
  federal grand jury and, 265–267;
  Fischetti and, 76–78; funeral of,
  272–277; generosity of, 67–68,
  236–237; goes to Mexico after release

from prison, 269–270; hatred of Bonanno, 156–159; hatred of Castro,
  18–20, 22–24; hatred of Kennedy family, 247–251; income of, 9–10;
  increased power of, 143; international
  Mafia operations and, 197–208; IRS
  and, 69, 70; and Italian Welfare Council of Chicago, 99–107; Jones
  kidnapping and, 70–72; Ladywood
  School administration and, 121,
  122–123; learns about Antoinette's affair with Nestos, 165; life-style of,
  42–43, 69–70; McClellan committee
  and, 175–196; Mafia background of,
  16–17; on Mafia's commission, 158;
  Marcy and, 247; Martin and, 107–109;
  moves family to Oak Park, 84–86;
  murders ordered by, 9, 75–76; Nestos
  and, 165–166; physical appearance of,
  14, 15, 60–61; plan to replace,
  267–268; and plot to assassinate Castro, 13–14, 15, 18–20, 23–25; politics
  and, 102–104; power in entertainment
  world, 83–84, 86–88, 94–96, 104–105,
  107–109; prevents Antoinette from
  modeling, 133–134; in prison, 27–29,
  36, 37, 54–55, 261–262, 267, 268–269;
  reaction to Antoinette's divorce, 271,
  272, 277–278; reaction to birth of Antoinette, 41–42; reaction to FBI
  surveillance, 233–234, 251–259; reaction to poverty, 48–49; reasons for
  assassination of, 25; relationship with
  Adduci, 74–75; relationship with Antoinette, 7, 49–50, 63, 67, 96–97, 146,
  153–155; relationship with father,
  31–34; relationship with Father Joe,
  89–90, 91; relationship with Phyllis
  McGuire, 209–227, 234–235; relationship with wife, 51, 53–58;
  relationships with children, 57; relationships with women, 152–153,
  245–246; Ricca and, 131–132; rise to
  prominence, 72–73; secrecy on criminal activities, 30, 80–81; and Sinatra,
  112–114, 202–203; and strengthening
  of power base, 139; subpoena for Antoinette and, 179; subpoenaed to
  testify before Senate committees, 18,
  187; taped conversations with Roselli,
  223–225, 249–251; Tisci and, 125; tor-
  ture of Jackson and, 164; trips with
  Antoinette, 150, 151–152; Valachi's
  testimony before Senate subcommittee
  and, 262–264; Villa Venice and,
  109–115; wedding of, 55–56

Giangana, Antonio (grandfather), 30,
  31–34, 43, 59–60, 143
Gioe, Charles (Cherry Nose), 88, 102, 104,
  295–296
Glimco, Joseph Paul (Joey), 34, 45, 72,
  143, 191, 296
Gonzalez, Pancho, 241
Guzik, Jake (Greasy Thumb), 34, 73, 139,
  143, 150, 151

Hanrahan, Edward, 261, 266, 269
Hoffa, James Riddle, 225–226, 262, 264, 298
Hollywood. *See* Movie industry
Hoover, J. Edgar, 67, 205, 208, 212, 213,
  215, 248–249. *See also* FBI
Humphreys, Llewelyn (Murray the
  Camel), 72, 74, 139, 142, 151, 194,
  200, 201, 246, 268, 296

Inglese, Charles. *See* English, Charles Carmen
Internal Revenue Service (IRS), 69, 70, 154
Italian American Civil Rights League, 106,
  294
Italian Welfare Council of Chicago,
  99–107, 117, 122, 138, 177

Joliet State Penitentiary, 53, 54
Jolly Boys and Girls Summer School Camp,
  100–101, 106
Jones, Edward, 29, 39, 70–71
Jordan, Georgianna, 89, 93, 94, 188

Kefauver, Estes, 102, 117
Kefauver committee hearings, 117,
  121–123, 130, 148
Kennedy, John F., 18, 143, 161, 184; and
  plot to assassinate Castro, 25
Kennedy, Robert, 111, 155, 175–178, 245,
  250–251, 266; Giancana's efforts to
  reach, 255–259; Giancana's fall and,
  262; letter from Hoover on Giancana
  and, 248–249. *See also* McClellan
  committee
Kennedy family, Giancana and, 223–225,
  247–251
Kruse, Lester, 206, 296

Ladywood School, 89–90, 91–92, 118,
  120–126
Lansky, Meyer, 19, 176, 197–198, 296
LaRocca, Sebastian John, 157–158,
  296–297
Leavenworth prison, 27–29
Leonetti, Tommy, 101, 210
Lewis, Joe E., 232–233
Libonati, Roland V., 22, 104, 122, 125,
  142, 193, 252, 266

Life magazine, 164, 201
Lucchese, Thomas (Three-Fingers Brown),
  157, 158, 159, 297
Luciano, Charles (Lucky), 77, 176, 297
Lytton, James M., 271–272

McClellan, John, 39, 155
McClellan committee, 151, 159; Giancana
  and, 175–196; subpoenas Antoinette,
  178–183
McGuire, Phyllis, 143, 226–227, 266, 288;
  FBI subpoenas, 213–217; relationship
  with Antoinette, 230–231, 236–243;
  relationship with Giancana, 209–227,
  231–235, 276
McGurn, Jack (Machinegun), 16, 44–45,
  294
Mafia; Apalachin meeting, 155–159; background, 7; and Catholic Church, 59,
  60, 118–119; and death of Caifano, 40;
  international operations, 197–208; loss
  of interests in Cuba, 21–22; and publicity over Giancana and Phyllis
  McGuire, 229–230
Mafia's commission, 157–158
Magaddino, Stefano (Steve), 155, 156–159,
  297
Manno, Carmen, 183–190, 236, 238–239,
  243, 272, 281
Marchone, Pasqualino. *See* Marcy, Pat
Marcy, Pat, 246–247
Martin, Dean, 107–109, 111, 114, 115,
  195, 222
Metro-Goldwyn-Mayer (MGM), 83–84, 95
Moretti, Salvatore, 74, 75–76, 80, 118, 264
Mortimer, Lee, 28–29, 77
Movie industry, underworld influence in,
  83, 86–88

Nelson, William. *See* Bioff, Willie
Nestos, Dr. William, 151–155, 159–160,
  161–166, 183, 194
Nevada State Gaming Control Board, 107,
  112–113
"Night of Stars" benefits, 101–102,
  104–105, 122
Nitti, Frank, 16, 21, 77, 86, 87, 297
Nixon, Patricia, 160
Nixon, Richard, 159–160

Ogilvie, Richard B., 258, 268
Olsen, Leonard A. (Leo), 109–110, 114

Parillo, Emilio, 131–132
Parrilli, Dr. William, 147–148, 181
Pasternak, Joseph, 84, 95–96
Perno, James, 155, 184, 202, 203

Perno, Marie, 128, 202, 203
Pinelli, Anthony, 138, 192
Pistilli, Anthony, 103, 104
Prio, Ross, 34, 118, 142, 143, 247, 297
Profaci, Joseph (Giuseppe), 157, 195,
    297–298

Rebozo, C.G. "Bebe," 160–161
Ricca, Paul (The Waiter), 17, 21, 45, 59,
    77, 86, 87, 88, 91, 99, 101, 102, 103,
    109, 117, 121–122, 130, 131–132, 135,
    142, 176, 198, 216, 229–230, 234, 259,
    263, 264–265, 267–268, 271, 294
Roberta, Sister, 65–66
Roselli, John, 18, 24, 88, 113, 156, 157,
    210–211, 217, 223–225, 249–251, 275,
    298
Rowan, Dan, 217–218
Ryan, Marianne (Mrs. Gus Alex), 151, 152
Ryerson, Howard, 279

Salinger, Pierre E.G., 192, 249
Siegel, Benjamin (Buggsy), 197–198, 296
Sinatra, Frank, 8, 76, 81, 94, 95, 101, 107,
    111, 115, 161, 184, 194, 195, 210,

220–221, 232, 257; Cal-Neva Lodge
    and, 226, 227; Giancana and, 112–114,
    202–203, 222–225; Kennedy family
    and, 248–249
Smith, Keeley, 232, 234, 276
Smith, Sandy, 90, 164, 189, 204, 252–255
Stark, Mrs. Wally, 94, 95, 96, 97
Stark, Wally, 89, 94, 95, 96, 97
Sulwk, Alan W., 135–137

Teamsters, 225–226, 264
Terre Haute federal prison, 27, 28, 39, 90
Time magazine, 83, 87
Tisci, Anthony, 22, 124–125, 135, 146,
    193, 195–196, 253, 255, 256–257, 266,
    268–269
Trafficante, Santos, 15, 158, 198

Valachi, Joseph, 42, 262–263
Villa Venice, Wheeling, Illinois, 109–115,
    202, 222

Warner Brothers, 87, 94
Wilson, O.W., 262, 264

Zerilli, Joseph, 158, 298